PEOPLES OF ROMAN BRITAIN

General Editor: Keith Branigan
Professor of Prehistory and Archaeology
University of Sheffield

PARISI

CORNOVII

CORITANI

ICENI

SILURES

DOBUNNI

CATUVELLAUNI

TRINOVANTES

ATREBATES

BELGAE

REGNI

CANTIACI

DUROTRIGES

DUMNONII

0   50
⊢—⊢—⊢—⊢—⊣ miles

THE
CANTIACI

Alec Detsicas

Honorary Editor, *Archaeologia Cantiana*

ALAN SUTTON
1987

First published in 1983
by Alan Sutton Publishing Limited
17a Brunswick Road,
Gloucester

Cased ISBN 0 86299 117 X

Typesetting and origination by
Alan Sutton Publishing Limited.
Printed in Great Britain.

For
my wife,
children and grandchildren.

Preface

This volume has been in preparation much longer than I envisaged when I was first invited to contribute to this series. Fifteen years of excavations on Kentish sites and elsewhere as well as my editorial commitments are offered as my alibis. I owe a large debt of gratitude to Professor Keith Branigan for his understanding forbearance.

Such is the wealth of the archaeological evidence found in the area of the *civitas* that, within the limited scope of the *Peoples of Roman Britain*, much has either had to be altogether omitted or given more cursory treatment in this volume than I would have chosen.

A survey of this nature relies heavily on the work and advice of many others, and I pay grateful tribute to all friends and scholars alike who freely placed material at my disposal, often in advance of its publication, and answered my numerous queries. My indebtedness to them will become apparent in the following chapters, but I alone remain responsible for the conclusions drawn from such information. However, I am very glad to mention my teachers, *non solum per lineam Valli*, Professor Eric Birley and Mr J.P.Gillam, who first led me into archaeology; Professor A.L.F. Rivet for his advice on ancient authorities; Lt.-Col. G.W. Meates for help with sites in the Darent valley; Mr A.C. Harrison for assistance with Rochester and other sites; and Mr T.W.T. Tatton-Brown, Mr J. Bradshaw and Dr F. Jenkins for material on Canterbury and east Kent sites. Finally, I am very grateful to my daughter, Mrs. K.M. Browne, for deciphering my manuscript into a respectable typescript.

Ardaneaskan, Wester Ross,   A.P.D.
August 1982.

Contents

List of Illustrations

Line drawings by Jennifer Gill

1

Tribal Territory and the Pre-Roman Iron Age

The political and socio-economic organisation, during the century between Caesar and Claudius, of the area which was to become the *civitas* of the Cantiaci is imperfectly known; however, it is becoming increasingly clear that the area formed part of a larger region centred on the Thames and stretching as far north as the East Anglia rivers, west to the Chiltern ridge and south to the High Weald of Kent and Sussex.

Very little is known of the people inhabiting the area of the later canton, apart from Caesar's celebrated reference[1] to four tribes, certainly hostile to the Romans, with their own rulers but unspecified tribal areas. The names of these rulers were known to Caesar but, oddly enough, not the names of the tribes over which they ruled and which he described as *ei qui Cantium incolunt* and *humanissimi*. The absence of tribal names – for if they existed, it is very unlikely that Caesar would not have recorded them – suggests local groups of people of no more than regional consequence and that their chieftains were flattered by their description as *'reges'*.[2] There are, however, indications that not all of these peoples belonged to the same ethnic group. Differing ceramic traditions and the distribution of the hill-forts at least suggest that Belgic penetration did not extend beyond the Medway, and that non-Belgic people were settled west of the river, with the so-called 'Wealden' people and their distinctive pottery styles further south.

Commercial links with the Roman world had already been established by the first century B.C., and a money market developed using Gallo-Belgic coinage as well as the locally-

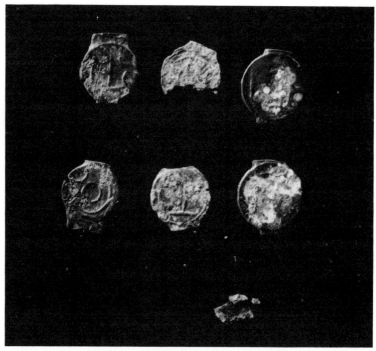

Fig. 1.   Greenhithe: *Potin* coins (1:1)

struck *potin* coins of north Kent (Fig. 1). This economic development brought about the establishment of settlements at strategic points on the routes used by this trade. The hill-fort at Bigbury, the precursor of Belgic Canterbury, controlled the crossing of the Stour, and the *oppidum* at Quarry Wood, Loose, anticipating Belgic Rochester, controlled the crossing of the Medway. Further west, the hill-fort at Oldbury, perhaps the staging centre between the Belgic and the non-Belgic peoples on either side of the Medway, controlled the Darent valley. All these three sites can be archaeologically shown to date to the early first century B.C., and Bigbury was almost certainly reduced by Caesar on his way to the Thames. Quarry Wood, Loose, is probably the latest and may indicate a shift of emphasis in the strategic control of the region from the smaller hill-forts to the larger area of the more open *oppidum* settlements.[3]

The hostility of the Kentish tribes to the Romans and their defeat by Caesar undoubtedly affected the subsequent economic development of the area. By contrast the Trinovantes north of the Thames profited by their treaty of friendship with Caesar and expanded their direct commercial links with the Roman world as seen in the importation of luxury goods like wine from the Mediterranean along an overland route ending on the Thames and the Essex coast, and in the richness of the grave-goods in burials north of the Thames; only the Aylesford cemetery in our area shows a comparable degree of wealth. It seems that the price of being anti-Roman was for the area to become a commercial backwater.

Settlement sites and casual finds of Iron Age date abound in the area, but often little survives to justify more than their general description as farmstead sites. There are many such sites with short lengths of rectilinear ditches filled with Belgic pottery, as for instance at Borden; others are rectangular or curvilinear enclosures, as at Dumpton Gap, Broadstairs and Highstead, Chislet, or circular enclosures surrounding a hut, e.g. at Fordwich, Greenhithe and Faversham.[4] The vague picture that emerges is generally of isolated farms barely above the subsistence level. The river crossings of the Medway and the Stour naturally attracted considerable Belgic settlement and some sort of communal living is to be expected at Canterbury and Rochester. The evidence for Belgic Rochester, just as for its Romano-British successor, is very sketchy; however, the discovery of fragments of coin moulds (Fig. 2) and a few coins, still to be fully published, within the post-holes of a structure that may have been a mint, clearly suggests a settlement of considerable importance. Most of the Belgic structures at Canterbury were swept away during the building of the Roman town, but enough survives to demonstrate much settlement of the site. Recent excavations by the Canterbury Archaeological Trust have recovered evidence for a round hut with porched entrance, parts of the concentric ditches of a defended enclosure and a clay mould, perhaps used for minting coins.[5]

In the years after Caesar's departure and his attempt to secure by treaty a foothold in Britain, the area became inextricably embroiled in the dynastic upheavals taking place

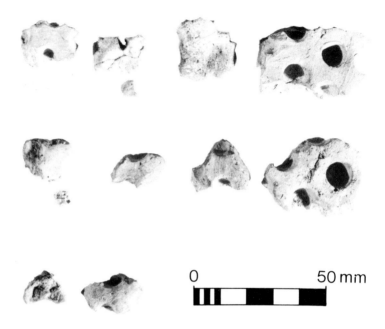

Fig. 2.   Rochester: Coin pellet moulds

north of the Thames and to west as a result of the power
struggles between the philo- and anti-Roman factions. The
only evidence for this involvement is the coin distribution of
various non-Kentish rulers, even allowing for the limitations
of such indirect evidence. It is noteworthy that, apart from a
few coins with the name of VOSE[NIOS], a coin with the
name VODENOS and another with SA[....], which is probably a mint mark, there are no known coin series belonging
exclusively to this area, and this may indicate how complete
the disorganisation of the 'tribes' of Kent may have been after
their defeat by Caesar. The distribution of coins of Tasciovanus suggests that he held sway south of the Thames and west
of the Medway. On his death, he was succeeded by Dubnovellaunus, whose coins have been found in both Essex and
Kent, mostly east of the Medway. Dubnovellaunus issued two
distinct series of coins in Essex and Kent but, though one of
his Essex coins has been found in Canterbury, none of his

Kent issues has so far occurred in Essex; moreover, it is not established whether the two series are contemporary or subsequent. This has led to suggestions of two different but synonymous kings ruling separately in Essex and Kent,[6] which seems implausible, that Dubnovellaunus was a Kentish king who seized the kingdom of Tasciovanus or even that he was somehow related to Cunobelinus who, on succeeding his father, Tasciovanus, offered the kingdom of east Kent to Dubnovellaunus rather than dispense with him.[7] Be that as it may, Dubnovellaunus' rule over east Kent appears short-lived; for, about A.D. 7 according to the *Monumentum ancyraneum*, he and Tincommius had sought refuge with Augustus. The power struggles to the west between the various Atrebatic factions about the end of the first century B.C. also affected the political stability of the area. After the death of Commius, Eppillus, having expelled the rightful heir Tincommius from Calleva, was in turn expelled and arrived in east Kent to supplant Dubnovellaunus for a time. A temporary unification of the area north and south of the Thames came about with the accession of Cunobelinus (Fig. 3) whose coins are distributed mostly east of the Medway and who, during the later years of his rule, placed his son Adminius in control of east Kent. Cunobelinus' policy sought to contain the anti-Roman elements in his court, but on his death about A.D. 40, the anti-Roman party, led by Togodumnus and Caratacus, returned to power. Subsequently, first Adminius sought the protection of Caligula, then Verica afforded Claudius the diplomatic pretext for his invasion of Britain.

Fig. 3. Eccles: Coin of Cunobelinus (2:1)

The Tribal Name and Boundaries

Unlike other Romano-British *civitates*, which retained under the Romans the tribal names by which they were already known before the invasion, the inhabitants of this canton appear to have belonged to rather small ethnic groupings of Belgic as well as non-Belgic origins, lacking a tribal identity. These people were brought together by the Romans, no doubt for administrative convenience, to form a new *civitas peregrina*, as in the case of the Regni, a *civitas* created within the tribal area of the Atrebates. The only additional question to determine is whether the members of this new canton were known as Cantii or Cantiaci. The evidence bearing on their name is overwhelmingly in favour of Cantiaci, as first proposed by Rivet,[8] and against Ptolemy's Cantii, followed by other authorities.

The name *Cantium* (Κάντιον) seems to have been known to the Massaliote traveller Pytheas (*c.* 320 B.C.). This probability is based on the fact that both Strabo, in his *Geography* compiled between 58 B.C. and A.D. 21, and Diodorus Siculus, in his *History* published between 36 and 30 B.C., though parts of it must have appeared by 49 B.C., occasionally refer to Pytheas, albeit not specifically in the case of *Cantium*. Both these sources, however, make it plainly obvious that *Cantium* was a geographical feature, *not* an area: Strabo refers to *Cantium* as 'Κάντιον ὅπερ ἐστί τὸ ἑῷον ἄκρον τῆς νήσου' and Κάντιον . . . ἑωθηνοτάτου σημείου',[9] and Diodorus Siculus describes it as 'ἀκροτήριον, ὃ καλοῦσι Κάντιον'.[10] The earliest use of *Cantium* to denote an area seems to be by Caesar who, writing before 44 B.C., not only refers to '*ei qui Cantium incolunt*', but also reports that the area was divided into four distinct regions ruled by their own kings known to him by name.[11] The conclusion seems inescapable that the people living in Caesar's *Cantium* were not known by a collective tribal name, but that there existed in the area several small groups of people, probably referred to simply as 'the people of Cingetorix', etc.; hence, it would appear that Caesar had no option than to encompass them all together in his circumlocution. For it seems both unnecessary and unthinkable, particularly in view of his direct involvement in the area and other specific references to British tribes by name,[12] that Caesar should have known and not used the name for the people of his *Cantium*, if they had one at that time. Nevertheless, Ptolemy, writing in the second century although his sources for Britain are mainly Flavian and earlier in date, first refers to 'τὸ Κάντιον ἄκρον', i.e. the South Foreland, and then, quite inexplicably, to 'Κάντιοι' and 'τοῖς Κάντιοις',[13] with a variant reading 'Κάντικοι' occurring in another group of manuscripts.[14] Did Ptolemy find it more convenient to coin this tribal name rather than use Caesar's indirect reference? For there is no other known evidence to support Ptolemy's Cantii.[15] However, Cantii was accepted, seemingly without question, by Haverfield and, following him, Dessau and Collingwood and Wright in expanding CI·CANT, on the only known inscription referring to a *civitas* member, into *ci(uis) Cant(ius)*, which still finds acceptance.[16]

On the other hand, there is very strong evidence in favour of Cantiaci. This was the tribal name so far as the compilers of the *Ravenna Cosmography* were concerned as, in common with other cantonal capitals, it was used there to describe Canterbury *(Duroavernum Cantiacorum)*; that this was the tribal name, at least from the second century onward, is very likely because the *Cosmography*, though compiled in the seventh century, seems to be based, so far as Roman Britain is concerned, on a second-century source in that it includes the Antonine Wall. There can be no doubt that Cantiaci is accurate; otherwise, why not *Duroavernum Cantiorum?* Cantiaci reflects the emergence of the 'new artificial creation of the Romans' into a *civitas peregrina*,[17] from the anonymity of Caesar's *'quibus regionibus'* into a Roman-made confederacy of the people living in the hinterland of *Cantium* and reflecting their new collective name (Cantiaci).[18]

The northern, eastern and southern boundaries of the canton are obviously determined by its geography and only its western limit is conjectural (Fig. 7). Cunliffe, in his discussion of the northern and eastern boundaries of the Regni adopts as a boundary 'the watershed between the rivers flowing north to the Thames and those flowing south to the Channel'[19] and excludes, in consequence, virtually the whole of Surrey from their *territorium*. Where the canton of the Cantiaci is con-

cerned, it is similarly impossible to be more precise than
Cunliffe's rule of thumb about its western boundary. This
may have lain somewhere to the west of the Roman road from
London towards Lewes, perhaps as far west as the line of the
Roman road from London towards Brighton, turning to
south-east around East Grinstead, the watershed of the
Medway and the Eden, in order to follow the high ground of
the Downs before reaching the Channel between Hastings and
Pevensey. It has long been noticed that temples in Gaul are
often situated on or near tribal boundaries; as the Titsey
temple lies close to this conjectural boundary line, between
two Roman roads, this may be thought as supporting evidence
for the proposed boundary. The clear connection between the
temple and the nearby building does not invalidate the
probability that it was built on or close to the boundary
between the two *civitates*. To north of the canton, there is no
direct evidence to show conclusively that its area reached,
along the south bank of the Thames, quite up to Roman
London, and the probable temple in Greenwich Park may
again indicate the canton's approximate boundary.

Geology

The geology of the area which was to become the canton of the
Cantiaci has dominated its settlement pattern from early Iron
Age times into and beyond the Romano-British period.
Broadly speaking, the canton forms a compact unit. At its
centre rise the heavy soils of the Weald, Wadhurst Clay and
Ashdown Sand, with their heavy vegetation and dense forest
and enclosed by the peripheral rims of Tunbridge Wells Sand.
To north of this land mass lies a thick bed of Weald Clay and
Lower Greensand, rimmed with Gault Clay, before the
ground rises again with the Chalk of the North Downs and its
Clay-with-Flints capping, dipping down once more to the
Thames estuary overlaid by London Clay and the Thanet and
Woolwich Beds. The Wealden land mass is well drained by
several rivers and their tributaries; to north by the Medway,
cutting through the chalk to flow into the Thames beyond
Rochester, the Darent and the Cray, whilst the Stour and the
Rother river-systems drain out to north-east and east, respec-

tively. The gradual rise in sea-level, which has taken place since Romano-British times,[20] has meant the deposition of much alluvium on the northern shores of the *civitas*, resulting in considerable changes in its coastline, nowhere more evident than at the extreme eastern tip where the silting up of the Stour estuary and the Wantsum Channel has connected the Isle of Thanet to the mainland. Likewise, owing to various geological changes, the indented coastline between Hythe and Hastings, which afforded several creeks and safe anchorages during the Roman period, has become land-locked by the alluvium of Romney Marsh. This geological formation explains why the central land mass of the Weald remained largely unsettled in Iron Age and Romano-British times, except for the exploitation of its mineral resources. Most settlement occurred away from the Weald, on the less intractable and lighter soils of the northern coastal belt, the gently undulating slopes of the North Downs and the fertile soils of the river valleys (Fig. 7).

Pattern of Settlement

The settlement of the canton of the Cantiaci during the Romano-British period owes its pattern to a combination of closely-related factors. Romanisation of the area, at its simplest and certainly for the large majority of the inhabitants, entailed little more than a rise in their standard of living or, rather, in the degree of its comfort. Few could have abandoned their traditional Iron Age way of life, their round huts and native farmsteads in favour of rectangular, stone-built houses and well-planned towns, but the material comforts, steadily trickling into Britain before the invasion, could now be had by all according to their purses. The gradual organisation of the whole province into one organic unit in the place of the earlier tribal units brought about a boost to economic expansion which was reflected in the new *civitas*. Political unification and the diffusion of the fruits of *Pax romana*, accelerated by the development of a road network initially built for the maintenance of military supply lines, resulted in the greater exploitation of existing resources, such as agriculture and mining, as well as the expansion of established but local industries, such as pottery manufacture. In turn, this economic expansion brought about a greater and better use of the land, the development of new industries close to areas of suitable raw materials, such as the clays in the valley bottoms or the coastal belt and the iron-bearing deposits of the Weald, better communications, certainly by road and very likely by water, the investment of capital, some perhaps from Continental sources, and the upsurge in communal living indicated by the development and prosperity of the towns and country.

Politically, the new *civitas* appears to have been composed of two *pagi*, divided by the Medway and the road from Rochester towards Hastings;[21] one in east Kent centred round the new cantonal capital, Canterbury, the other in west Kent was administered from Rochester. Settlement and industrial activity appear more concentrated in the western *pagus*, though evidence is now accumulating to suggest an analogous settlement in the Stour valley and to east of Canterbury.

2

History: A.D. 43–367

The expeditionary force, about 40,000 men, sailed from Boulogne under the command of Aulus Plautius: it consisted of one legion, the IX *Hispana*, drawn from Pannonia, and three, the II *Augusta*, the XIV *Gemina* and the XX *Valeria* from the army of the Rhine, with a fifth legion, Legio VIII, forming the strategic reserve; no doubt, auxiliary troops would have been part of the invading force, but there is no direct evidence for their presence in 43. The primary objective of Plautius' task was to break up the Catuvellaunian power in the south-east and to capture Camulodunum; to achieve this, the Romans had first to effect a landing in force and cross the natural barriers on their way to Camulodunum.

Speed was essential. The necessity to land his troops as soon as possible must have been foremost in Plautius' planning; apart from the well-known aversion of the Romans to sea-voyages, precious time had been lost before embarkation by the mutinous soldiers who were only pacified by the despatch from Rome of one of Claudius' ministers. There can be little doubt that, whilst troops and supplies were being assembled at Boulogne, intelligence would have reached across the Channel to warn of the impending invasion and much of the element of surprise would thus have been lost though, unbeknown to the Romans, this very delay was probably a blessing in disguise as it may have allayed the Britons' fears, particularly in view of Gaius' ill-starred venture, and accounted for the lack of opposition at the landing.

The invading forces landed at Richborough. The choice of the site testifies how far the Roman staff had learnt Caesar's lesson and indicates careful planning on the basis of intelligence undoubtedly available at army headquarters; in this intelligence gathering, it is not too difficult to imagine the importance of the commercial contacts existing between Britain and Roman Gaul in the years before the invasion. Richborough not only affords the shortest route from Boulogne but also a safe anchorage protected to east by a sand-bar; no sailing up and down the Channel in search for a harbour this time, but a direct landing at a pre-selected beach-head.

There have been suggestions in the past that the Roman army may have landed at three separate points, on the east Kent coast and elsewhere, that 'two forces – main and decoy' were involved, with a third one landing further west still.[1] This is based on a misinterpretation of Cassius Dio's account of the invasion,[2] and support for this theory has been sought in the Roman road system from the Channel ports to Canterbury and the size of the Claudian bridgehead at Richborough. Apart from the fact that the roads converging on Canterbury from Richborough, Dover and Lympne must clearly be of later construction, there is no known over-riding reason why the invading forces should have converged, across the difficult terrain of the Downs, on Belgic Canterbury where no military presence of this period is so far attested. The size of the Claudian bridgehead at Richborough does, however, pose a problem: the area (about 4 ha.) enclosed by the double Claudian ditches is manifestly too small for a force of about 40,000 men and supplies, assuming that no other military installations of the invasion period are awaiting discovery in the vicinity of the later Saxon Shore fort and that the army was to be landed at Richborough in one wave, clearly a major undertaking on any account, even if the landing were to be unopposed. Yet, Dio speaks of three divisions to avoid the delays in landing which might be occasioned by the ferrying over of a single force, but it does not necessarily follow from this that these three divisions were landed at three *different* places (it was bad enough to have to find *one* good anchorage!). However, what is not improbable is that a first wave landed at the chosen beach-head, consolidated the ground won and moved forward on the arrival of the second division which would, in turn, make way for the third wave;[3] this would mean, of course, that at least one, possibly two more camps would have been needed for the accommodation of the whole force – that such camps are not yet known does not prove that they never existed. On the other hand, this interpretation makes better sense of both the historical and archaeological facts, for Dio speaks of avoiding delays and this must have been uppermost in the minds of the staff officers; given a confined beach-head, it makes better military sense to land and establish a force before more troops are landed, it makes for better strategy to concentrate rather than disperse one's initial effort. Furthermore, no sooner than the landing of the first wave, news would have reached the headquarters staff that there was surprisingly no opposition, hence no need even for a diversionary landing in the hope of dispersing enemy forces.[4]

What happened immediately after the initial landing phase and before the crossing of the Medway can only be conjectured. Belgic Canterbury seems to have presented no problem worth even a mention by Dio though, in accordance with normal Roman military practice, it is not unlikely that a fortlet may have temporarily guarded the crossing of the Stour.[5] Dio only mentions the defeat of Caratacus and Togodumnus who, after their inexplicable failure to oppose the landing at Richborough, were no doubt trying to retrieve the situation by fighting a rear-guard action until the Romans reached the next natural obstacle which, unnamed by Dio, must be the Medway. The only remaining question is the line of advance of the Roman army.

There is no direct, conclusive evidence bearing on this line of advance before the Medway. Dudley and Webster, following Burn,[6] suggest that the Romans advanced along the North Downs Trackway until they arrived at the Medway somewhere between Aylesford and Rochester; however, this line would appear a rather indirect route as it would have involved a march from the Canterbury area down the Stour valley, across hilly country suitable to guerilla attacks before joining the prehistoric trackway, a detour for which there is no evidence. On the other hand, military logic and speed of advance dictate the more direct route along the northern foothills of the Downs and the fairly open ground beyond them, which is the line of the post-conquest Watling Street. Moreover, as Frere has already pointed out,[7] Belgic Rochester, where fragments of coin moulds have recently been found, may have been a worthwhile military objective, assuming that there were no pre-Roman bridges at Rochester which might have been captured intact.[8] Some archaeological support for this line of advance has been provided by the recent discovery at Bredgar, near Sittingbourne, of a hoard of 34 Roman gold coins, probably the savings of an officer, hidden before an engagement; though this hoard does not conclusively prove that the Roman army passed through this area, at least it is a pointer which is so far totally lacking along the North Downs Trackway.

The Romans found the Britons in position along the west bank of the Medway; if there had been a bridge, or bridges, at Belgic Rochester, none was found. The events of the two-day battle of the Medway, described somewhat confusedly by Dio, are too well known to warrant their repetition here; what is in doubt, however, is the precise location of the ford forced by the specialist troops, recruited in the Low Countries, under the command of Vespasian. Almost certainly, this ford must have been upstream, nearer Rochester than Aylesford and unobserved by the Britons; partly, because such a location would have been more in direct line with the more likely Roman approach route ending on the high ground above Chatham, partly because there could not have been much time for the army to camp on the east bank and reconnoitre the ground in search of a suitable ford.[9] Dudley and Webster[10] suggest the site of the modern Rochester motorway bridge as the location for the opposed crossing on the grounds that the river, below Aylesford, is unsuitable, though this objection could equally well apply to the whole course of the Medway between Aylesford and Rochester. However, there is so far no direct archaeological evidence, on either bank of the river, to indicate the exact location of this crossing. Nevertheless, after two days' pitched battle, directed from the high ground above the Medway, the river was crossed by the Romans in strength and the defeated Britons fled.

Beyond the Medway lay the Thames, and clearly the routed

Britons must have sought refuge and a chance to re-group their battered forces beyond this natural barrier. It is not unreasonable to suppose that, during this period, the Roman army may have used Rochester as a supply port, which would have avoided difficult overland communications from Richborough across territory still lacking a good road-system.

The only source for the events that followed the battle of the Medway is again Dio who describes the crossing of the Thames without specifying where, apart from a vague reference to 'a point where it enters the sea and forms a large pool at high tide';[11] in fairness, it is difficult to see how else, short of fixed geographical points, could Dio have referred to this crossing. Yet, the location of this crossing point presents an even greater problem than that already discussed with regard to the crossing of the Medway. It has always been assumed that Plautius, following in the steps of Caesar, crossed the Thames in the London area after awaiting for Claudius himself to arrive with his elephants for the triumphal entry into Camulodunum; there is, however, again no archaeological evidence to support this location or along the route towards it. For Caesar, aiming towards Wheathampstead, it was logical to follow a direct route and cross the Thames at Brentford; but for Plautius, marching on Camulodunum, crossing the Thames in London would have meant a considerable detour, let alone that it suggests a lack of military intelligence relating to the hinterland of south-east Britain, which is clearly unlikely. An alternative theory has recently been put forward,[12] which suggests that the Thames may have been crossed between Higham in Kent and East Tilbury in Essex, a much more direct route to Camulodunum. Though this theory is mainly based on the logic of the more direct approach, it lacks supporting evidence on the north Kent coast, apart from the fact that a ferry was in use at a much later period between Higham and Tilbury; on the other hand, the existence of a probable military site at Mucking, on the high ground of the Essex coast above East Tilbury,[13] may lend some support to this line of advance: for here the Thames widens into its estuary, which could be Dio's 'pool'. It is not impossible that both alternative theories may be right; for it would be tactically advantageous, after the routing of the

Fig. 4. Richborough Roman fort from the air

Britons on the Medway, to divide the invading force into two
groups in pursuit of the Britons fleeing towards their heart-
lands in Hertfordshire and Essex. This division of the army
clearly did take place, but it is not known how soon after the
Medway battle Vespasian's group drove westward; this could
have happened before the Romans reached the Thames in
London, again in order to avoid unnecessary detours.

Consolidation

In the rear of the army advancing beyond the Thames, peace
was quickly re-established. The only evidence for continued
military activity in the canton in the years immediately after
43 concerns the development of the original Richborough
bridge-head into a supply base and, subsequently, into the
main port of entry into Britain (Fig. 4). It is not impossible
that the putative fortlet at Reculver continued to be manned,
at least for a short time, and that Rochester may have
remained an advance supply port, but in both cases direct
evidence is so far lacking.

At Richborough, in the years between 44 and 85, considerable military activity continued and the original beach-head was developed into a large supply depot, extending beyond the area of the later Saxon Shore fort, which was excavated between 1922 and 1938. First, the site was cleared of any temporary Claudian installations and the ditches of the invasion encampment were filled in. Next, a regular grid of metalled roads was laid over the site, with the main east–west road pointing towards Canterbury:[14] here was the beginning of the main Roman road to London and beyond, which became known as Watling Street. South of this road, other roads divided the site into regular *insulae*, containing many timber buildings. In *Insulae I–III* were sited at least ten large granaries or store-houses, with others perhaps lying beyond the excavated area. North of the main east–west road, in *Insula IV,* there was recovered a complicated sequence of timber buildings which seem to have succeeded one another fairly rapidly; clearly, Building A is another granary, but the series of Buildings B–E is difficult to interpret, though they may probably have functioned as the administrative block of the site, possibly as *mansiones*, too. However, the latest of these structures, Building F, was a large courtyard building, and much of its west and south ranges, as well as some of its east range, was excavated. The rooms of this building were arranged in pairs, a main room and a smaller ante-room round an internal courtyard measuring 28.7 m. from east to west, though its longer north to south dimension is not fully known. Again the function of this building is not fully understood; it could have combined the functions both of an administrative headquarters and a *mansio*. On the other hand, its dating to 75–85 is more precise as Building F lay over a Vespasianic pit and had obviously been dismantled before the construction of the *quadrifrons*. The timber buildings in *Insulae V* and *VI* are also less well understood; partly because of site clearance in Roman times, partly because the complicated series of construction trenches for timber sleeper-beams was not fully appreciated at the time of the excavation.

The military phase in this period of occupation at Richborough seems to have come to an end about 85 but, even before that date, some reduction in the military importance of the site seems indicated by the demolition about 70 of at least some of the granaries, particularly those in *Insula IV*. This is only to be expected because, with the army already operating in Brigantian territory, supply bases are likely to have been established nearer the front-line; moreover, in the thirty years since the invasion, fewer corn supplies would have been needed from the Continent as some at least of the quantities required by the army would have been provided by the province. The general picture that emerges at Richborough is one of a gradually scaled down military presence, as shown by the demolition of the early-Flavian timber buildings, and an increasing development of civilian life before the site became the main port of entry into Britain. This transformation was heralded by the construction of the Monument, of which only a cruciform remnant of its foundation survives at present.[15]

No effort or expense, in labour, materials or expertise, seems to have been spared in the building of this great structure. The timber store-houses were demolished and the site for the Monument, lying across the original *Insulae I* and *IV*, was cleared in the late-Flavian period. A large pit was excavated to a depth of about 9 m. through the sandy subsoil, which was disposed of by means of two ramps leading to the surface. It has been estimated that some 93,330 cubic metres of sand were laid on the area north of the main east–west road. Into this large pit was built the foundation of the Monument; it consisted of a mass of coursed flints set in white mortar and, at ground level, a flange was bonded into this massive foundation. The overall dimensions of this construction, including foundations and flange, were 44.4 × 31.9 m.[16] On top of the foundation was laid a hard layer of packing and a solid concrete platform, cruciform in shape originally though now badly eroded, was built upon this foundation; its longer and narrower arm extended north–south, whilst its east–west arm was shorter and wider. This cruciform base survives to a present height of *c.* 1 m. and is interpreted as 'a filling put in to raise the level of the passages above the surrounding ground level and to provide a bed for the paving.'[17] Clearly, this raised level of the *quadrifrons* passages would have necessitated steps leading up to them, but no direct evidence has survived; likewise, there is no direct evidence, apart from the layer of hard packing, for paving round the central structure, but this is very likely. A wall enclosed the whole area, though it now survives on three sides only of the cruciform foundation.

The Monument has been interpreted as a *quadrifrons* and its total height, excluding any statuary at the top, has been restored to 26.2 m. This interpretation is based on the examination of the structure by Sir Ian Richmond which was completed by Professor D.E. Strong following Professor Richmond's main conclusions. According to this interpretation, the *quadrifrons* was built rather 'to symbolise the *accessus Britanniae*' than as a triumphal arch.[18] The main elevation of the *quadrifrons* consists of arches calculated to be 7 m. wide, supported by columns, fluted fragments of which were found in the excavations; the height of these columns has been estimated at 11 m., including base and capital. No fragments survived, however, to show the order of the columns. The side elevation to east–west had arches estimated to be lower than those of the main elevation.

The whole structure was encased in marble veneers, mainly from Carrara though some Pentelic marble fragments have also been recovered, fastened to the masonry by bronze cramps. The decoration of the *quadrifrons* does not seem to have been elaborate, and apart from fragments of decorated mouldings, only two indeterminable fragments of marble sculpture have been found. Likewise, virtually nothing survived from the dedicatory inscription but, on the basis on one surviving letter, it is probable that this dedication consisted of applied bronze letters. However, fourteen fragments of bronze sculpture did survive and, though this is slight evidence, they indicate that an equestrian statue or group, apparently larger than life-size and in military uniform, once stood on the attic of the Monument.

The date of the Monument, begun between 80 and 90 and completed a few years later, and the bronze equestrian statuary suggest that the *quadrifrons* was erected under Domitian, and it may well be that the bronze figure in military costume represented the emperor commemorating the new conquest. If so, Domitian's figure would have had to be replaced after his fall. However lacking in decorative elabora-

tion compared with other monumental buildings, the Richborough *quadrifrons* would have presented the traveller from
Gaul with a magnificent entry into the province as soon as he
landed on its soil, a fine piece of propaganda proclaiming
perdomita Britannia.

With the building of the Monument at Richborough, the
military occupation of the site appears to have come to an end
at the beginning of the second century, and Richborough,
though continuing as a port which is shown by the building in
Insula IV interpreted as a *mansio*, developed into a civilian
settlement. Why, unlike other Romano-British towns with
military origins, it failed to develop fully into a town is
discussed in Chapter 3. However, military activity did not
cease altogether in the canton during this century and this
concerns the operations of the naval unit known as the *Classis
Britannica*.

Coastal Defences (Figs. 4 and 5)

It has long been assumed that the fleet was assembled as a
new formation in the years immediately before 43, perhaps
during the abortive preparations of Gaius in 40, though there
is no direct evidence for such a date. It is logical, however, to
expect the formation of such a naval unit, if only for the
transport of the invasion troops across the Channel, and there
are parallels for such a formation in the case of the campaigns
during the early Empire. Clearly, this fleet would have needed
a base in Gaul before the invasion, and the presence of tiles
stamped CLBR at Boulogne indicates that it must have been
based at the embarkation port of the invading force. Following
the landing at Richborough and the consolidation of the
South-east, it is again to be expected that, in order for the fleet
to continue with its support role of the army, a naval base
would be necessary on the coast of the canton. However, no
evidence has so far come to light to indicate where such an
early base may have been located, unless it was at Lympne,
close to the site of the later Saxon Shore fort. That a naval
installation existed at this site during the second century is
shown by the well-known altar found re-used in the construction of the fort, erected by Aufidius Pantera, an officer attested

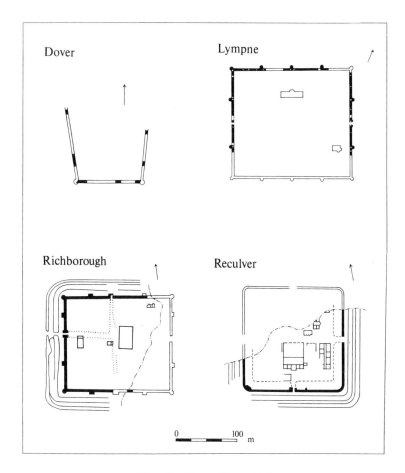

Fig. 5. Saxon Shore forts

during the Antonine period, who is described on this altar as *Prefect(us) Clas(sis) Brita(nnicae).*[19] The altar was encrusted with barnacles when found and obviously derived from an installation on the coast; a rise in the sea-level of the Channel, activating springs in the Gault Clay and causing the landslips that continued to beset the site at Lympne beyond its Roman occupation, may have brought about the abandonment of this presumed naval base in the second century and its transfer to Dover, with another probable base in the Richborough area.

The light-houses on the heights above the modern town of Dover, coupled with finds suggesting harbour installations, have long indicated a major port and the recovery of stamped tiles suggested a connection with the *Classis Britannica*. However, speculation came to an end in 1970 with the discovery of two forts about 260 m. west of the approximate coastline in Roman times. The earliest of these forts was not completed, and the construction of both dates to Hadrianic times.[20]

Whatever other roles the fleet was called upon to play, it is clear that it was connected with some at least of the iron-working sites of the Weald as attested by finds of stamped tiles at two such sites within the canton and another two sites which may have been connected with the transport of iron. The implications of this probable involvement of the *Classis Britannica* are discussed elsewhere, but it may be significant that at none of these sites, or at the Folkestone villa where stamped tiles incorporated in its walls have led to the suggestion that the house may have been the official residence of the fleet's commanding officer,[21] no military associations or items of equipment have so far been found.

Again, it is impossible to say what happened to the *Classis Britannica* after it disappeared from the historical record about the middle of the third century. It is about this time that stamped tiles no longer occur, which suggests that the fleet was either disbanded or based elsewhere at a hitherto unknown site. If the hypothesis of a new location were to be accepted, it is strange that the practice of stamping its tiles ceased, unless the hypothetical new base was located in an area of abundant building stone. Even so, some traces of the *Classis Britannica* should certainly have survived. On balance, it seems more probable that the fleet was disbanded about the middle of the third century when its role of policing the Channel may have been transferred to the coastal forts, Reculver and Brancaster, being built at this time.

Some time early in the third century, it is probable that the east coast of Britain was becoming already unsafe as a result of the piratical raids that were to beset it during the remainder of the Roman occupation of the province, and to afford it a measure of protection two forts were built, one at Brancaster on the Wash, the other at Reculver, at the mouth of the

Thames estuary.

The fort at Reculver *(Regulbium)* was constructed on a spur of land facing north into the Thames estuary and east, across the Wantsum Channel, towards the Isle of Thanet. The site, which shows traces of Belgic occupation,[22] was originally about 1.2 km. inland, but coastal erosion has reduced the surviving area of the fort to rather less than two-thirds of its full size. At the beginning of the seventeenth century the sea had encroached to about 165 m. and, soon after 1784, by which time the north-west angle of the fort had already disappeared, all the northern side of the walls had been eroded away; however, it is likely that the fort occupied an area of about 3 ha. (7½ acres). The fort walls, with rounded corners and angle turrets, were built of ragstone and flint, without any lacing courses of bonding-tiles. At foundation level, the walls measured about 3 m. thick, reducing to a width of *c.* 2.5 m. above two offsets. The total height of the walls is not known; a maximum height of *c.* 2.7 m. survives along the west side of the fort,[23] but it is probable that the perimeter wall may have originally stood to a total height of some 6 m.[24] The fort walls were internally buttressed by an earth rampart, whilst externally, the fort was defended by two ditches. The inner ditch had been cut to a depth of 2.7 m. and was 7.9 m. wide whereas the outer ditch was shallower (*c.* 2 m.) and narrower (5 m.). Of the four presumed gates, only the south and east gates have survived and been shown by recent excavation to be both *c.* 2.7 m. wide, with a single carriageway and a single guard-room projecting into the fort area. The east gate faced towards the Wantsum Channel and the main road through the fort connected it with the lost west gate where began the Roman road from the fort to Canterbury. Excavations[25] inside the fort area have established, south of the *via principalis*, the plan of the *principia*, facing the south gate. This headquarters building had a 10.7 m.-wide cross-hall *(basilica)* flanked by smaller offices, and an underground *sacellum*. To east of the *principia*, another building and two barrack-blocks have also been established. North of the *via principalis*, the south-east corner of a building probably belongs to another barrack-block and, to its south, there are two more masonry buildings. The southernmost is a hypocausted building, clearly a bath-house, 'proved to be the fort bath-house', and further north there is another and larger hypocausted building, interpreted as 'probably another bath-house',[26] though its plan is not that of a baths. However, the close relationship of these two buildings and the small size of the bath-house suggest that the larger structure is likely to have been the commandant's house and the smaller building its baths suite.[27] Traces of a civilian settlement (*vicus*), have been found on all sides of the fort, except to the east, and a large hypocausted building, probably a corn-drier, south-east of the fort.

The Reculver fort was built in the third century, probably before 250, but a more precise date is at present impossible. Apart from the evidence of the shape of the fort, its lack of bastions and the internal lay-out which hark back to the first and second centuries rather than to the later Saxon Shore forts, this dating is confirmed by fragments of a building inscription found in the rubble filling of the *sacellum*, which refers to the construction[28] of the *basilica* and mentions the name of the governor under whom this work was undertaken. Unfortunately, only fragments of this name survived, and Sir Ian Richmond's expansion to Triarius Rufinus, who may have been appointed governor of Britain about 210–12, is not now generally accepted. It has been shown that it is 'most improbable that the governor ... is Triarius Rufinus' but more likely that he was Aradius Rufinus, who may have been governor in the period 238–44.[29] All that can be said with certainty is that this building inscription may be dated 'to any time in the third century after the reign of Severus', and the construction of the fort to 'the early decades of that century.'[30]

The unit stationed at Reculver is known from the *Notitia Dignitatum* and stamped tiles found at the fort as the *Cohors prima Baetasiorum,* a quingenary cohort, which is attested in northern forts and at Old Kilpatrick during the second occupation of the Antonine Wall sometime during the second century, though it is not improbable that other units may have also been stationed at Reculver, perhaps auxiliaries or marines of the *Classis Britannica.*[31]

Some time during the third century, perhaps about 250, the Richborough site was re-occupied by the army; it is not known how much of the earlier civilian settlement had survived by that time, but an area of less than $\frac{1}{2}$ ha., centred on the ruined *quadrifrons* was cleared and enclosed by a triple ditch. At the north-east corner of this area the middle and outer ditches were not continued beyond the line of the second-century building in *Insula IV* and the inner ditch was slightly diverted to avoid its south-west corner, which shows that the *mansio* had not only survived but also that it was important enough to preserve it during this military re-occupation. To east, the ditches have not survived subsidence but the whole of the remaining circuit has been excavated. The inner and middle ditches were both slightly deeper than 2 m., but differed in width, being 6.7 m. and 4.6 m., respectively; the outer ditch was slightly deeper (2.3 m.) and 5.2 m. wide. Inside the inner ditch, there was a clay rampart, but no evidence was found for revetting or a palisade. Three timber posts on either side of a causeway which carried the main east–west road into the defended area, clearly formed a timber gate at this point. The area enclosed by these defences was about 91 m. sq., but nothing is known of any internal buildings.[32]

This earth fort has been interpreted as 'a defended look-out post',[33] and the ruined *quadrifrons* is thought to have been the base for a timber tower used for signalling purposes, but the date of its construction is difficult to determine. Clearly, 'it could have been erected any time between 200 and 280',[33] perhaps about the time the Reculver fort was built. It may have been at the approximate centre of a system of signalling, embracing Reculver, Richborough and the eastern light-house at Dover (Fig. 6), to warn of the approach of sea-borne raiding parties in the Wantsum Channel. Whatever its function, the earth fort must have had a fairly short life as its rampart was dismantled and the ditches filled in before the construction of the Richborough Saxon Shore fort either under Carausius or, possibly, under Probus.[34]

Forts of the Saxon Shore

The last phase of military activity in the canton of the Cantiaci concerns the defence of its Channel coast against the increasing attacks by raiding parties across the North Sea by

Fig. 6. Dover: Roman light-house

the system of fortifications collectively known as the Saxon Shore forts and extending from the Wash to the Solent. The forts located in the *civitas* are at Reculver, Richborough, Dover and Lympne, a large proportion of the whole system clearly due to the exposed geography of the cantonal coast and its proximity to the source of danger.

At Richborough,[35] apart from the foundation of the *quadrifrons*, the site of the earth fort was cleared and its ditched perimeter filled in before the construction of the Saxon Shore fort, which occupied an area of *c.* 2.5 ha. The perimeter wall of the fort was between 3.2 m. and 3.5 m. wide at its base; it had been built of stone rubble set in concrete and faced with squared masonry, with lacing courses of bonding-tiles at intervals. The exact height of this wall is not known, but the south wall survives to a height of 7.6 m. which suggests an original height of about 9 m.

The main gate of the fort, through its west wall, had a single portal spanning the 3.3 m.-wide carriageway, with two flanking gate-towers and guard chambers. A small postern gate opened through the north wall and was protected by a stone *clavicula*, and another such gate may have been through the south wall. Nothing survives, however, of the east wall. At the two surviving corners of the fort there were circular turrets, bonded to its wall and 5.5 m. in diameter. Bastions were also regularly spaced between the corner turrets; these bastions were rectangular, *c.* 6 m. long and projected 3 m. from the wall face.[36] Beyond the walls were two defensive ditches of the standard V-shape; the inner ditch measured 9.1 m. wide and 3 m. deep, the outer *c.* 4 m. wide and 2.4 m. deep. To west, a causeway had been left through the outer ditch to carry the road from Canterbury, which passed on a timber bridge over the inner ditch.

Internally, the fort was divided by a road connecting the north and south postern gates, and this area was further sub-divided by the west road terminating at the foundation of the destroyed *quadrifrons*. Little survived of the internal accommodation of the fort, and it is likely that most of its military installations were of timber; even so, only in the north-east corner the area of four timber buildings, possibly barrack-blocks, can be recognized. The *principia* may have been located on the foundation of the *quadrifrons* but this is not certain. The only surviving buildings are a small bath-house, consisting of the standard rooms *(praefurnium, caldarium, tepidarium* and a combined vestibule- *apodyterium/frigidarium)* and used at least by officers, and two other masonry buildings which have been interpreted as military guilds *(scholae)*.[37]

Excavation outside the fort area has been much less intense, but there is some evidence for a civilian settlement *(vicus)*. Roads branch off Watling Street to north and south. To north, about 88 m. from the north wall of the fort, there was found evidence for two lime kilns, possibly in use at the time of the building of the fort, and traces of a building, which may have been part of the harbour installations. To south, at 130 m. from the fort's west wall, part of a building was excavated in 1887. South of the fort crop-marks seen from the air suggest another building and, at about 85 m. south of the fort wall, were excavated parts of another building and beyond it part of a cemetery. Two Romano-Celtic temples were excavated further south of this area, and to their west a structure, partly examined in the 1840s by Rolfe and variously interpreted as an amphitheatre or a military *ludus*.[38] Its arena measured 61 by 50 m., with entrances to north, south and east, and the evidence suggests that this structure was contemporary with the building of the fort. There is no doubt that much remains to be discovered in the fields surrounding the fort.

The garrison of the fort is given by the *Notitia* as *Legio II Augusta*, though undoubtedly only a *vexillatio* of the legion could have been stationed at Richborough.

The Saxon Shore fort at Dover *(Dubris)* was found in 1970, though the mention of its garrison in the *Notitia* and work before and after the last war pointed, albeit inconclusively, to its presence there. A portion of the fort's south and west walls has so far been excavated. The walls were *c.* 3 m. thick, had a rubble core and were faced with squared masonry, with corner turrets and bastions, some of which were added to the original construction. A single ditch, *c.* 12.2 m. wide and 3 m. deep, has also been found. The area of the fort has not yet been established, but its shape does not appear to be rectangular. Not much is known to date about its internal lay-out, though it seems to date to the second half of the third century[39] and, to judge from its plan, late in that period.

The garrison of the Dover fort is listed in the *Notitia* as the well-known *Milites Tungrecani*, though there are good grounds for believing that another unit may have been stationed at the fort in the years before 367, if the *Tungrecani* came to the fort after the barbarian conspiracy.[40]

The fort at Lympne *(Portus Lemanis)*, located at the head of rivers draining the Weald to east, was built close to an area previously occupied by the presumed *Classis Britannica* base, materials from which had been incorporated in the fort's building. Apart from the Aufidius Pantera altar, other masonry had been re-used in the fort's construction, including some of the fleet's CLBR-stamped tiles found lying around the site as if to underline the change-over from a naval base to an army fort. The whole of the site has suffered considerable land-slips which have made very difficult the planning of the surviving remains. Excavations in the late nineteenth century have shown that the fort's area may have been about 3.5–4 ha. The fort wall was *c.* 3.2 m. thick and survived in places to a height of 6 m.; it had the usual lacing courses of bonding-tiles, corner turrets and cylindrical bastions. The main gate opened through the fort's east wall, was arched and 3.15 m. wide; it had projecting towers, 3.2 m. in diameter, and two guard chambers. The shape of the fort may have been pentagonal but recent work at the site[41] indicates that the fort may well have been rectangular in plan and not unlike the forts at Richborough and Portchester. Very little is known of the internal arrangements of the fort; the rear portion of the *principia*, whose cross-hall had a polygonal *sacellum*, has been examined and, close to the east gate, a small baths, possibly for the use of officers.

The unit stationed at Lympne is given by the *Notitia* as the *Numerus Turnacensium* and the known evidence indicates that the fort was built in the late-third or early-fourth century, its occupation lasting into the middle years of the century.[42]

The fortification of the east coast of Roman Britain and the English Channel has long been discussed,[43] but two main questions remain unresolved: the meaning of the term *Litus Saxonicum* and the purpose of these coastal defences.

With regard to *Litus Saxonicum*, the question is whether the adjective was intended to refer to a coastal strip settled by Saxons or to a shore threatened by and protected against Saxons. *Litus Saxonicum* is the description used in the *Notitia Dignitatum*, which dates from the very late fourth century, perhaps slightly earlier. If this was a *de facto* reference to conditions obtaining along the eastern sea-board and the Channel coast of Britain in the late fourth century only, there would be some justification for accepting it as meaning 'settled by Saxons', as there is mounting evidence to suggest the settlement of Germanic *foederati* in the *civitas* as well as elsewhere. However, as the Saxon Shore forts are much earlier than the date of the *Notitia*,[44] it is very doubtful, if not unlikely, that there was enough Saxon settlement in the area defended by the forts during the third century to warrant its description as *Litus Saxonicum* at such an early date. Moreover, the undoubtedly earlier date for the construction of Reculver and Brancaster, the forerunners of the whole system, as well as the Richborough earth fort, suggests not only that the coasts were becoming unsafe as early as about the middle of the third century, but also that their security deteriorated sufficiently in the following decades to bring about the building of the later forts of the system – after all, Carausius' commission was to 'pacify the sea . . . which Franks and Saxons were raiding.'[45] Initially, at any rate, it is more likely that *Litus Saxonicum* referred to a shore to be defended against raiding Saxons though, by the end of the fourth century, sufficient Germanic settlement would have justified the alternative interpretation of a shore 'settled by Saxon'.[46]

The purpose of the Saxon Shore forts has also been much debated and, though in all probability they need not testify to anything other than coastal defences, views have differed. White has proposed that, in general terms, the whole system had been established by Carausius, albeit inheriting Reculver and Brancaster, and developed after his usurpation as a sort of widely-scattered line of defence against a Roman attempt, expected by Carausius, to recover the province. This is a thesis which has not met with general acceptance, for in this case, and apart from the manpower required for the full manning of these forts at a time when the army was fully committed elsewhere, it is difficult to accept that Carausius could really hope to oppose for long a landing in force once he had lost control of the sea approaches to Britain, which is precisely what happened after the fall of Boulogne in 293 with the consequent ability of Maximian to invade Britain across the Channel. More recently, Johnson has sought to interpret the Saxon Shore forts as a *Limes* analogous to the fortifications along the Rhine; his thesis is mainly based on apparent similarities between town walls in Gaul and forts on the Gallic side of the Channel on the one hand and the Saxon Shore forts on the other, though the sites in Gaul are not either as methodically excavated or as closely dated as the British forts. According to this newer interpretation, the Saxon Shore system would comprise both sides of the English Channel and the North Sea, and the function of the system, which could not prevent a piratical landing on the extended coast-line, would have been to recoil upon and seek to destroy the raiding force on its return journey through the Straits of Dover or across the North Sea.[47] However, what can be safely concluded on the whole vexed question of the Saxon Shore forts is that their immediate concern was the protection of the towns and the countryside, which can be legitimately inferred from the location of these forts mainly at or near river estuaries[48] offering a natural route inland to raiders. That, in most cases, the forts replaced fleet bases, as clearly shown by Dover and, possibly, Lympne, would have meant that the *Classis Britannica*, under unified command with the army, lost its identity. Furthermore, it is probable that naval detachments may have been incorporated in the garrisons of the forts, for some time at least, as the evidence from Pevensey shows. Moreover, the forts may not have been permanently occupied, either, but used as places of refuge in troubled times or manned by a local *militia*, as shown by the evidence for women and children and industry at Portchester. Professor Richmond long ago interpreted these forts as defended harbours and this role cannot be denied to the Saxon Shore forts.[49]

3

Communications and Urban Settlement

The road network of the canton (Fig. 7) was initially dictated by military needs and later by its geography and pattern of settlement. The Roman roads appear to have developed independently of the existing North Downs Trackway and any other Iron Age tracks, though there is evidence that they were in fact incorporated into the Roman road system. Basically, the new roads connected the Channel ports and the Wealden hinterland first with Canterbury and Rochester, ultimately with London, and attracted road-side settlements, such as Springhead and *Durolevum*. Roman roads are notoriously difficult to date by themselves, but what is known of the history of the canton and the development of its towns and other settlements points to the gradual extension of its road system.

The earliest road is clearly the highway, known as Watling Street, from the Channel to London and beyond; that this was the case soon after the invasion is underlined by the building of the Monument at Richborough. Watling Street is the longest route *(Iter II)* of the *Antonine Itinerary* and played a major role in the communicatins system of Roman Britain. According to Margary, Watling Street began at Dover; though this has the advantage of a shorter route from the Channel, it is unlikely to have happened before the second century when Dover replaced Richborough as the main port of entry into the province. Beginning at Richborough, the road reached Canterbury by easy stages and a slight deviation in the Ickham–Wingham area to avoid low-lying marshy ground; an existing Iron Age trackway, running through

Fig. 7. Romano-British settlement of the canton

Wingham, was incorporated into the line of the Roman road. Leaving Canterbury in the area of the later west gate of the town, Watling Street continued towards Rochester in a series of remarkably straight alignments, probably following the line of the army's advance. Reaching Rochester on the high ground and descending Chatham Hill, the road entered the town near its later east gate, and the present-day High Street follows approximately the course of the Roman road to the Medway. Originally, the road through Rochester was *c.* 2.8 m. wide; later, however, it was widened to *c.* 6.7 m. and had a dual carriageway, with a central drain, though the south-western carriageway seems to have soon gone out of use and only the north-eastern one, which was re-metalled several times, was used thoughout the Romano-British period. The site of the Roman bridge across the Medway is not exactly located, but it is likely to have been north of the medieval bridge, where evidence suggesting bridge-works was found in 1850, and approximately on the line of the bridge built in 1856. There is no evidence to show how the Roman bridge was constructed. On the Strood side of the river, Watling Street was carried across the low-lying ground on a causeway and followed the line of the High Street to the top of Strood Hill where begins a series of alignments bringing the road across the Darent and the Cray, towards London until positive traces of it are lost near Greenwich Park. A deviation through Deptford and New Cross would have been inevitable because of the bend in the Thames and this would have brought Watling Street to the Peckham area where it was joined by the London–Lewes road.[1]

Apart from Watling Street, there is also a network of roads, two of which appear in the *Antonine Itinerary*, the *Peutinger Table* and the *Ravenna Cosmography*. The road from Dover to Canterbury *(Iter III)* connected the port and town with the cantonal capital; except for deviations in the Dour valley, this road reached Canterbury by the most direct alignments. Similarly, the road from the Lympne site *(Iter IV)* reached Canterbury on an almost direct alignment across the high ground of the Downs. Though there is no direct dating evidence to indicate when these roads were built, they were both in use from the very beginning of the second century when naval presence is attested both at Dover and Lympne.

Dover was also directly connected with Richborough by a straight road to Woodnesborough and thence to Ash where it connected with the Richborough–Canterbury section of Watling Street. At Woodnesborough Church a short branch road points in a north-easterly direction towards Sandwich and suggests that a small port may have existed there.[2]

Communications between Canterbury and the north-east corner of the *civitas* were effected by a road leaving the town towards Sturry and traced to the old coast-line a little beyond Upstreet; a ferry across the estuary must clearly have existed in this area to connect with the Isle of Thanet. A short distance beyond Sturry another road branched off the Thanet road towards Reculver, which it reached on an almost straight alignment as far as Hillborough where it turned slightly to east to avoid marshland before reaching the fort. Margary argues that the Canterbury–Thanet road is earlier than the Reculver road, though this needs more direct evidence than the fact that their junction is 'sufficiently far beyond Sturry'. The early fort at Reculver would have had to be connected with the main road from Richborough to Canterbury and the road to Reculver was probably in being before a branch road towards the Isle of Thanet was constructed, for there is no evidence to show that there was an immediate military necessity in that area. It is probable that another road, shown on maps of the area about 1630, left the west gate of the Reculver fort along the coast towards Herne Bay, but this area has now been lost to coastal erosion.

Just as Canterbury was the nodal point for the communications in the eastern part of the canton, Rochester was the starting point of a main road, serving the eastern part of the Weald and the iron-working areas to the north of Hastings, from which branch off two other roads. Leaving Watling Street above Rochester, the Hastings road continued along Blue Bell Hill before descending to the Maidstone area and thence to Amber Green, a road junction, and Staplehurst, crossing a small stream on a ford of large stones at Iden Green. The southern part of the line of this road was of necessity less direct as it had to avoid the ridges and steep valleys of the Weald, but it has been traced to the crossing of

the Rother at Bodiam Station, where a small port serving the
Wealden iron-works has been suggested,[3] and as far south as
Westfield. Here a short length of road from the Brede estuary
joined the main road and continued it as far as the trackway
on the ridge at Ore above Hastings. There is no evidence at
present to indicate that the road continued beyond this point;
furthermore, it seems unnecessary for evidence of a settlement
at Hastings is also lacking. There is little doubt that the
purpose of the road south from Rochester was to link the town
with the iron-producing sites of the Weald, and the presence
of iron-slag metalling at various points along its southern
course amply demonstrates this function.

From the junction at Amber Green, another road was laid
on a direct alignment towards Lympne and reached the high
ground in the Aldington area; from there the alignment
became shorter because of the nature of the ground, and the
road reached West Hythe, the presumed site of *Portus Lemanis*.[4]
As it was clearly important to have a road-link between
Lympne and Dover, the road was continued towards Dover.
Though this coastal road is shown on the *Peutinger Table*, its
course is not certainly established, but it probably followed
the terraces towards Dover Hill, as shown by the distribution
of Romano-British finds along the coast.

Another branch road, which shows much evidence of
iron-slag metalling, left the Rochester road at Hemsted Park
in an easterly direction and skirted the estuary inland from
Tenterden, whence two short lengths of road branched off to
the shore, before it resumed a more north-easterly direction,
crossing the Rochester–Lympne road near Ashford and
proceeding to Godmersham Downs where it crossed the
Stour. From there, the road follows the line of a pre-existing
trackway from Wye over the Downs to Canterbury.

At the extreme western limit of the canton a main road
ensured communications between London and the south
coast. Branching off Watling Street in Peckham, its course
through the south-eastern London suburbs has been traced on
two direct alignments as far as the zig-zag descent of the
North Downs above Titsey and Crockham Hill near Eden-
bridge where it resumed its earlier alignment. There is a slight
change to southward in the area where the modern Groom-

bridge–Maresfield road now crosses the Roman road and a
further deviation to south-east at Duddeswell from which
point it continued on a direct alignment beyond the proposed
boundary of the *civitas* towards Lewes.[5]

Though the western part of the canton was served by only
two north–south roads (London–Lewes and Rochester–Hastings), the area contained between them was criss-crossed by
several minor roads or ways, which have been recorded
mainly by Margary.[6] The purpose of the majority of these
tracks was to afford communications from east to west across
the southern part of the Weald and its iron-working sites.
However, one of these ways continued in a northerly direction, virtually bisecting the area between the two north–south
roads, through the Tonbridge crossing of the Medway as far
as Ightham where it met the North Downs Trackway. One of
the two branches of this way may have continued beyond the
Iron Age trackway and reached Watling Street in the Springhead area, but direct evidence for this is so far lacking.

Urban Settlements

Following the Roman organisation of the province into administrative units based on either existing tribal areas or newly
formed groupings of smaller tribes, Canterbury *(Durovernum
Cantiacorum)* was promoted from a Belgic settlement to the
status of cantonal capital; this is made clear by the addition of
the name of the new tribal confederation to the name of the
town. Rochester *(Durobrivae)*, already an Iron Age centre
important enough to possess a mint (Fig. 2), was the other
main settlement of the canton. The reasons why Canterbury
was preferred to Rochester as the tribal capital can only be
conjectured as little is known of the Belgic occupation at either
town. A case for Canterbury's greater importance can be
made out on the grounds of its location nearer to the Channel
ports and trade routes. An area as large as that of the Cantiaci
may well have needed administrative sub-division into two
pagi in which case Rochester could obviously act as the
administrative centre for the area west of the Medway. It is
none-the-less true to add that, however logical and advantageous such sub-division may have been, there is no direct

evidence to confirm it. Both Canterbury and Rochester were defended by walls in the third century and appear in the *Ravenna Cosmography*, the *Peutinger Table* and the *Antonine Itinerary*.

Other minor settlements developed either at the Channel ports or alongside Watling Street. Dover *(Dubris)*, Lympne *(Portus Lemanis)* and Richborough *(Rutupiae)* are mentioned by the ancient authorities. Recent excavations at Dover are beginning to produce evidence for the civilian occupation alongside the military installations, though work at Lympne and Richborough has almost exclusively been concerned with the fortifications. A minor settlement *(Durolevum)*, perhaps a posting station, remains to be located in the Faversham–Sittingbourne area, and a road-side settlement developed at Springhead *(Vagniacae)* along Watling Street whilst another such settlement is mentioned at Crayford *(Noviomagus);* other minor civilian settlements have been postulated at Dartford, Maidstone and Hastings.

The Tribal Capital

Roman Canterbury *(Durovernum Cantiacorum)*, 'the walled town by the alder swamp'[7] (Fig. 8), a graphic description of conditions in its vicinity, is mentioned in the *Antonine Itinerary (Itinera II, III* and *IV)*, the *Peutinger Table*, the *Ravenna Cosmography* and Ptolemy's *Geography*. The Roman town was established in direct succession to the Belgic settlement; it lay at the nodal point of the east Kent road network and had direct access to the sea through the Stour estuary. Like most modern towns with a continuous sequence of occupation from Roman times, Canterbury's Roman deposits lie buried beneath those of succeeding periods and, consequently, its internal layout is only partially known. An earlier opportunity to secure evidence of the Roman town occurred in 1867–68 when the whole modern city was trenched to a depth of nearly 5 m. for the laying of a drainage system; however, excavations at bomb sites after the Second World War and recent work, still in progress, by the Canterbury Archaeological Trust, have significantly added to what is so far known of the Roman town.[8]

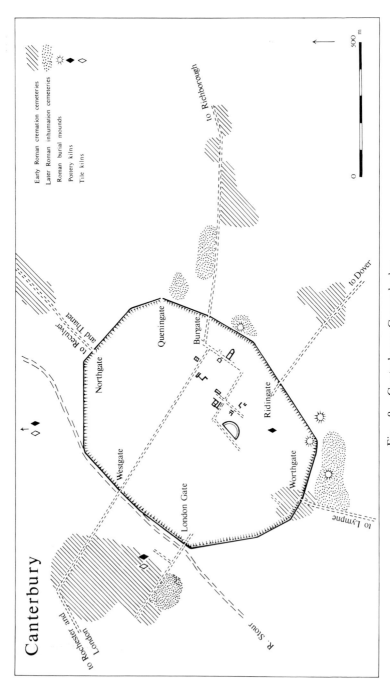

Canterbury

Early Roman cremation cemeteries

Later Roman inhumation cemeteries

Roman burial mounds

◆ Pottery kilns

◇ Tile kilns

to Rochester and London

R. Stour

London Gate

Westgate

Northgate

to Recuiver and Thanet

Queningate

Burgate

to Richborough

to Dover

Ridingate

Worthgate

to Lympne

500 m

Fig. 8. Canterbury: General plan

The early Roman occupation of the site suggests that, in common with other Romano-British towns developing from their pre-Roman settlements, Roman Canterbury was founded very soon after the landing in east Kent. The location of the site close to the Claudian base at Richborough, surrounded by intensively farmed land, already noted by Caesar in the preceding century, and the sprawling Belgic settlement would have attracted the Roman town-planner with its potential for methodical development. The pottery from post-war excavations shows a mixture of Belgic wares and early-Claudian vessels and clearly demonstrates that the site was being developed very soon after the Richborough landing with the removal of Belgic huts and the filling-in of their gullies and pits before the laying out of a grid of regular streets.

So far, there is little direct evidence of a military presence at Canterbury intervening between the Belgic settlement and the foundation of the Roman town, apart from a bronze fitting which was found in the filling of an early ditch and may belong to a legionary cuirass; this fitting by itself need not be more than a stray survival.[9] An early fort is probable, but conclusive evidence is mainly lacking. According to standard Roman military practice, a fort would have been essential either at Canterbury or downstream on the Stour in order to guard the crossing of the river and to police the important Belgic settlement until the *civitas* was established; but it is very doubtful that such a fort could also have served as a forward supply base after the main army had moved to the Medway. For, as the Roman advance beyond Canterbury is likely to have been rapid and virtually unimpeded by the retreating Britons, it is also probable that army supplies would have been ferried from Richborough to the Medway much more quickly by sea, through the Wantsum Channel and any of the numerous creeks of the Thames estuary, than overland from Canterbury and across terrain lacking any roads other than trackways and risking harassment by the enemy. On the other hand, there must be a reason to account for the reference by Ptolemy, writing about the middle of the second century but using Flavian material, to *Darouernon=Durovernum* (the *walled town*) when it is clearly established that Canterbury was not enclosed by a stone wall until the late third century. There is no secure evidence for an earth rampart preceding the wall or to suspect that Ptolemy was referring to such an earthwork rather than the stone wall; however, Canterbury in the first century could well have been surrounded in part by dykes as at Colchester, which may account for Ptolemy's reference.[10]

Following the decision to lay out a Roman town on the site of Belgic Canterbury, a gradual clearance of the Belgic dwellings must have begun. This demolition and preparation of the site for new structures clearly occupied several decades as shown by the Belgic hut in Whitehall Gardens, which is thought to have continued in use until about 60. Presumably, priority would have been given to the clearance of that part of Belgic Canterbury where it was intended to erect the public buildings of the Roman town, yet the site of the theatre remained still occupied till 60.[11] In any case, it is unlikely, even if physically possible, that the barely Romanised Britons abandoned their huts almost overnight and built new timber-framed houses, whatever official Roman policy decreed, whatever inducements may have been offered. Without the restrictions of a pre-Roman defensive perimeter and only considerations of town planning, such as the most advantageous siting of the public buildings and the street grid, to be taken into account, it would have made for efficient re-development to begin with the nucleus of the Roman town and allow for further expansion in later years. That this must have happened is clearly shown by the existence of at least one kiln and the Dane John burial mounds not far from the centre of the town as well as by whole areas where clearance had taken place without subsequent re-development – even so, clearly several years elapsed before even the central part of Canterbury was re-developed as the earliest public buildings are almost certainly of Flavian date. Thus, a picture emerges of new Roman structures erected in the midst of Belgic dwellings and co-existing with them for at least some time during the later first century.

One of the difficulties in considering the town plan of Roman Canterbury (Fig. 9) is that neither the location of its forum nor the layout of its streets and *insulae* is established beyond doubt. The forum is thought to lie under the area of the County Hotel, but its dimensions and date of construction

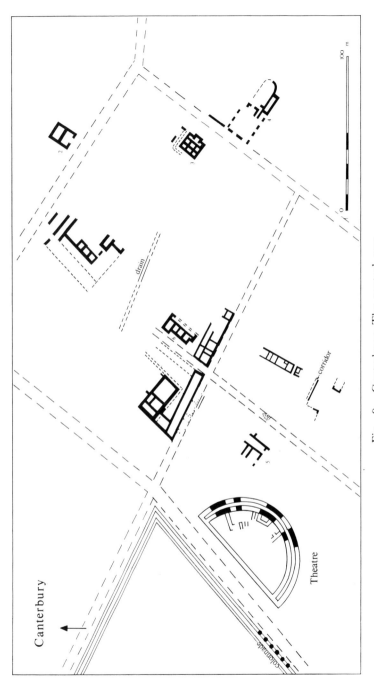

Fig. 9. Canterbury: The central area

are not known. Several streets have been sectioned and recorded, mostly in very restricted sites. The earliest of these streets lie generally over deposits containing Belgic and early-Claudian pottery, or Belgic ploughsoil, which makes it clear that a start in laying out the grid system had been made by the middle of the first century. Frere, on the basis of the limited areas available in his immediately post-war excavations, has attempted a tentative and partial reconstruction of the Roman streets in the central and eastern part of the Roman town and this has been followed by Wacher.[12] However, there is now evidence to show that most of this reconstruction is doubtful. Excavations in 1976–77 by the Canterbury Archaeological Trust have brought to light a wide Roman street aligned with the rear wall of the Roman theatre which is itself out of alignment with the streets thought by Frere to form its *insula*. A street is shown as passing between the presumed site of the forum and the theatre and directed towards the south (Worthgate) gate of the town and to north towards the probable site of the Roman north gate, though recent excavations have disproved its existence. Another street is shown as passing beneath St. Margaret's Street and Rose Lane beyond the public baths site, but excavations in 1967 at the south corner of Rose Lane and Gravel Walk showed that the Roman street ran along its postulated line. On the other hand, a wide street with central drain was found in 1979 further north-west at the Marlowe site between the public baths and the theatre.[13]

Although the known gates must date from the construction of the Roman wall in the late third century and the walled enclosure reduced the defended area by leaving out the area north of the Stour where there was much Belgic and early Roman occupation, the location of the gates must obviously have related to the roads constructed at least two hundred years earlier. It is logical to expect the methodical Roman town planners to ensure that the lay-out of a street grid system bore some relation to existing roads converging upon Canterbury; and, though it is not certainly known when the internal lay-out of the town was begun, it is fairly safe to assume that this did not happen before the construction of Roman Watling Street. The course of Watling Street as it approached Canterbury from the east is open to discussion. According to Wacher,[14] the road entered the town through the Queningate, presumably because part of the Roman arched opening can still be seen embedded in the medieval wall, and left Canterbury through the London Gate, another known Roman gateway; but, if so, Watling Street would have run an indirect course from one gate to the other, through the internal street grid. On the other hand, a more direct course would be for Watling Street to have entered the town through the Burgate and left it by the Westgate. This course means that the road descended the higher ground above Canterbury to the south of St. Martin's Church in an area occupied by both early and later cemeteries, which are normally to be expected alongside a main road close to a town. Entering through the Burgate, Watling Street would have only needed a slight deviation along a south-west to north-east street before joining another street beneath Butchery Lane and Iron Bar Lane which aimed directly at the Westgate. Wacher rejected the strong likelihood of a Roman predecessor to the Westgate because 'there seems no good reason to have an extra gate, in addition to the London Gate in this sector of the wall',[14] though he admitted the difficulty of the St. Dunstan's burials, 'as if a street ran out of the town in that direction,'[14] which is precisely what Watling Street must have done before turning on its westerly course beyond the cemeteries. Moreover, the very presence of the cemeteries at St. Dunstan's, which Wacher dismisses in that 'most of them predate the construction of defences',[14] is an argument in favour of Watling Street leaving Canterbury through a Roman gate at the Westgate. A late Saxon/Norman Church of Holy Cross is recorded on the Westgate before it was rebuilt in 1380, which strongly argues for its Roman origin.[15] Without such a Roman gate, there would be no gateway along the long sector of the defences from the London Gate to the site of the Northgate, which is very improbable. The Dover road entered Canterbury through the Ridingate and, with a slight deviation, its projected line would have reached the London Gate. A street is known leaving the London Gate to north-east of Rheims Way, but it is more likely that it was part of the street system beyond the Stour before the walled *enceinte* reduced the size of Canterbury.

Thus, it seems probable that there were in the town two axial streets, running approximately parallel to each other and linking, albeit with a slight kink, the Burgate with the Westgate and the Ridingate with the London Gate, respectively. It is also likely that another street connected the Burgate with the Ridingate; and that a fourth street slightly deviating from the Northgate, continued towards the centre of the town to pass to the rear of the theatre and reach the main street found in 1979 in the area of the public baths, which may have interrupted its course towards the Burgate–Westgate street.

The earliest buildings of the new Roman town were of timber construction. In all post-war excavation reports there is some evidence of construction trenches for sleeper beams, finds of the wattle-and-daub filling between the timber frames, pits, gullies and associated early pottery. However, in view of the demolition and reconstruction in the following years and the great restrictions of the excavated areas, little can be said of the plans and purpose of these early buildings; in any case, it is likely that some of these timber-framed houses must have existed alongside their more substantial stone-built neighbours.

The forum complex was naturally the most important public building; unfortunately, virtually nothing is so far known of this structure. Even its actual location has not yet been established beyond doubt, though it is probably not too far away from the centre of the medieval town. Most probably, the forum and *basilica* lie to west of High Street Parade beneath the area occupied in part by the County Hotel. Work in the cellars during alterations to the hotel has produced evidence for a layer of rammed gravel, which continued to west beyond Stour Street; this gravel could have been laid on the area of the forum's internal courtyard. In this general area under the High Street, finds of several architectural fragments testify to the demolition of an important building nearby. Also, under the former Fleur de Lys Hotel, parts of a large building have been found with obvious signs of importance indicated by the imported marble veneers used to decorate it and suggest that this opulent structure may have formed part of the forum complex, perhaps its *basilica*, or the north-west main frontage of the public baths. Wacher finds it difficult to accept this area as the likely site of the forum mainly because these fragments of buildings do not seem to relate 'to the known street plan'. If, however, Frere's tentative street plan needs modification in the light of current work, the forum site may in fact have lain further to east of its presumed location and astride the High Street. In this case, the forum complex would have faced on the street from the Burgate area, which aimed at the Westgate; the size of the *insulae* is not known, and there is no reason to anticipate a difficulty in that the forum site appears to occupy 'two adjoining insulae.'[16] The problem cannot, of course, be resolved until the opportunity arises for excavation in the relevant areas.

On the other hand, there is no doubt at all as to the location of Roman Canterbury's theatre at the intersection of St. Margaret's Street and Watling Street (Fig. 9). This is due to Frere's monumental achievement in archaeological detection and interpretation on the basis of a few fragments of walls and Pilbrow's account of his observations during the laying of the drainage system. As a result, two successive theatres have been established on the site, though their plans are different. The earlier theatre, probably constructed in Flavian times and 'not later than *c.* A.D. 80–90', was Romano-Celtic in type. Its seating consisted of a gravel bank retained by a curving outer wall, which measured 1.2 m. in thickness. If circular, the diameter of this wall (*c.* 100 m.) would seem too great; thus, it is more probable that the *cavea* wall had a radius different from that of the orchestra wall and that the Flavian theatre was elliptical in plan. One entrance was probably through a wall found under St. Margaret's Street, with the main *vomitaria* on either side of the stage. The later theatre is confidently dated to *c.* 210–20 and was a complete rebuilding with a more classical plan; this third-century theatre was semicircular, with a diameter of 71 m., and its two concentric walls (3.7 m. and 2.4 m. thick, respectively) enclosed an ambulatory.[17] The construction of the later theatre partly incorporated portions of its Flavian predecessor, but the structure of its stage is not yet known, though it could not have been very wide because of the Roman street, running parallel with Castle Street, recently found and upon which the theatre is clearly aligned.[18]

A large open courtyard was discovered in 1976 and 1978 north-west of the Roman theatre; it was surrounded by a colonnade at a higher level than the courtyard. The destruction deposits of this courtyard contained several thousand fragments of imported marble veneers, part of a bronze inscription and fragments of a very large Corinthian capital, possibly from a classical temple at the centre of the courtyard.[19]

Of the other public buildings, the first candidate is the baths found under the Marlowe car park (Building 1) (Figs. 10 and 11). This building had a large hypocausted room, measuring about 7 × 9 m., a cold room (about 4.6 × 6.1 m.), another heated room of unknown dimensions further to north and other rooms running under and alongside St. Margaret's Street. A substantial drain ran along the southern and eastern walls of the large hot room and carried water perhaps from another drain found at the junction of Rose Lane and St. George's Street. It is worth noting that the baths drain runs approximately on the same alignment as the street to the rear of the theatre as if to conform with a street plan. Even though this baths building is very partially known, the size of its recorded rooms alone and its location so centrally in the town strongly suggest its likely function as a public baths, with its main entrance perhaps in the White Horse Lane area, where a possible *laconicum* was found in the seventeenth century.[20]

The only other building (Building 2) for which a public function has so far been suggested was excavated in 1945 to south of Burgate Street and immediately north of the Roman street from the Burgate to the Westgate. Built in the late second century over a demolished earlier structure, this building occupied an area of 10.6 × 6.7 m.; its walls were very solid (between 0.8 and 0.9 m. thick) and formed clasping buttresses at the north-east and north-west corners. Internally, the building was laid with a substantial floor, surviving as a foundation material at the north-west corner, and divided by a slighter partition wall into two compartments of about the same size. The south wall, facing onto the Roman street only 6 m. away, was pierced by a doorway, and a short length of wall projected beyond the south-west corner, and this suggested a portico or walls flanking the entrance. Whatever

Fig. 10. Canterbury public baths (first phase)

its true function, this building seems too small, too substan-
tially built and too isolated to have been a shop or store-house
and, as Lewis has suggested,[21] may have been a small temple.

There are numerous references in recent excavation reports
to some of the private houses of Canterbury, which were
constructed both of masonry and timber and/or clay walls.
Masonry buildings would naturally survive longer and leave
more obvious signs of their existence than timber-framed
houses, though it is clear that both types co-existed. Some
stone-built houses can be shown to have superseded timber
buildings, but that does not necessarily mean that all timber-
framed houses were earlier. Of those that have so far been
recorded in detail, the most complete is the baths suite in St.

Fig. 11.　Canterbury public baths (second phase)

George's Street (Building 3) consisting of twelve rooms, two of which served as plunge-baths to adjacent hypocausted rooms, with cold rooms and a probable changing-room to the east; a drain flanked the baths along its north and west sides. Clearly, this bath building must have been a wing to a large house, and a wall, projecting to south, as well as part of the original construction, suggests that this house may have been in that direction and fronted onto a known street in this area. Near this bath-house to the east of the Roman street and close to St. George's Church parts of another house have been recorded, with one room having an apsidal end (Building 4). To south of Burgate and across the Roman street from the probable temple, there is a record of a timber-framed building, originally consisting of two separate units, built in the second century. Other partly known houses, nearer the centre of the town, have been found in the Rose Lane area to north and south of the Marlowe Theatre; one of these had a mosaic floor but their fragmentary plans preclude further comment. Another house has been recorded in the former Simon Langton School yard and, very recently, buildings have been traced north of Watling Street and a hypocausted building in Castle Street close to the theatre site (Building 5).

Fig. 12.   Canterbury: Mosaic panel from a private house

The largest house (Building 6) so far known was found under Butchery Lane and dates from the first century, with additions probably during the second century, which may have involved the construction of a baths wing; further additions took place towards the end of the third century, when tessellated floors with mosaic panels were laid (Fig. 12). The interesting feature of this house is again its alignment with the drainage of the presumed public baths, itself in apparent alignment with the Roman street to the rear of the theatre site, as if to emphasize the probability of a street between the public baths and the Butchery Lane house.[22]

Canterbury was apparently not defended before the late third century when its stone wall was constructed; thus, the Roman town, probably already smaller than the Belgic settlement, was further reduced in size to about 48 ha. (120 acres) as the area north of the Stour was excluded from the walled enclosure. It is strange indeed that the cantonal capital apparently remained undefended for so long when Rochester was already protected by an earth rampart in the late second century. The possibility must be examined that there also existed at Canterbury such an earthwork which has so far totally escaped detection. A possible clue to such an earth boundary or defensive perimeter may be the location of the cemeteries and a kiln in the southern part of the town, which would normally have been sited outside the town limits; both the kiln and the cemeteries are not later than the third century. Yet, whereas in the eastern part of the town the wall carefully excluded such cemeteries, to the south the kiln site, the Dane John burial mound and part of an early cemetery at the Worthgate were left out of the *enceinte*. This suggests that the town area was extended in this direction as if to compensate for the ground lost north of the Stour, and so enclosed an area easier to defend in the third century. Again, it is conjectural why Canterbury did not apparently possess a stone wall until about 275. If the citizens of Canterbury felt in earlier centuries too far away from the troubled North to seek to defend their town, clearly this did not apply to towns at least as remote as Exeter and Ilchester, to Rochester which had replaced its earth rampart by a stone wall some fifty years earlier than Canterbury, or Aldborough in the North which remained undefended. If civic pride was the motivation for wall building elsewhere, as probably expressed at Verulamium in the construction of monumental gateways before the building of the wall circuit, it is stranger still that it did not find such expression during, say, the Antonine period in a cantonal capital which, at least in the erection of its Flavian theatre, seems to have surpassed Agricola's celebrated injunction.[23]

The line of the Roman wall, enclosing an irregular octagonal area, was followed in the late fourteenth century by the reconstruction of the medieval city wall, which follows exactly the Roman perimeter. The evidence shows that, at that time, the Roman wall was either reconstructed or refaced with its medieval successor. A section at the south of the circuit has shown that the base of the Roman wall had been built on a plinth with two internal offsets. The wall itself was about 2.3 m. thick and constructed of whole coursed flints set in buff pebbly mortar, without any lacing courses of bonding-tiles. The height of the Roman wall is not known for certain; at St. Mary Northgate, there are indications to suggest that the wall was almost 9 m. high. Internally, the wall was supported by a clay bank, perhaps 7.6 m. wide, but the cutting of the medieval ditch has removed most of the evidence for the Roman ditches. Excavations to the west of the White Cross bastion have shown parts of a ditch, with a half width of about 9 m. and a depth of 5.5 m., though this may not be a section of the Roman ditch. There is some evidence for internal towers, too; one of these, near St. George's Street, was contemporary with the wall, square and measured 4.8 m. across. Likewise, there are indications of external bastions at the corners of the Roman wall, but most, if not all, of these bastions can be shown to be of medieval date.[24]

Four gates are so far known: the Ridingate at the end of the Dover road, the Worthgate at the end of the Lympne road, the London Gate facing across the Stour the undefended part of the town and Queningate; another gate would have been needed in the area of the medieval Northgate to serve the Reculver and Thanet road. Other gates would also have been required, as argued above, at or near the sites of the medieval Burgate and Westgate to carry the Richborough road through the town. All the known gates, except for the Ridingate, seem to have been single-arched openings through the curtain wall, quite utilitarian in aspect and unlike the elaborate gateways of

other Romano-British towns. The Worthgate was almost
cetainly flanked by internal towers and the Queningate
appears to have been of similar construction. The London
Gate, only a postern, was 2.4 m. wide, with walls to its rear
retaining the wall-bank and probably supporting a tower
above the gate. The Ridingate is at present the only known
gate that had a double portal and carriageways, which
suggests the volume of traffic on the Dover road, though it is
quite possible that the other gates (Burgate, Northgate and
Westgate) also had such double portals and carriageways.
The Ridingate was flanked by internal towers, about 6.1 m.
square, which contained guard-chambers.[25]

Canterbury was ringed with cemeteries; apart from the
burial mounds in the Dane John area and another one close to
the Burgate, early cremation and later inhumation cemeteries
are known astride most Roman roads leaving the town (Fig. 8).

Rochester

Rochester *(Durobrivae)* was the second largest town in the
civitas; its name, 'the walled town with bridges',[26] is certain, as
it appears in the *Antonine Itinerary, (Itinera II, III* and *IV)*, the
Peutinger Table and the *Ravenna Cosmography.* The reason why
Rochester was not chosen as the *civitas* capital can only be
conjectural. Whether a temporary fort of the invasion period
to guard the crossing of the Medway, which would not be at
all unexpected, ever existed in Rochester cannot be demonstrated as the most likely site is now occupied by the medieval
castle. Again, there is no evidence for pre-Roman bridges,
likely though they are, or defences in the town to account for
its name but, as Frere has pointed out,[27] this name may have
been transferred to the new Roman foundation from the
postulated fort. Watling Street passed through Rochester on
its way to cross the Medway, and it would be normal for a
settlement to develop alongside it as it did elsewhere, e.g. at
Dartford/Crayford, even if it did not have a Belgic predecessor.

It is presumed that Watling Street entered Rochester in the
area of its medieval east gate and then continued north-
westward towards the Medway bridge whose exact location is

not known, though it cannot have been too far away from the sites of its successors. The alignment of Watling Street through the town is likewise not exactly known, but it is likely to have been slightly further to north-west than the line of the present High Street. Excavations in 1961–62 at a site near the Old Corn Exchange have established that the road was *c*. 2.8 m. wide, with a single carriageway; in the late first century, however, it was widened to *c*. 6.7 m. and had two carriageways with a central gutter. It seems that, at a later date and after two re-surfacings, the south-western carriageway was abandoned and only the north-eastern one continued in prolonged use requiring a total of seven re-surfacings.[28]

The original Roman settlement alongside Watling Street is scarcely known. However, there is some evidence for timber buildings found during the 1961–62 excavations. This settlement cannot have been much smaller than the area enclosed later by the circuit of the stone wall; yet, its importance was underlined by the construction of an earlier earthwork round it. This consisted of a clay rampart which was virtually destroyed when the stone wall was built; the rampart has survived to heights from 1–1.9 m. and a width of 7.2 m. A ditch had been dug in front of this early defensive perimeter but, as the front of the rampart had been cut away by the construction of the stone wall, it proved impossible to establish the width of the berm. The ditch, however, has been estimated to have measured *c*. 5.2 m. wide and 2.5 m. deep, and traced to north-east for some 5.5 m., beyond the edge of the modern High Street, at which point it was proved to end. Assuming that this ditch continued uninterrupted below the modern roadway, its ending has been interpreted as an indication that the gateway into the defended perimeter may have been close by; on the other hand, the clay rampart continued uninterrupted beyond the end of the ditch. The later stone wall was found to be continuous at the point where the early ditch ended, which must inevitably mean that the gateway through the stone wall must have been on the same site as the medieval gate. This is almost certain but, in this case, the early ditch must have been interrupted, too, and dug again for a short length beyond the gate, probably for its protection. For there is neither reason nor necessity to suppose that an original gate through the clay rampart may have been superseded by a later one further to south-east when the stone wall replaced the clay rampart. Moreover, the line of Watling Street probably points to the area of the medieval east gate and, as the road antedates the earthwork, it follows that its alignment commanded the siting of the gateway at its presumed location, both through the clay rampart and the stone wall. To suppose otherwise would result in postulating a re-alignment of Watling Street from the third century onward, and all the evidence of several re-surfacings of the north-eastern carriageway is against such a hypothesis.

The clay rampart has been dated to *c.* 150–175 though a rather later date of *c.* 170–190 is more likely on the basis of the pottery stratified below the clay rampart, in the rampart itself and in the silt in the ditch.[29]

The stone wall enclosed a kite-shaped area of *c.* 9.5 ha. and was internally buttressed by a wall-bank. Built with a core of ragstone and flint rubble with some tile debris set in hard brown mortar, it had been faced externally with dressed, internally with undressed ragstone courses (Fig. 13) and survives at several places around its circuit. The maximum surviving height of this wall is 4.9 m.; it was 2.4 m. thick at foundation level and reduced, by successive offsets, to a thickness above ground of 1.5 m. No secure evidence has been found for any internal or angle towers. The wall circuit has been established along most of its perimeter, except for the section facing the Medway beyond Rochester Castle, but there is no direct evidence for any of its four gates, known from Saxon charters. Apart from the almost certain location of the east gate discussed above, the west gate must have faced the Roman bridge on the Medway, and two other gates have been postulated at right angles to Watling Street at or near the sites of the medieval Northgate and South Gate, but the slight evidence is inconclusive. Likewise, and in spite of its location, the size and form of the Roman east gate can only be conjectural, as it was totally removed by the construction of its medieval successor. However, the evidence of the 1961–62 excavations strongly suggests that a single-portal gateway, contemporary with the earthwork, must have been widened to a double-portal gate when Watling Street itself was widened

Fig. 13.   Rochester: The south-west angle of the Roman wall

to a double carriageway, only to be later reduced to a single
portal again by the blocking of the south-west portal when the
south-western carriageway ceased to be used.[30]

The date of this stone wall has not been securely established, though it must clearly fall well into the third century. If
the earthwork was not built much before 200, which is
indicated by the facts of its excavation, it follows that the stone
perimeter must be dated rather later than hitherto. The
dating of the Reculver fort, which has been considered as
supporting evidence for the fortification of Romano-British
towns under Caracalla, is not now thought to be quite so
early, and Frere's suggestion of 'a programme of wall-
building' under Alexander Severus or Gordian III at the
earliest would seem to fit the evidence from Rochester. If the
east gate through the clay rampart was of the double-portal
type, which is demanded by the double carriageway of
Watling Street, it would probably have been reduced to a
single portal when the stone wall replaced the earthwork later
in the third century at a time when concern was felt for the
security of the towns. It may well eventually be proved that
the Rochester stone wall was contemporary with the Canter-

bury wall, which would not be unexpected seeing that these were the only walled towns in the *civitas*.[31]

So far as the internal layout of Rochester is concerned, Wheeler's comment is still generally valid; for, in spite of several recent excavations, 'almost nothing has been discovered of the buildings' within the defended area, and Rochester still remains a sort of Romano-British ghost-town. The main reason for this is the siting of the cathedral and its precincts, the location of the medieval castle, the unbroken occupation of the town and the almost total lack of redevelopment in modern times; moreover, even when excavation on a fairly large area was possible, it was found that medieval and later works had almost entirely removed the Romano-British layers. Assuming that the four gates were at their presumed locations and the roads connecting them, the centre of Roman Rochester would have been close to the Old Corn Exchange. So far, no evidence has been secured for any of the public buildings to be expected in this area, except for a structure, probably a bath-house, partially recorded during the 1961–62 excavations and built, in part at least, over the disused south-western carriageway of Watling Street – whether this was the public baths, as seems likely, it is impossible to say. Other remnants of buildings have been imperfectly recorded, but neither planned nor accurately located, mainly to the north-west of the road likely to have connected the Roman north and south gates. Foundations were recorded in 1897 in the police station yard, but, as there is no plan of even the restricted area excavated, this building cannot be more precisely located. Other foundations have been found in front of the King's Head Hotel, close to the site of the 1961–62 excavations, behind Barclay's Bank in the High Street and close to the bridge. Likewise, other remains of foundations have been found during restoration work in the cathedral, suggesting a substantial, probably public, building of indeterminable function, and another wall was exposed south-west of the cathedral in Boley Hill Street. Very recently, another length of wall was recorded below the castle curtain wall and the associated evidence, which included numerous late fourth-century coins, suggested a probable market area. Nothing structural has been recorded in the area south-west of the cathedral and in the Deanery Gardens.[32]

Once again, virtually nothing is known of internal roads. The length of road recorded west of the probable site of the north gate may not be Roman. Elsewhere, a length of road, which may be Roman, has been found between College Green and Boley Hill Street, and only in the north-eastern section of the town where several straight lanes connect the High Street and the Common, there appears to have survived a reminiscence of internal Roman roads.

The cemeteries of Roman Rochester are also imperfectly known. A reputedly large cemetery has been known on Boley Hill, beyond the south-west wall, but dating evidence is not at all conclusive; another cemetery was found at Borstal, c. 1.6 km. south of Rochester, which appears to be later than the Boley Hill burial ground. The two cemeteries at Strood, on the Medway bank opposite Rochester, found during the nineteenth century may belong to the Roman town as there is no evidence for a settlement at Strood and, in view of the shortage of space nearer Rochester, it would not be surprising to have cemeteries located across the river.[33]

The importance of Belgic Rochester has been made clear by the discovery of coin moulds (Fig. 2), though the size and nature of the occupation is not known; there can be no doubt that as a Roman town, however overshadowed by Canterbury as the *civitas* capital, Rochester retained this importance, demonstrated by its defensive fortifications and occupation throughout the Roman period and beyond. But for the continuity of occupation since the fifth century, it is not improbable that much would have survived; that this evidence is not available is no proof that Rochester was not a thriving Romano-British town. Its role as the administrative centre for the western part of the *civitas* if, as seems likely, it were divided into two *pagi* for administrative convenience, cannot be demonstrated in the absence of direct evidence for public buildings and their function, but that it must have served as a civilian port is circumstantially clear. As such, Rochester would have been used as a transit harbour, clearly not for travel to and from Gaul, but at the head of the road from the industrial Weald and on the confluence of the Medway and Thames.[34]

Springhead

Springhead *(Vagniacae)* (Fig. 4), 13 km. west of Rochester, is a
typical case of Romano-British ribbon-development along
Watling Street. The settlement does not appear to have
developed into a regularly-planned small town with a grid of
streets dividing it into *insulae*. *Vagniacae* is mentioned in *Iter II*
of the *Antonine Itinerary* where its distance from Rochester is
given as 9 Roman miles; Crayford is next shown at a distance
of 18 Roman miles from *Vagniacae* which, as Rivet has recently
demonstrated,[35] must be due to a scribal error for 8 Roman
miles, the correct distance. Sporadic finds during the last
century, which included a milestone whose Romano-British
authenticity is not beyond doubt, and in the years before the
Second World War had clearly pointed to a settlement of
some sort at the point where Watling Street crosses the valley
of the Ebbsfleet, a small tributary of the Thames, and this was
confirmed by a series of excavations since 1950. Though
several excavation reports on individual features have already
been published, including a general plan of the area, the
piecemeal reporting of the excavation makes for several
difficulties in its interpretation and calls for re-assessment.
Moreover, a recent re-surveying of some of the excavated
features has resulted in a number of amendments to the
generalised plan of the area, where several features have been
shown without much supporting evidence.[36]

The earliest evidence of Roman occupation seems to be a
ditch at the eastern limit of the examined area and sectioned
on either side of Watling Street; this ditch was found to be
about 3 m. wide and 2.8 m. deep. The corner of the sectioned
lengths must lie beneath the modern road (A2), which made it
impossible to confirm whether it was rounded or rectangular.
This ditch has not been sectioned much further to the west
beyond the new carriageway (M2), nor in the area of Building
16 to justify the suggestion that it turned 'a right angle' at that
point and enclosed 'a square approximately 420 feet square'.
Likewise, there are no published sections to judge the nature
of the ditch from their outline, nor pottery or other published
finds to support that 'it is certainly of first century date and
may be early.' However, as Watling Street passed through the

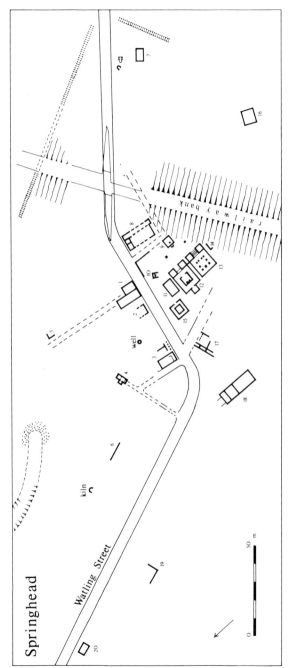

Fig. 14. Springhead: General plan

east corner of the enclosed area, it must be earlier than the road. It would be consistent with military practice for a small temporary fort to have been established here during the invasion period for the purpose of guarding the small creek to its north which may have been used for supplying the army at an early stage of the conquest. There is some inconclusive evidence for this suggestion, but to call it a 'Roman harbour'[37] is stretching the hypothesis. Apart from this possibility, considerable settlement has been proved in the area to north and south of the railway embankment. There is at that point a deviation in the course of Watling Street before it reverts to its former alignment further to west and most excavated features are concentrated on either side of this deviation.

Watling Street itself was partially sectioned at the eastern beginning of the deviation where it was found to have had several re-surfacings, and reported as being 7.6–8.2 m. wide at a point beyond the deviation, though the position of the section is not given.

North of Watling Street and facing the temple compound, evidence was found for at least five buildings. The eastern-most of these structures, Building 1, was built of flint walls fronting directly onto Watling Street and measured 16 × 11 m.; originally, it consisted of three rooms, with clay floors over an accumulation of earlier debris layers. The building dates from about the middle of the second century, as the clay floor in one room contained an illegible coin of Hadrian. Whatever the original function of this building, and the long room suggests a workshop with a probable dwelling-house attached, it underwent a reconstruction in the third century. There is some evidence for iron-working, but the insertion of a corn-drier suggests that the whole building may have been used for the drying and storage of grain. A curious feature in the long room, during its latter phases, is a tiled 'platform', with much evidence of burning, and a pit, lined with chalk at the bottom, which has been oddly interpreted as a *mausoleum* on the basis of a burial in it and another inhumation adjacent to the 'platform', just south of the pit. The area to the south of this platform contained red burnt clay which, though it does not quite reach the 'platform', must be associated with the burning of its tiles. It is not improbable that this may be a partly-demolished tiled partition, confining industrial activity to its south and causing the red burnt clay. According to the excavation report, a chalk road 'was built over the east side of the building' (actually about its middle) in the late fourth century when the structure was derelict and probably used for the deposition of the burials it contained. In the absence of more evidence, however, this carries little conviction, as this chalk could equally have been used as a sealing layer over the debris filling the rooms of Building 1 – furthermore, the excavation report does not produce the evidence for the projection of this 'road' towards Building 5 at such a late date.

Immediately to west and about 5 m. away was Building 2. Only a short length of a flint wall was found in trench-digging for a drain, and there is no published evidence for the plan of this building as previously shown. A coin hoard found outside the wall of this structure clearly indicates that the building, or its ruins, was still in existence during the last decade of the fourth century.

Building 3 was located at the corner junction of Watling Street and a minor roadway leading north, at about 20 m. west of Building 2. Little is known of this building, too, but its plan suggests a shop, fronting onto Watling Street, and a workshop, possibly with dwelling accommodation attached to it.

Building 4, to north of Building 3 and at the end of a path leading east from Watling Street, was a small bath-house; originally correctly identified by Penn as a bath-house, this description is not used in the later excavation report. However, it is a standard bath-house, consisting of a *caldarium*, *tepidarium* and *frigidarium/apodyterium*; a plunge-bath was later added to the *tepidarium*. The walls were of flint reinforced with bonding-tiles, and the report records that the 'floor was well made with concrete', and presumably had underfloors of *opus signinum*, which is fairly standard practice for a hypocaust; however, as the plan shows such a floor in the *frigidarium/ apodyterium* only, this is not quite certain. Clearly, a hypocaust was meant to heat this bath-house but, as neither traces of *pilae*[38] nor any fragments were recovered, it must follow that the building was either not completed or commissioned, which is further supported by the lack of any burning of its

walls and the absence of ash and soot in the debris filling it. It
certainly lacks a furnace-room, too, which would normally
have been sited outside the *caldarium*, though provision had
been made for at least a stoke-hole by leaving a tile-reinforced
flue through the external wall of this room. It is not reasonable
to suggest that this bath-house 'was in use for a time even
without heating'; that a plunge-bath was added to the *tepidarium* does not necessarily mean that a long period must have
elapsed since the original construction of the baths. Another
reason advanced for such a use is that a chalk path leads from
the baths to Watling Street and this is shown in the published
plan as starting from exactly where the stoke-hole should have
been built. Though it would have been very convenient to
have direct access for fuel from Watling Street to the baths,
Plate IV in the excavation report shows this area as a hollow,
presumably after the chalk had been stripped, and it seems at
least possible that a stoke-hole may have been at best all that
was intended for the heating of such a small bath-house. Built
about 150, this building was in ruins by 350 when a chalk floor
was laid over the debris filling its rooms, though again the
possibility must also be considered of whether this was a mere
sealing.

Building 6, some 30 m. north of the baths, lies buried
beneath the A2 and only about 6 m. of its south-west wall
were exposed in a trench on the verge of the modern road and
0.3 m. of an inner wall parallel to it, which gave a corridor,
about 3.6 m. wide and laid with a wooden floor. Little can be
said on such slender evidence of the nature of this building,
and an association with the bath-house has been suggested on
the basis of similar mortars used and some tessellation debris
in both Buildings 4 and 19.

Building 5 is represented by a wall-corner, some 50 m.
north of Building 1, for which no other published information
is available.

A well was excavated to the rear of Buildings 1, 2 and 3. It
was over 4 m. deep and lined with flint to a depth of 3.5 m.;
circular in shape, though wider towards the bottom than at
the lip, it became square at about 0.6 m. from the bottom and
timber-lined. This well was probably dug during the second
century and was still open in the fourth century as its filling

contained a coin of Allectus.

To the north of the site of Building 6, a small pottery kiln was found in 1922; though destroyed and unplanned, it is reported to have measured 1.2 m. in diameter and been lined with clay. No details of the pottery found in this kiln are recorded other than 'typical specimens . . .' and 'for the manufacture of "Upchurch" pottery', which presumably refers to black-burnished wares and should tentatively date this kiln to the second century.[39]

South of Watling Street were recorded three features. One of these, Building 7, has yet to be reported in detail, but was constructed of wattle and daub presumably on a timber frame, had a baked clay floor and was partly burnt down. Because of the large amount of samian ware found on its floor, it has been suggested that it may have been a pottery shop. This interpretation does not seem likely, for as a structure (c. 9 × 6 m.) it appears too small and insubstantial to allow for the storage, display and sale of pottery. Close to this building and to north-east two other structures have been reported as a corn-drier and an oven. As shown in the published plan, the so-called corn-drier has all the appearance of an incomplete small tilery (4.3 × 2.5 m.); a substantial flint surround enclosed two chambers and a long central flue, which had walls made of chalk. There was no stoke-hole, but the lumps of chalk shown at the mouth of the central flue could have been laid for the floor of such a stoke-hole before rendering it with mortar, which could equally well apply to the internal walls of this structure; the suggestion of poles and straw over the flue in order to support drying corn would be to invite a conflagration. There is little secure evidence to date the construction of this feature; the 'poppy-head' beaker, containing an intrusive cremation within one of the chambers, is of a type that survived quite late into the second century. This would agree with the samian sealed by the flint surround and indicate that the beaker is contemporary, not later as suggested in the report, with the building of this probable tilery in the latter part of the second century. It is not possible to suggest why this structure was neither used nor completed. The other structure described as an oven is even more problematical. Cut into the clay and lined with a thin skin of chalk, it looks like an elongated rubbish pit. It may have been intended for some other purpose in conjunction with the probable tilery nearby and used as a rubbish pit after the fire which clearly swept through this area – both the published sections show immediately below the topsoil a thick layer of burnt daub, clearly deriving from the burning of Building 7. It is not impossible that Building 7 may have been intended as a shed for tile-making, its tiles to be spread for drying in the open space between it and the probable tilery, and that the burning of this workshop brought about the abandonment and filling-in of the other two features. The layer with samian ware need not be other than a rubbish deposit already spread over this area at the time of the tile-kiln's construction and subsequently carried onto the floor of the destroyed Building 7.

Further to east, Building 8 has been only partly recorded; with overall dimensions of about 17 × 10 m., its plan suggests a shop fronting onto the main road, with workshop and living accommodation to the rear. Originally a timber-built construction dating to the late second century, it had been reconstructed after a fire early in the third century.

The area occupied by Building 8 is delimited by two roads at right angles to each other. To south is a road leading east from the entrance of the temple compound. This road could have joined Watling Street and afforded direct access from it to the temple compound by avoiding the deviation in Watling Street. On the other hand, it could have turned to north alongside Building 8, but there is no direct evidence either way. To west of Building 8 ran the road known in the Springhead reports as the *'Temenos Road East'*. This was a well-made road of flint and had been re-surfaced once. Its width for a branch road is surprising; originally, 8.2 m. wide, with a re-surfacing of 7.6 m.,[40] it was further reduced to just over 3 m. by the construction of the *temenos* wall which cut through the road surface, a width seemingly more appropriate to a branch road. Whether it continued, and how far, beyond the entrance of the temple compound in a southerly direction is not known because of the railway embankment.

West of Building 8 lay the temple compound. Springhead has long been claimed as the site of seven Romano-British temples. This is demonstrably not the case, as only three of the structures within the compound can be rightly described as temples where some form of communal worship could have taken place, and a fourth can be best considered as a small shrine. Another three structures within the compound are clearly associated with the two main temples, but that does not allow them to be called temples. Indeed, the term 'temple' has obviously been used for the sake of convenience; Penn himself says of 'Temple III' that it was a 'sacred pool', that 'Temple V is a small room' and describes the entrance to the compound as 'Temple VI/Gateway' with 'certain temple features.' Building 15, clearly a temple of Romano-Gaulish plan, was excavated since Penn put forward his suggestion of seven temples, others may still come to light, but, so far, Penn's theory cannot be supported by the facts of his own excavations.

The earliest religious building in the temple area (Temple I) was Building 15, which was demolished and superseded by later buildings. Though only its foundations mainly survived, the plan of Building 15 is that of a typical Romano-Gaulish temple, 8.3 × 8.9 m. in overall dimensions, and with a *cella* measuring 3.8 × 4.5 m.; 'it appears to be of late-first or early-second century date.' At about that time, the whole area was cleared not only of Building 15 but also of any other existing structures and laid with a chalk raft[11] (in some parts at least as this raft does not appear in all the published sections) and the temple compound built in stone.[12]

The temple compound was surrounded by a *temenos* wall which was robbed out in fairly recent times, though it survived as foundation material against the east side of the entrance where there should have been a gate. Nevertheless, it has been established that this wall had been built of flint to a maximum width of *c*. 0.6 m. and ran at least as far as the east corner of the entrance into the compound. The robber trench of the *temenos* wall has been traced up to and alongside Watling Street for some 9 m.; the western limit of the compound was probably enclosed by a *'Temenos Road West'* (Penn's road 4) at about 52 m. from its eastern corner. If so, the *temenos* wall would be expected to turn south in this area, but the only evidence so far known is for 'a well defined ditch

and bank.'[43] If the obvious symmetry of the architectural
arrangements within the temple compound were to be used as
a very tentative guide, its southern limit should lie to south
beyond Building 14 and entirely beneath the railway embankment.

The entrance into the temple compound was built about 21
m. from the east corner of the *temenos* wall. At this point, there
must have clearly centred a gate, but no traces of it survived at
all. The entrance was a building (Building 9), 6.7 m. square
externally, with walls of flint and 0.9 m. thick; however, as
only the chalk foundations of these walls remained, it is likely
that the walls of the entrance were slighter. The latest floor of
this building was surfaced with gravel above a foundation of
flint and blocks of chalk. Below this flooring are reported a
number of roads; yet, a study of the published section makes
this interpretation rather difficult to accept because the layers
described as roads appear to be a mixture of debris layers
beneath levelling deposits of gravel upon which had been laid
the earliest floor of the entrance.[44] Moreover, a section cut only
15.4 m. north of the entrance section shows a completely
different stratification. Internally, the walls of the entrance
had been rendered with painted wall-plaster, and at its centre
there was a tiled base, probably supporting an altar or statue.
Immediately west of this base, a trench, 0.6 m. deep and cut
through the flooring, has been interpreted as a 'votive pit'.
Apart from its appearance, the filling of rubble and in
particular the lack of any stratification in the 21 coins it
contained strongly suggest that this 'votive pit' may well be a
recent excavation trench. Furthermore, it is not plausible that
a devotee 'would have made an offering . . . into the votive pit,
before entering the temple area' for, in that case, it would be
perhaps more logical to have such a pit *in front* of the base, not
behind it. Two steps led from the entrance into the courtyard
in front of the temples, which was 0.9 m. lower than the floor
of the entrance. These steps were flanked by a column
pedestal and an altar base completely in symmetry facing the
two main temples.

Temple II (Building 12) had originally been constructed
following the typical Romano-Gaulish plan, except for a room
projecting at its rear, with an ambulatory round a central *cella*.

It is not reasonable to postulate that 'there may well have been wooden temples' before the construction of Temple II because some material was found ante-dating its construction; some post-holes at least should have survived and been recognized. Moreover, it is now known that Temple I had been demolished before the construction of Temple II. Temple II measured[45] externally 10.8 × 10.5 m. and the *cella* 5.7 m. square; the ambulatory was slightly narrower (2.1 m.) facing the entrance into the temple than round the *cella* (2.2 m.), and the room at the rear measured 3.2 m. square. A pebble path led to a step upon which had been laid a coarse geometric mosaic with *tesserae* cut from tiles, and immediately behind this step was a vestibule partitioned from the ambulatory by slight walls which did not survive. Another mosai had been laid on the vestibule's floor, but it has been almost completely removed, except for a few *tesserae* surviving near the step. The ambulatory, whose walls were faced with painted wall-plaster, had a standard tessellated floor. The projecting room, interpreted as 'the store or strong room' had 'no signs of a door into it.' However, the gap in the west wall of the temple is obviously the site of a doorway; if the door was of wood, which seems probable, it would not have survived. There is no evidence to show how this room was floored. Penn mentioned a destroyed mosaic in this room without giving the grounds for this assertion but, if it was a store-room, it is very unlikely that it would have had a mosaic floor. More probably, this room may have had a clay floor, perhaps with a mortar surface. The *opus signinum* bedding of the ambularory tessellation does not continue into this store-room, and it is extremely unlikely that both such a presumed mosaic and its *opus signinum* bedding would have been removed – this has certainly not occurred in the ambulatory. The *cella*, with walls internally faced with painted wall-plaster, also had a tessellated floor and a small mosaic panel, laid *c.* 0.6 m. from its entrance. This mosaic was similarly made of coarse *tesserae* cut from tiles with a simple diamond pattern of varying colours. An apsidal *suggestus* had been built against the western wall of the *cella*. Beneath this feature was a deposit of 'burnt earth, charcoal, etc.', interpreted as a hearth with ritual significance. It is difficult to understand this explanation and it may be wondered whether this layer of burnt material may be no more than evidence for the disposal of material during the construction of the temple, which had been conveniently and carefully swept under the *suggestus*. An uninscribed altar was found lying between the *cella* mosaic and the *suggestus* and, as it lay closest to the latter, it is almost certain that the altar must have stood in front of the *suggestus* but, as it was 'certainly not higher than the altar placed in front of it', it is clear that the altar was the focus of the cult and the *suggestus* served as a background to it. The roof of the temple was hung with standard tiles, but little other evidence survived to indicate the superstructure of this temple. It is clear, however, that the ambulatory must have been open and protected by a pent-house roof, supported by columns or beams on dwarf walls,[46] to allow for light to enter into the *cella* through clerestory windows. Though Penn rejected this even as a possibility, the existence of such clerestory windows is made abundantly clear by a *croisillon* from a window *grille*, found on the floor of the vestibule but not recognised as such. Two projecting wings were added to the original plan of the temple on either side of the pebble path.

The structural sequence of Temple II as reported by Penn calls for a detailed re-consideration, but it is demonstrable that the building was erected rather later than indicated, probably *c.* 120, if not later. It continued in use until the middle of the fourth century, when it appears to have been in a ruinous condition and given over, in part at least, to some sort of industrial activity, probably connected with iron-working. There is little secure evidence to point at the cult involved in this temple, though the finding of a bronze thumb in the debris filling one of the projecting wings, unless deriving from elsewhere, suggests a healing cult. Much has been made of a clay Venus-figurine, found on the *cella* floor, of a type common enough throughout the western Roman world in ordinary domestic contexts, and some seeds of *Atriplex patula* on the *cella* floor and presumed to have fallen out of 'a small incense cup'.[47] For all this, there is no certainty that Venus, or a like deity, was worshipped in this temple and the question must remain unresolved.

Building 11 was found north of Temple II at an average

distance of 0.9 m., as it is not quite aligned with the temple and had been erected on the chalk raft laid over the area of the temple compound; its external dimensions are given in the report as 8.8 × 5.9 m.[48] The walls of this building were 0.9 m. thick and built of flint. They are thought to have been lower on three sides and higher on the western side of the building because on this side alone there was much wall debris, though this is not conclusive as it assumes that no such debris, since dispersed, existed on the other three sides. Externally, Building 11 may have been faced with wall-plaster, but the small amount found need not have derived from its walls; no rendering of any sort has been reported internally. Instead, the report mentions 'the remains (in the north-western corner) of a four-inch thick layer of opus sig.' *(sic)*, without making it clear whether this 'layer' was present elsewhere within this building.[49] There were no internal structural features, and the whole area had been filled with light soil, clay and dark soil containing much pottery. This 'building was not strictly a temple since neither the priest nor the worshippers entered it' but, as it was within the temple compound and 'its exact purpose . . . unknown', it is 'conveniently called Temple III.' The excavator, having considered and dismissed the possibility that this was a priest's dwelling, sought to interpret this building as 'a sacred pool' into which pottery offerings were made. If this structure was indeed meant to contain water, for whatever purpose, it would be logical to expect it not only to possess walls of sufficient thickness to withstand the water's outward thrust, but also to be impervious internally; the walls are thick enough, but this is the only factor in favour of Penn's interpretation. If the *opus signinum* in the north-west corner is not a lump of debris, then it is surprising, in view of its well-known durability, that it did not survive anywhere else, either sealing the walls or as debris, if it had fallen off. The walls survived to a height of *c.* 0.8 m. above foundation level, so the question of robbing does not arise at all. Likewise, an *opus signinum* lining would be expected at the bottom of such a pool; instead, 'there was no floor of solid construction', only 'a spread of clay' later described as 'a clay floor lining . . . for retaining water'. However, the drawn section shows that this layer (Layer E) can hardly be described as a lining, for it is shown as lumpy patches of clay, hardly solid, even less impervious, over layers of light soil, flint and chalk (Layers D and C), scarcely suitable in themselves to retain water. Nor is it very probable that Layer F was a deposit of 'pottery offerings' (why were two decorated samian bowls found incomplete?); for, in this case, such pottery should have compacted into a more or less homogeneous deposit at the bottom of the pool, and not become interspersed in the dark brown soil making up this layer. It should have contained a greater number of complete vessels than the two found. Whatever the purpose of this building, and it is not impossible that it may have been intended to contain water, it does look unfinished which may explain the lack of internal features, such as doorways, to be eventually constructed at a level higher than that of the walls. If it was indeed unfinished, Building 11 may well have been used as a dump for soil and pottery from another part of the site, which could have been appropriately sealed and since ploughed out. Built c. 175, perhaps even in the early third century, this building was being filled in with material[50] containing some fourth-century sherds which, though dismissed out of hand, must mean that this deposit had been collected elsewhere and dumped at a time when the structures within the temple compound were no longer used for their original religious purpose.

Building 13 is the second of the two main temples, Temple III, and was built to south and c. 2 m. away from Temple II. Externally, the main part of Temple III measured 11 × 10.1 m., increased to 11.9 m. when the projecting wings were added. The outer walls of the ambulatory had been totally robbed, but they were probably of the same width (0.5 m.) and flint construction as those of the wings and faced with red painted wall-plaster. Because of the robbing, it is not certain that the wings were part of the original plan of the temple; it is more likely that, as for Temple II, they were additions but, in any case, they are thought to have been similarly ornamental. Access to the temple was by means of five steps built between the flanking wings. The ambulatory was wider on the east and west sides of the *cella* and narrower on the other two. At the junction of the ambulatory walls and its floor had been laid a 'concrete strip' (0.2 m. wide), interpreted as a seating for worshippers, a suggestion for which there is no evidence. Except for its width, no information is given in the report about the height of this 'bench', nor does it look anything other than a surround to the floor. A tessellated floor on a bedding of chalk had been laid on the ambulatory and, though mostly ploughed out, enough survived *in situ* to show that this tessellation had floored the *cella* as well. The area of the *cella* (13.2 × 15 m.) was enclosed by nine tiled column bases, which were substantial enough to bear the weight of columns supporting the roof, but nothing remained above floor level to indicate whether these columns were of stone or, more probably, tile.[51] Facing the entrance to the *cella*, two bases placed within the corner ones formed the doorway into it; a base at the centre of the western side has been considered as 'presumably serving as a cult statue base' because it was larger than the rest and evidence was lacking for an altar or statue within the *cella*. It is, however, difficult to see how this large base could have both supported the roof and something else. There were no traces of walls connecting the bases to enclose the *cella* area, and this has led to an interpretation of the architectural arrangements within this temple which, however plausible, carries little conviction. Even allowing for the absence of walls connecting the bases, there is no proof that the spaces between them may not instead have been filled with wattle-and-daub, built level with the inner faces of the bases, and the weight of the superstructure carried on the columns. This alternative suggestion, at least, accounts for the absence of masonry walls and eliminates the need to consider an 'open plan' and its complications for the ambulatory. If so, such slightly built walls would have been constructed on the tessellated floor and demolished in the wholesale dismantling of this temple. In addition, such an arrangement would allow for an enclosed *cella* surrounded by an ambulatory with the usual penthouse roof, supported by columns or beams on outer dwarf walls. A curtain wall, beyond the north corner of the main part of the temple, closed the gap between Temples III and II; as this curtain wall was integral with the building of the Temple II wings and abutted on to Temple III, it means that this temple had already been built by the time the wings were added to Temple II some time after 150. It is impossible to judge with much certainty the date of construction of Temple III, but it is not improbable that it is contemporary with Temple II.

South of Temple II and mostly under the railway embankment, parts of another structure, Building 14, were examined. This is 'a small room connected to a larger building',[52] with very slight walls of flint (0.5 m. wide) finished internally with painted wall-plaster. This building is reported as measuring 4.8 × 3.3 m., but this is not certain because of the restricted area examined. Clay filling within this building suggested a wooden floor and the coins stratified in it pointed to a fourth-century date. There is no justification, however, for the statement that this was 'yet another temple', and the conclusions drawn from the finds close to its west wall, particularly those based on the pottery, are not at all secure for all their plausibility. In the circumstances, it is impossible to interpret the purpose of this building, but a connection with Temple III is likely.

In the courtyard facing Temple III, a tiled base was found 'a few feet'[53] from the temple steps and 'a recessed stone altar base' adjacent to it. Its counterpart faced Temple II though, at c. 7 m., a little further away into the courtyard; it was 'solidly made' and, from a few fragments found, it is probable that it supported a free-standing column with a Corinthian capital.[54]

Building 10, in the eastern corner of the temple compound, was a small shrine measuring 4.2 × 2.8 m., its mostly robbed walls made mainly of chalk blocks with some flint. A cross-wall divided this shrine into a front room where a tiled base had been placed against the partition wall, and a narrow back room, both rooms being faced with painted wall-plaster. The shrine had been twice floored with rammed chalk, and a series of post-holes inside the front room and its robbed southern wall suggest a doorway at this point with a wooden screen across it. Though, clearly, the larger room contained the altar placed on the tiled base and would have served for cult purposes, the function of the smaller room is not known. Four burials of children under the floors of the shrine were thought to be 'sacrificial foundation deposits'. Built after 120, this shrine was still in use in the early fourth century; the cult may have been connected with fertility or healing, but this is not certain.

Other religious buildings may still await discovery within the temple compound, whose complete area is not yet known, but at present the temple area is striking for the symmetry of its internal arrangements, at least from the middle of the second century. The traveller or worshipper, on entering the compound through the entrance building on its higher level, would have been confronted first by two altars or columns, then two temples, almost identical in size and apprearance, flanked by ancillary buildings.

A crop-mark seen on an aerial photograph led Penn to postulate the existence of a road to west of the temple area, his *Temenos Road West*. Recent excavations have recovered traces of metalling in this area, but on a different alignment to Penn's road and at a sharp angle to the Watling Street frontage of the temple compound. If this road and the road to east of the entrance into the compound (Building 9) continued on their known alignments, they would intersect beyond the railway embankment and delimit a trangular area for the religious enclosure, unless another road lies beneath the railway embankment.

Building 16, a small rectangular structure with flint walls, has been located about 800 m. south-west of the temple area beyond the railway embankment; though 'almost completely ploughed away', it had 'substantial walls' within 'a large enclosure.' It may prove to be another temple, but only excavation can establish this and its implications for the whole of the Springhead religious site.

Fronting for some 10 m. on the road west of the temple compound, part of a structure (Building 17) was recently recorded. It consisted of a large room and other smaller ones, which may be additions, and had been built partly of timber on footings of dressed chalk blocks and/or flint, but insufficient is so far known of the plan of this building to suggest its probable function.

Building 18, excavated in 1951–52 at about 151 m. west of Temple I, was a buttressed building 'tentatively identified as a bakery.' Built upon an earlier chalk floor, this building

measured 22 × 7 m. and was subdivided into three compartments by cross-walls; its walls were 0.5 m. thick and had
internal offsets 'to support a wooden floor'. Externally, all
corners and the long walls had substantial buttresses, usually
associated with granaries. Two ovens were recorded inside the
two larger rooms, and the smaller, front room has been
interpreted as probably a shop where the bread baked in the
ovens would have been sold, hence the building's interpretation as a bakery. However, the plan of the building and its
suspended floor clearly indicate its role initially as a granary
until it became derelict at which time the wooden floor must
have collapsed and allowed for the insertion of the ovens
below offset level.[55] A re-examination of the finds suggests[56]
that this building was constructed during the first half of the
second century and became derelict some 75 years later.

Building 19, west of Watling Street after it had resumed its
previous northerly alignment, is represented only by a corner
containing a tessellated floor; it was destroyed, before recording, during road-making. Further north, Building 20, a 'presumed wooden building with chalk floor' observed during
trench-digging, has not yet been reported in any detail.

The main question still unresolved is why the Springhead
settlement was ever founded at the site. The temporal needs of
the traveller along Watling Street were clearly not the main
consideration as Springhead lies close to both Rochester and
Dartford/Crayford where the facilities usually associated with
posting stations must have existed. It would seem probable,
therefore, that the attraction of Springhead must have initially
been the springs close to which was built Temple I as a
roadside shrine, if there is no earlier temple still to be found. It
would further appear that, whatever was the cult practised, it
proved sufficiently popular to bring about the development of
the temple compound and the ribbon development around the
religious site.

Other Urban Settlements

Dover *(Dubris)* at the end of the *Antonine Itinerary*'s *Iter III* and
mentioned in the *Peutinger Table*, was probably Ptolemy's
Novus portus. It lies at the mouth of the Dour and, in Roman

times, the area would have afforded a natural anchorage at the shortest distance from the coast of Gaul and a safe harbour in the lagoon formed at the mouth of the Dour and protected on either side by high cliffs. The existence of a Roman settlement beneath the modern town had long been suspected and evidence for buildings and cemeteries was recorded before the last war. Post-war excavations in bombed sites in the town have added more information, and 'an inventory of discoveries' was published more recently by 'plotting the distribution of Roman finds'[57] before excavations in advance of road works brought to light the discoveries discussed in Chapter 2.

The Roman harbour at Dover was protected by two light-houses, one each on the Eastern and Western Heights, respectively. Of the western *pharos* (Bredenstone) only a fragment of masonry has survived but, as it contained re-used material, including stamped tiles of the *Classis Britannica*, it is of much later date than the light-house on the site of Dover Castle (Fig. 6). The eastern *pharos* now stands at a total height of 18.9 m., of which 3.1 m. are part of the original Roman structure, the rest being medieval additions; this light-house had 'a stepped or telescopic outline' and its total original height must have been about 24.4 m. Octagonal in plan and built with a rubble core set in stiff white mortar, the *pharos* was externally faced with sandstone and tufa, with lacing courses of bonding-tiles at regular intervals. Internally, it was provided with several stages floored with planking: the lowest of these, with a doorway through the south side, was at a height of 5.4 m., the other three recorded at heights from 2.3–2.4 m. Though no internal evidence was found to indicate the light-houses's date of construction, the absence of any re-used material in its fabric and 'grounds of general utility' indicate a date during the first century, which would be consistent with its counterpart *pharos* at Boulogne.[58]

Of the civilian settlement that grew alongside the Roman harbour, following the establishment of the naval fort and continuing beyond its abandonment, only remnants of the harbour mole, parts of buildings and the lines of the Dover–Richborough and Dover–Canterbury roads have been recorded. However, some of these buildings must have been fairly large and opulent as clearly shown by the recent discovery of a substantial hypocausted building internally faced with painted wall-plaster, some of which survived to a height of *c.* 1.8 m., and built about 200.[59] But, in the absence of published plans, little more can be said about the lay-out and probable size of the civilian settlement; nevertheless, it is undoubted that the decline of Richborough in Hadrian-Antonine times brought about the development of Dover as the main gateway to Roman Britain.

The status of urban settlement has been claimed for Maidstone and Hastings, but evidence does not support this suggestion for communal living at those two modern towns.

According to the Ordnance Survey *Map of Roman Britain* (1956), Maidstone is the site of a major settlement because of the presence of 'substantial buildings with stone foundations'. But this criterion alone is not incontrovertible evidence for the kind of communal living implied by a settlement of any size and, moreover, there are other concentrations of such buildings in the Medway valley for which the status of settlement cannot be claimed. However, two years after the publication of the Ordnance Survey map, Maidstone was reduced to 'a settlement of some kind'.[60] Even so, when the known evidence is examined in detail, not even that much can reasonably be claimed. Ignoring early attempts, to identify Maidstone with *Vagniacae,* the arguments for a Romano-British town at Maidstone are now worth only a curiosity value for their attempt to identify a Romano-British settlement on the basis that present-day Week Street is a corruption of Anglo-Saxon *wyke,* which is equated with Latin *vicus.* Canon Scott Robertson went even further[61] and argued that this postulated *vicus* would have been located on the north side of Maidstone, on both banks of the Medway, because of the presence of buildings at the Mount and Little Buckland, with another building a little farther north at Allington. The Rochester–Hastings road passes through the centre of modern Maidstone, yet none of the ribbon development associated, for instance with Watling Street at Springhead, has so far been recorded; nor is there any evidence for minor roads or tracks branching off the main highway, which would clearly hint at a roadside settlement of some sort. There are several burials, coins and various finds from a number of locations around Maidstone, but no more so

than anywhere else in the countryside. Certainly, no other
buildings are so far known, apart from those already mentioned, and it is well to the south of Maidstone, at Loose Road
and Combe Farm, that substantial Romano-British buildings
are again recorded. There is an analogous concentration of
buildings at Barming–Teston and Eccles which owes its
existence to the settlement of the countryside, not to communal living, and this is all that can reasonably be claimed for
Maidstone, too. In effect, nothing has changed in the fifty
years or so since Sir Mortimer Wheeler wrote that 'we must
remember throughout that, in speaking of 'Roman Maidstone', we are isolating somewhat arbitratily a unit which in
Roman times may have had no real corporate entity' and that
'Maidstone has no more than a slight claim to distinction as a
spot of exceptional convenience where this riverside population may have been a little more numerous than elsewhere.'[62]
Even this 'slight claim' can now be disputed as the population
in the Eccles area is likely to have been even larger.

The case for a settlement at Hastings rests on probability
rather than direct evidence as the logical terminus of the road
from Rochester to the iron-producing sites of the Weald. Rivet
has postulated an iron port at Hastings;[63] however, it is
difficult to accept that a permanent port, with its ancillary
installations and some sort of civilian settlement, could have
both existed in the area of the modern town and escaped
detection so far. For, even when allowance is made for coastal
changes owing to sea-erosion, there is a total lack of structural
remains, and only two small coin hoards, totalling fewer than
100 coins, are recorded from the area. Moreover, the total of
chance coin finds, scattered all over the Hastings district, is a
mere 26, ranging from Augustus to Theodosius, hardly the
number of coins to be reasonably expected from the area of a
harbour serving the Wealden iron industry over a prolonged
period of time. The Rochester road has been traced to
Westfield, its junction with a short length of another road
from the Brede estuary, which is known as far as Ore, above
Hastings. At that point, a ridgeway track continued to east in
the direction of the estuarine inlets, and it is more likely, in the
absence of any direct evidence for a settlement at Hastings,
that small harbours to the east of the modern town were used

for the maritime transport of the iron products whilst the Rochester road provided overland communications north-ward with the Wealden iron industry.

At Dartford there is some direct evidence to justify the existence claimed for 'a small Roman settlement in the vicinity of Watling Street'; for, apart from a tessellated pavement found in Lowfield Street, foundations of a building have also been recorded in the High Street and parts of another substantial building elsewhere in the town have been found during the last century. More recently, Romano-British pottery has been recovered from various sites as well as evidence for pits, ditches, timber buildings, part of another building near Central Park and other foundations spanning the entire Romano-British period. Two Romano-British cemeteries are also known in the general area of Dartford, at Joyce Green and East Hill.[64] Though this evidence is sketchy and much of it awaits full publication, it nevertheless points to a settlement at or close to the crossing of the Darent, and it is not improbable that it developed near the spot where Watling Street crossed the river.

Crayford *(Noviomagus)*, the last station on Watling Street before London, is attested by both the *Antonine Itinerary (Iter II)* and the *Peutinger Table,* and the evidence, however circumstan-tial, points conclusively to Crayford where the Britons fought against Hengist and Aesc. It is a natural enough site at the crossing of the Cray and its Roman name (=Newfield)[65] suggests a new settlement. However, except for several burials found on both sides of Watling Street in the general area of modern Crayford and some building debris, there are so far only two imperfect records of probable buildings, and it is likely that more substantial evidence for the settlement has been lost to modern development in the area.[66]

Durolevum, very probably a road-side settlement along Watl-ing Street, has so far escaped archaeological detection. Lo-cated in both the *Antonine Itinerary (Iter II)* and the *Peutinger Table* at 12 Roman miles from Canterbury,[67] it must lie somewhere between Faversham and Sittingbourne. For in this area, Watling Street crossed lower lying ground at the head of Milton Creek, an ideal situation for a settlement as in the case of Springhead and Dartford/Crayford. In fact, apart from several cemeteries in the Sittingbourne area and the Ospringe cemetery, near Faversham, structural evidence is virtually non-existent, and it is not improbable that the settlement consisted mainly of insubstantial timber buildings and huts, which have hitherto remained undiscovered. Traces of a masonry building were reputedly found in 1872 in the Milton churchyard and again in 1881, but these reports are inconclusive. At Radcliffe, about 2 km. east of Sittingbourne, there are again references to traces of Roman buildings and recently parts of a probable ditched enclosure have been excavated.[68] Clearly, Watling Street attracted much settlement in this area. The *duro-* element in the settlement's name suggests that it may have originally belonged to an early fort, which may have been sited on Milton Creek in order to protect the army's supply route by sea from Richborough before the battle of the Medway; if so, the site of *Durolevum* ought to be very close to Sittingbourne. On the other hand, the concentration of occupation material and the cemetery in the area of Ospringe suggest some sort of a settlement there, too, whose name may not have survived.

Other sites can lay claim to be minor settlements, but the evidence is, so far, inconclusive. Occupation has been recorded at Fordwich and Sturry, both sites probably serving Canterbury as ports. Likewise, harbour installations may have existed at the head of an inlet at Bodiam, and recent excavations at the centre of Gravesend have brought to light evidence for occupation within reach of the Thames and a road, which probably connected the site with Springhead.[69]

4

Rural Settlement

The rural settlement of the *civitas* (Fig. 7) during the Romano-British period developed from the pattern obtaining in the pre-Roman Iron Age. Towns developed from existing Belgic settlements or were newly founded in response to local needs and, in similar fashion, Iron Age farmsteads evolved into Romano-British farms, while others may witness to investment in the countryside by town-dwellers. This process of rural development was clearly very gradual. In some cases, Iron Age farmsteads would have sufficiently prospered to become farms boasting a stone-built cottage or even grow into a villa-estate, but this was exceptional; most farmsteads could not have progressed much beyond their Iron Age condition and the only visible sign of Romanisation was an increase in their material comforts.

For not every farmer could have had the means, even if he had the ambition, to move out of his round hut into a new rectangular house whatever his near neighbours could have afforded to do. The farmer's innate conservatism is more likely to have led him first to improve his farming methods and implements, then his home; and, if he could not afford a new house, he could at least compromise by introducing into his post-Belgic hut such luxuries as painted wall-plaster, glazed windows and hinged doors as well as better pottery.[1] Thus, it is not unlikely that refurbished huts were in the majority and continued throughout the Romano-British period to exist alongside the houses of the wealthier farmers and the absentee landlords.

The main settlement was concentrated in the river valleys

and the coastal belt of the Thames estuary and the English Channel, where lighter soils allowed for expanded agricultural development, and close to the network of roads built after the conquest. The central land mass of the Weald and its dense forest cover were largely unexploited, except for the extraction of minerals and supplies of timber. The distribution of the farms clearly underlines the importance of the towns as markets for the produce of the countryside and the close relationship between town and country. The farms of the Cray and the Darent valleys would depend on the civilian settlements in the Crayford/Dartford area; Rochester and its port facilities undoubtedly spurred on the settlement of the Medway valley. The same view can now be put forward with regard to the Stour valley, where the comparatively smaller number of buildings has been thought to indicate farming by the citizens of Canterbury. Although this must have happened, strange though it may seem in view of the buildings clustering close to towns elsewhere in Roman Britain, it certainly cannot be the only explanation. It has been suggested[2] that lack of archaeological excavation in the Stour valley may also explain this less dense distribution, and the recent examination of buildings at Charing and Wye and elsewhere where building debris indicates others,[3] has clearly justified it.

Four classes of settlements can be discerned in the countryside:

  (i)   farmsteads, usually with round huts and ditched enclosures;
  (ii) farms with timber-framed cottages built on stone foundations;
  (iii) the estates of the wealthy, usually referred to as villas; and
  (iv) the so-called isolated bath-houses.

(i) *Farmsteads*

Romano-British farmsteads, exploited by small farmers probably as tenants, were in the majority. The sites of such agricultural settlements abound in the *civitas* and occupy a broad band along its northern part from Greenwich and Charlton to Cliftonville and Broadstairs. That many more other farmsteads must have existed is abundantly indicated by the very large number of seemingly isolated burials. However, the very soils upon which such farmsteads depended have attracted much deep ploughing and development in recent centuries resulting in the virtual obliteration of most of the evidence. The huts used for dwellings, the fields under cultivation and the enclosures for stock animals have survived only in part. All that is usually recovered is a few, short lengths of ditch or shallow drip-gully and rubbish-pits, which is sufficient to indicate the site of a possible farmstead but precious little else. Though pottery and other associated finds normally suggest a dating for the occupation of such a site, there is seldom any other evidence from which to draw secure conclusions on the area of the farmstead, the type of agriculture and animal breeding that supported it or the number of people living on its land. Most conclusions often drawn, especially concerning population,[4] can at best be only generalisations or guesswork.

In spite of the incomplete material from any of these farmstead sites a generalised, composite picture can nevertheless be drawn by taking the evidence from several of them. The farmsteads were enclosed either by circular[5] or rectilinear ditches,[6] usually flat-bottomed or with a V-profile. Within these enclosures would be situated the dwelling hut, which was normally rounded[7] and presumably not different in construction from Iron Age round huts. Occasionally, a hut built late in the Romano-British period may be rectangular and with its timbers laid in deeper trenches and nailed together as at Addington. Other features are the ubiquitous rubbish-pits, hearths and ovens, as at Greenhithe. Rare suggestions of possible field boundaries have been recorded at Highstead.[8]

The Charlton site may be in a class of its own as the area it covers (c. 7 ha.) and the number of huts enclosed by one or two banks and ditches indicate a nucleated settlement approximating that of a later village.

In general, the picture that emerges is of a large number of small-holdings existing alongside the more prosperous farms in succession to the pre-Roman farmstead and continuing throughout the Romano-British period.

(ii)   *Farms*

At a social level above the farmsteads, if only because of their masonry and timber buildings, were the farms. Their sites cluster generally in river valleys and the lower slopes of the Downs and their distribution suggests a preference for the eastern part of the *civitas*, though the comparatively greater development west of the Medway may partly account for this pattern. The distinguishing feature of farms vis-à-vis the more modest farmsteads is the dwelling-house which was built on stone foundations, with elevations very probably carried on in timber-framed wattle-and-daub construction. These farms lack, in general, the combination of size and such amenities as baths and/or hypocausted rooms with tessellations or mosaic pavements, which would justify their inclusion among villa-estates. Naturally, there is much variation in the features exhibited by these farm-houses, depending on the prosperity of their owners. The whole range is typified by the houses at Burham, Cobham Park, Charing and Sandwich, which illustrate the dwelling-houses on farms that did not evolve into villa-estates.

Considerable occupation has been recorded in the Cray valley, no doubt depending upon the settlement at Crayford, but the extensive development of the area in the last two centuries has brought about the destruction of sites and only a few remnants survive such as the sites indicated at St. Paul's Cray and at St. Mary Cray.[9] The most substantial building in the area was at Orpington Station; it was virtually completely destroyed during construction work. What survived suggested a second-century corridor house covering an area of *c.* 30.5 m. × *c.* 15.2 m., with substantial walls and hypocausted rooms, some of which had been laid with tessellations. Occupation of the site appears to have begun in pre-Roman times and, to judge from coin evidence, continued into the late Romano-British period.[10] Further inland and to west a building was found under the church and yard at Hayes, but little more is known of this house apart from an *opus signinum* floor.[11]

Further to east the flood-plain of the Darent and the gentle slopes of the valley it cut through the Downs attracted considerable development. Undoubtedly, the urban settlements at Dartford and Crayford acted as outlets for the produce of the farming communites in the area. Apart from the villa-estates at Dareth, Farningham and Lullingstone, several other farms are known in the Darent valley.[12] South of Dartford, foundations were recorded in 1889 at Wilmington. Exploratory work in 1975 brought to light parts of a building with walls of flint and mortar covering an area of c. 15.25 × 21.35 m. Three bases of mortared tiles close to the south wall suggest that this structure may have been internally divided into two aisles and a central nave, the former probably further sub-divided into smaller compartments by timber partitions. Remnants of a channelled hypocaust, which appears unused as it lacks signs of burning, were also found outside the west wall of this building. The plan of the building as so far known, indicates a barn adjacent to a dwelling-house, probably lying under the unexplored area; this likelihood is further supported by fragments of painted wall-plaster found close to the hypocaust. Pottery and other finds indicate a third-century date for this farm. A substantial granary was recorded in 1972 at Horton Kirby close to the west bank of the river. This building of flint walls was longer than 18.3 × 30.5 m. and divided by dwarf walls into three parts, a central area and two aisles, some of which had been laid with clay floors or tessellations. More tessellation, associated with flint masonry to south-east of this large barn points to a house of unknown dimensions in the vicinity. The pottery evidence suggests a date for this granary in the second and third centuries.[13]

In the Darent valley itself, several buildings have been recorded on both banks of the river concentrated on Farningham, apart from the large houses (Farningham I and II, Fig. 15) to north and south of the village. There is a record of foundations at Farningham Wood and at The Folly where parts of a building were examined c. 92 m. east-south-east of Farningham I. A corridor building was located on this site, with walls of flint and tile, and the parts examined were c. 36 m. long and 11.6 m. wide; nothing more is known of the rest of this house or its initial foundation. However, at a date during the fourth century, as suggested by the few coins found, this part of the building was converted into a baths wing by the insertion of hypocausts and a plunge-bath. Materials from other parts of the house, probably partly demolished by the time of this reconstruction, were used in this conversion and included part of the base of a pillar shaft in oolitic limestone; this by itself indicates that the original building must have been of some substance.

A building (Farningham II) was recently excavated at Franks Hall, Farningham, on the west bank of the Darent (Fig. 15); its site lies on a bend of the river and a large portion of the house had been destroyed by river erosion before its excavation. Belgic pottery and *potin* coins found in gulleys on the site suggest a pre-Roman occupation. The original house, built about 100, was constructed of mortared flint and appears to have consisted of a large central room and a smaller one to its west. It proved impossible to determine because of river destruction whether a similar room flanked the central room to its east. A small projecting room beyond the south corner of the house and a fronting corridor were added about 170–200; it is probable that such a projecting room existed at the other end of this corridor beyond the lost east corner of the building. Finally, during the first half of the fourth century, a range of rooms was added to the rear of the house, and the western-most of these rooms contained a channelled hypocaust. In its final reconstruction this farm-house measured probably 30 × 19.5 m., including the projecting room(s). Pottery and coins indicate continuous occupation from the second to the fifth century when the farm was abandoned and the house gradually destroyed. Another farm building was partially examined recently close to the river ford at Eynsford. So far as could be ascertained from builders' trenches, this was a small house, measuring 8.2 × 18.6 m., with flint and mortar foundations; it was probably built late in the Roman period. Flint and chalk foundations as well as hypocaust and tessellation debris on the river bank at Shoreham indicate another building there, which may have been *c.* 36.6 m. long.[14]

Further inland, the existence of a number of farms is clearly indicated by much occupation debris in the Otford area. A building was explored in 1927–28 close to the railway station. Of the dwelling-house only parts of a corridor were recorded, though evidence was also found for the walls of other rooms adjoining this corridor. This house must have been fairly

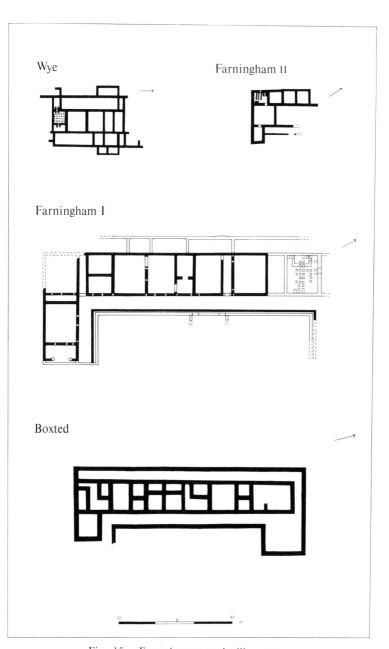

Wye

Farningham II

Farningham I

Boxted

0   5   10 m

Fig. 15. Farm-houses and villa-estates

opulent as suggested by much tessellation and wall-plaster debris; fragments of the latter were reconstructed to show parts of two male figures and an inscription reading BINA MANV, a reference to the Aeneid. To north-east of this corridor there was a rectangular structure, measuring 12.2 × 19.5 m., floored in part at least with flints and built over what appear to be the post-holes of an earlier round hut. This building was interpreted as a courtyard, though it is more likely that it was a barn. Outside the east wall was found a small kiln assumed to have been used for the firing of pottery. However, as apparently only one 'waster' was found in the pottery associated with it and, more important, the surviving floor was not pierced by vents, it is more likely that this kiln was intended for the drying of corn. A re-examination of the published evidence suggests first occupation about 100, perhaps a little earlier, and that the house succeeded an earlier round hut. According to the excavation report, the house 'was burnt down and never rebuilt' about 200 whereas the barn continued in use until 300. It is not clear what evidence led the excavator to this conclusion which is difficult to accept in view of the pottery evidence most of which belongs to the third and fourth centuries. For, even if the barn 'was still used as a refuge for cattle', the coins and pottery clearly show continued occupation. To west of this site, considerable quantities of building debris and pottery suggest further farms in the Twitton and Otford areas.[15]

Other farms existed on the higher ground between the Darent and the Medway valleys. A fairly substantial house was discoverd in 1914 in the parish of Ash. The structure (Fig. 16) consisted of a rectangular walled enclosure, measuring c. 30.5 × 15.2 m., with an entrance through its east wall; facing this entrance was a series of rooms and a small baths wing appears to have occupied the building's south side. Recent re-examination of the site has accurately established the dimensions of the walled enclosure and uncovered a small kiln, probably used for corn-drying. The major part of the structure may have been an open courtyard or an aisled house with rows of timber-posts supporting a roof over the courtyard. However, recent excavations showed that most of the building found in 1914 had been completely demolished soon-

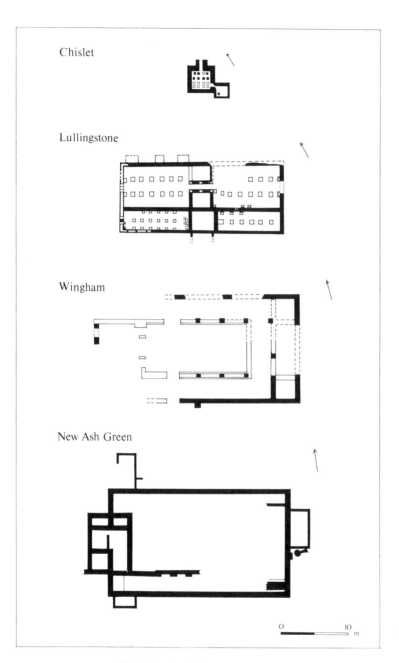

Fig. 16. Agricultural buildings

after its examination and only some slight indications survived for an internal lean-to roof and for timber outbuildings. Dating evidence is very scanty, but the pottery found suggests occupation from *c*. 150–250. Another building is marked on the O.S. map at Betsham, but recent trial-trenching has shown that this is more likely an industrial site. A building may also have existed at Ightham where foundations and occupation material were recorded in the early nineteenth century.[16]

To the north of the Downs and the lower ground to the Thames foreshore there is evidence for farms close to the Springhead site, but the buildings are either imperfectly known or destroyed. A farm was clearly located immediately north of Watling Street in the Stone Castle Quarry area to judge by rubbish-pits containing domestic refuse and much building debris, and a building probably existed here from 100 onward.

Further north another farm may have existed at Stone,[17] and a farm-house was found further to east in the grounds of Cobham Park and 91.5 m. south of Watling Street. The house (Fig. 17) which had foundations of mortared flint supporting a probable timber-framed construction, consisted of a series of five rooms behind a fronting corridor; the original building measured overall 9.1 × 29.3 m. During the late second century the north-easternmost room was reconstructed and probably converted into a small baths suite. Three more insubstantially built rooms, probably timber sheds on rubble foundations, were also added at the south-western end of the building. An outbuilding, probably a barn, with overall dimensions of 5.9 × 13.7 m., stood *c*. 18 m. further south-east. Pottery found in layers below the floor level of the house indicates occupation of the site during the last quarter of the first century. The house was very probably built during the second century and continued in use until at least *c*. 350 as suggested by stratified coins and a hoard of 836 coins found *c*. 107 m. further west.[18]

The Medway valley was extensively settled by farms and villa-estates from north of Rochester into the fringes of the Weald; the gently undulating ground of the valley floor and the slopes above it supported much agriculture and animal

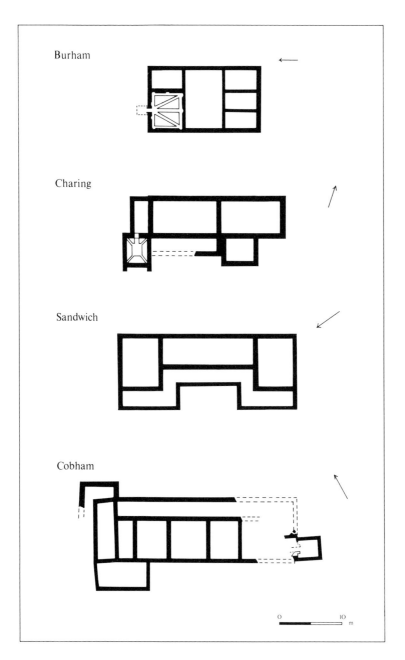

Fig. 17. Farm-houses

husbandry. Unfortunately, hardly any traces of field systems have survived. On the north bank of the Medway and close to Rochester, a building was located at Frindsbury where much occupation debris, including fragments of flooring and tessellation, over an area of 4.6 × 15.2 m., indicates a house of some size. Fragments of sculptured and inscribed stones, one of which bears a partial reference probably to Aesculapius, and a lead coffin underline the importance of this house, probably occupied from the second century onward, but nothing is known of its plan. Another building may have been sited further upstream at Cuxton where there is Roman building material and burials. On the other hand, the location of the site on a steep slope above the river may indicate a mausoleum. At Allington, building debris may point to another farm-house. Foundations of what is described as 'an apparently extensive Roman Villa' were observed at Little Buckland Farm about 412 m. west of the river, but this site has since been destroyed and must remain unconfirmed. At East Malling, recent work in the churchyard located the external north wall of a building and its fronting verandah, and a small outbuilding. Following on the Belgic occupation on the site, the house was built in the late first century and occupied well into the fourth. Further south two farms were located, within 804 m. of each other, at East Barming, but little is known of their plans. One of these buildings had a number of small rooms; the coins found would give it an occupation from the middle of the second century to the fourth. The second building is said to have been very substantial but, apart from two walls traced for a short distance and a deep tiled floor, which may have originally served a water-tank, nothing more is known of this structure.[19]

On the east bank of the Medway, two buildings were located in the Chatham area, though little is known of their plans. During the construction in 1779 of the Amherst Redoubt parts of a building were found, but only a small room projecting from a range of larger rooms, was planned. The occupation debris indicates a date from the second century onward. At Luton less that 400 m. south of Watling Street a second building was found but nothing is known of its plan; the finds suggest occupation from the second century onward.

South of Rochester, a building was probably situated at Borstal, but the main concentration of farms was further upstream where the valley floor becomes wider and the slopes of the Downs much less steep. A farm was located at Wouldham, but of its buildings only a small internally vaulted cellar, with three arched recesses in the east wall, is known. A chalk causeway from the entrance of the cellar led to the river bank where there was a timber wharf. It is now clear that the building was almost certainly used for the storage of corn or wine and oil transported by river. The presence of this depot on the river-bank clearly points to a building nearby and there were some indications of another structure further to the south. A number of sites were situated close to the modern villages of Burham and Eccles and on the slopes of the Downs. A small farm-house was excavated at Burham (Fig. 17) consisting of six rooms, with flint walls, and measuring externally *c.* 18.3 × 10.4 m. One of these rooms contained a channelled hypocaust, and another smaller room appears to have been laid with *opus signinum*. No dating evidence was found.

Apart from the villa-estate centred on Rowe Place Farm west of the village and close to the east bank of the Medway, there is no reliable evidence for a farm-house just to north of Eccles, although the site is so marked by the Ordnance Survey. Further inland, there is a strong possibility of a farm near Boxley Abbey where Roman building material was observed incorporated in the construction of the abbey, and it is probable that a farm-house existed on the slopes to north of the abbey. Upstream from Maidstone foundations were recorded just east of Tovil and another farm may have existed at Combe Street, East Farleigh.[20]

West of the Medway valley there is much evidence of occupation. No doubt several farms would have prospered on the fertile lower ground north of the Downs and bordering on the Medway and Thames marshes; but the records date mostly from the last century and many of these sites have not been confirmed by modern examination. Farms are indicated by building materials at Minster-in-Sheppey, at Otterham Creek, Rainham, and in the Lower Halstow area. This area is to north of the villa-estates at Boxted and Hartlip, and clearly supported considerable agricultural development in the hinterland of the pottery and salt-panning sites on the marshes. Further west, farms were probably located at Milton-next-Sittingbourne and in the Faversham area. Apart from the building recently excavated, foundations were seen below the churchyard at Faversham, a hypocaust and part of a tessellated floor at Luddenham and the remains of a building at Buckland church and other foundations in a field west of the Hog Brook. Of these probable farms, only the Buckland site provided any dating evidence, in this instance late in the Roman period. Further north and across the Swale, another farm is suggested by building debris and fourth-century coins at Harty on the Isle of Sheppey. Inland, three buildings were recorded last century in a field at Sutton Baron manor, near Borden; the record of their examination is, however, extremely confused, and it is not certain whether all these structures formed part of the same complex. The associated coins point to a date not earlier than the late third century.

To south, the soils were heavier and the forest cover increasing in density as it gradually merged with the Weald; naturally, rural settlement was less dense and the known farm-sites more scattered. In this area, too, the evidence is patchy and few sites have recently been examined and recorded. During the construction of the M20, the foundations of a small building were exposed at Hollingbourne. The discovery of a hoard of about 5400 double *denarii* of late third-century date near this site further reinforces the probability of a farm in this general area. A building was excavated behind the church at Chart Sutton about 1950. It had ragstone foundations and consisted of a corridor and three small rooms; it measured overall 18.3 × 8.2 m. Coins and pottery suggest a dating from Hadrian to Constantine, and the considerable amount of iron slag found on the site as well as hearths in two of the rooms indicates iron-working. Building material and lumps of *opus signinum* in Frittenden church indicate a farm-house nearby. Further north-east at Charing, a small farm-house was excavated in 1975. The building was constructed of ragstone foundations set in yellow mortar and measured overall 24.6 × 10.6 m. Originally, it consisted of one large room, probably with a fronting corridor. More rooms were later added on both sides of this large room, and one of these rooms contained a channelled hypocaust. Dating evidence was scanty, but a coin of Elagabalus indicates occupation during the third century. The plan of this building (Fig. 17) suggests a small farm in this area gradually becoming comparatively more prosperous as denoted by the new rooms.[21]

Further west, the rural settlement of the Stour valley was dominated by Canterbury and no farms have so far been located in the immediate vicinity of the cantonal capital. However, evidence of farms in the Great Stour valley is beginning to accumulate and its settlement may prove in future years to have been analogous to that of the river valleys in the western part of the *civitas*. A farm may have been located near Crundale where foundations were recorded in the churchyard. On the west bank of the Great Stour, much settlement was centred in the Wye area. Apart from evidence for iron-working and smelting hearths, dateable on coin evidence to the third century, a probable farm-house is suggested by building debris about 80 m. from Kempe's Corner, Boughton Aluph, with occupation from the second to the fourth century. About 1.5 km. south-east of this site a large building was partially examined close to Wye racecourse on the river-bank. This building originally measured at least 6 × 19 m. and had additions to north and towards the river, with a hypocaust at its south end (Fig. 15). Only the flint foundations of its walls had survived deep ploughing and its present plan suggests a house, with easy access to riverine transport. It is not improbable that this building was connected with the Boughton Aluph site. Further south foundations and parts of a tessellated floor near Aldington indicate another farm building, and a farm-house is suggested by foundations and building debris west of Saltwood. A farm (Folkestone II) appears to have been located at Folkestone about 55 m. southwest of the villa on East Cliff, but the published evidence does not allow for a coherent plan. However, a substantial building seems to have been at the centre of the site. Only an angle of this structure was exposed and consisted of a thick wall traced for only 8.2 m. To north of this corner was found a small hypocausted chamber, which may have been a corn-drier. To south was another hypocaust and stokehole, close to which was a circular structure which may have been connected with it and formed part of a baths suite. There were also signs of other foundations nearby. Two probable farms are so far suggested north of Canterbury. Near Whitstable, a small cellar was partly examined; it was 2.44 m. wide, probably in use during the second century and its presence argues for a farm nearby. At Chislet, a building consisted of a small hypocausted room, measuring 3.8 m. sq., with a smaller compartment adjacent to it and heated by the same hypocaust (Fig. 16). The function of this structure has not yet been determined, but it is probable that it was part of a larger building destroyed by deep ploughing. To the south of this building, another small structure, probably used for drying corn, was recently found at Hoath; the use of building debris in its construction, including *opus signinum* fragments, points once again to a farm building in this area. To east of Canterbury, foundations at Littlebourne indicate another building.

A concentration of settlement is clearly indicated by building debris in the Wickhambreaux-Ickham-Wingham area. Apart from the Ickham industrial complex, much debris and coins have been found slightly further south-east of Wenderton. There is also a large area on Britton Farm further east where building debris, including hypocaust tiles, pottery and coins have been found. A small farm was found in 1978 during road-works in Sandwich. The building (Fig. 17) was a simple house consisting of a long, central room and two other projecting rooms (Fig. 18); all these rooms could have been sub-divided by wooden partitions, but no evidence survived. The house was fronted by a verandah and measured overall 27.5 × 11.6 m., and the associated pottery suggests a rather short period of occupation from *c.* 200–300, perhaps a little later. Another farm-house is suggested at Sholden by foundations and occupation material. The northernmost farm seems to have been situated at Margate where four rooms of a house were observed during road-works.[22]

Fig. 18. Sandwich: Foundations of the building

(iii) *Villa-estates*

At the top of the social scale were the estates of the wealthy, usually referred to as villas. Some of these estates may have been owned by absentee landlords and the day-to-day management left in the hands of farm managers, and others may well represent investment from beyond Roman Britain; but many of these large houses must have been occupied, for some of the time at least, by their owners. Otherwise, there seems to be little economic justification for the large expenditure involved in the construction of these 'stately homes', their internal decoration, the laying of tessellated pavements and mosaic floors and the maintenance of their luxurious baths.

'Villa' is a convenient term, which has been indiscriminately used for all Roman buildings; this tendency still persists in spite of the classification of villas and other buildings in the recent Ordnance Survey maps of Roman Britain. There have been several attempts to define the term 'villa'; others have posed the question without proposing an answer.[23] The difficulty lies in that the term 'villa', as understood by classical writers and demostrated by the extensive Continental villas, such as Anthée, Chiragan or Montmaurin, has little practical application in Roman Britain so far as the vast majority of Romano-British buildings is concerned. Clearly, to describe both the Sandwich building and Folkestone as villas is to liken Knole with a modest farm-house.[24] The plans of Romano-British buildings themselves show the differences between a farm-house and a villa-estate and the distinction adopted here is that of size and luxury, as proposed by Rivet.[25]

At the extreme west of the canton a villa-estate was located at Titsey. The house was not a large structure, measured 39.9 × 17.2 m. overall and was constructed on foundations of flint and sandstone blocks. The main part of the house consisted of a central suite of rooms, flanked to north and south by corridors. The excavator supposed that this central range was an open courtyard, but the presence of tessellation *in situ* argues against this, and evidence for partition walls may have been so thoroughly removed as to escape detection. The eastern end of the house was occupied by a large room, heated by a channelled hypocaust served by a furnace to its north. Apart from its heating, its size and a remnant of mosaic floor, almost certainly found in the debris filling this room, suggest that this may have been the dining-room of the villa. At the western end of the house was a baths wing consisting of a number of heated rooms and a *caldarium* with an apsidal plunge-bath. Internally, to judge from surviving fragments, the house was decorated with painted wall-plaster of simple panels outlined by borders of different colours. It is probable that later the baths wing was converted into a fullery and the dining-room used as a drying-room; if so, the house itself must have been abandoned as a dwelling and the site converted to industrial use. On the basis of the inadequately published pottery and the coins found, it would seem that the house was built during the second century and continued in occupation beyond *c.* 350 when it may have been destroyed by fire. By itself this building would not be classed as a villa, but its provision of a substantial baths wing and the presence of tessellated and mosaic floors indicate a more luxurious estab-lishment than its excavation report suggests; moreover, the temple and pottery manufacture nearby point to a villa-estate close to the Roman road from London to Lewes.[26]

About 8.5 km. further north another villa-estate was situ-ated at Keston. A small detached house was excavated in 1854 and re-examined in 1968 at the southern part of Lower Warbank field; it measured overall 18.4 × 10 m. This building consisted of at least five rooms, with walls of mortared flint and tile courses, flanked by corridors to north and west; the associated pottery and coins support an occupation during the third and fourth centuries. To west and within 30 m. of this house lay another building only partly examined. From what is so far known, this structure was built over a Belgic hut and was at leat 30.5 m. wide facing to east, with a corridor clasping a range of rooms to west whose plan is not known in great detail; this house was probably built at the beginning of the second century. Close to the site of the cemetery was a substantial but undated corn-drier, measuring at least 9.1 × 12.2 m., with three drying chambers built of chalk blocks, flint and tile fragments. To west of this corn-drier and built on a mound was a circular mausoleum (Fig. 19). The structure had an external diameter of at least 9.1 m. and six external buttresses which may have supported columns. The walls of the mausoleum were 0.9 m. thick and built of ragstone with string courses of tile; externally, the mausoleum was wall-plastered and painted dark red. The primary burial was not located in 1828, but a secondary burial was found in 1967, between two buttresses on the western side of the mausoleum, contained in a lead coffin inside a cist-like tomb. Re-examination of the mausoleum suggests construction *c.* 200. About 0.6 m. to north-west another stone-built tomb (3.4 × 3.7 m.) contained a stone coffin and two other graves were located further to north-west.

The evidence so far recovered clearly points to a large villa-estate on this site, with a main house still to be examined

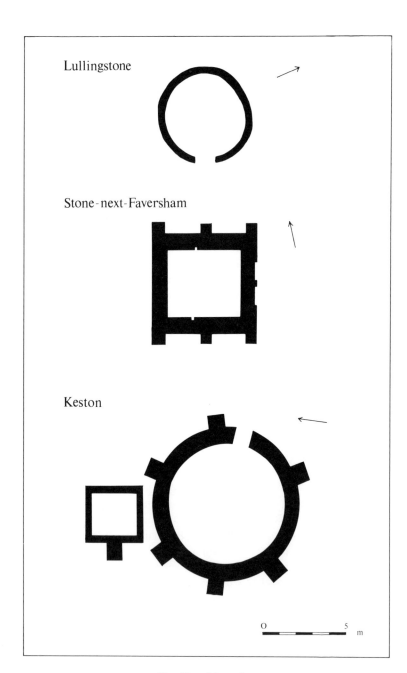

Lullingstone

Stone-next-Faversham

Keston

0   5 m

Fig. 19.   Mausolea

in detail flanked by agricultural buildings of which the small corridor house may have been occupied by the farm bailiff, and a walled cemetery. The occupation of this estate, developing directly from an Iron Age hut within a ditched enclosure, is likely to have lasted until the closing decades of the Romano-British period.[27]

The major villa-estate of the western part of the *civitas* was undoubtedly located at Darenth. The site (Fig. 20), which covers an area of at least 1½ ha. at the mouth of the Darent valley below the foothills of the Downs, was excavated in 1894–95. The interpretation of the site has suffered from the excavation methods of that time. It is now quite clear that the structures found were not those of a single house, but that the villa originally consisted of two buildings and had undergone several modifications and additions before all the domestic accommodation was grouped together behind an open courtyard. However, a partial re-interpretation of these buildings in 1905 and further excavations in 1969 beyond the dwelling-house have added much to the understanding of this villa-estate.

At the centre of the site was Building A, a fairly modest structure, measuring overall 37.8 × 18.3 m. and consisting of a main range of rooms, with fronting and rear corridor, and projecting wings to east and west of the central rooms; the western wing was probably a baths suite. About 15 m. west of this house was another structure, Building B, which measured 15.2 × 2 m. overall and had its own baths projecting beyond the north-western corner. In plan, this house looks similar to Building A, with corridors to front and rear clasping the central rooms; the baths suite appears additional to the original plan of this building. Building C was constructed *c.* 16 m. east of Building A; it measured 14.2 × 23 m. and had several hypocausted rooms. A new corridor, connecting Buildings B and C and fronting Building A, was also constructed and all three buildings were now to the rear of an open courtyard (26.5 m. wide). An entrance into the compound was at the centre of the courtyard's south wall and immediately to north was found a semicircular, solidly built and probably lead-lined cistern, 1.5 m. wide at the centre and 0.41 m. deep. The cistern was flanked by massive walls extending through

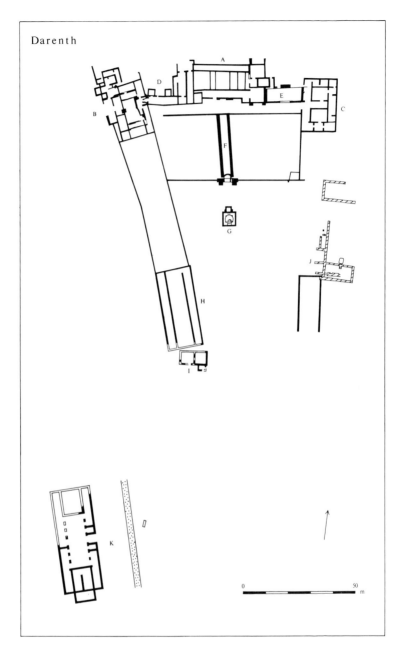

Darenth

Fig. 20.   Darenth: Plan of the site

the whole width of the courtyard and up to the new fronting corridor of the villa. This narrow (3.4 m.) compartment, dividing the courtyard into two parts, was interpreted as 'a large hall'; however, it is not unlikely that it served as an ornamental basin fed by the cistern to its south, even if its original purpose may have been that of a water-tank for industrial processing. The solidity of the tile-lined walls, clearly indicating that they were meant to withstand outward pressure, the remnant of 'yellow concrete' floor (10 cm. thick) found at the northern end which is likely to have been of *opus signinum*, and a small bronze lioness head, probably part of a water-fountain, found in the filling of this compartment, strongly point to water being contained within its flanking walls. Facing the courtyard entrance and 9.2 m. to south was a well (G).

According to Fox's interpretation of the house, part of its accommodation was converted into a *fullonica*. This conversion affected mainly the baths suite in Building A and necessitated the construction of Building D to house the fulling tanks and connect Buildings A and B. It is clear, from the fact that the new fronting corridor ran straight to Building B, that Building C was erected during this second phase of the villa's occupation; this new building may have served as a drying block for the fullery. Certainly, it contained many hypocausted rooms which could have been used for this purpose; in particular the hypocaust in Room 27, which resembles the arrangement of a tilery requiring much more heat than for domestic rooms, supports this interpretation. In a later re-organisation, Building A was converted into a dwelling-house once again, with its western wing reverting to its original function as a baths suite. Building C ceased to be used for industrial purposes. It may have become a private suite of a smaller number of heated rooms as clearly indicated by tessellated floors, which must obviously belong to this post-industrial phase. Building E, measuring 14.4 × 4.9 m., was constructed during this period to connect the main house (Building A) with the converted Building C, as shown by the west wall of Building E, which was built up against the west wall of Building A, and by buttressing at its north-west corner. Internally, Building C had been laid with *opus signinum* and its walls decorated with frescoes. Its function is uncertain, but evidence of burning on its floor suggests that this building may have been a dining-room heated by braziers. Building B is thought to have continued serving as a fullery until the end of the site's occupation.

Projecting beyond the south wall of Building B was an open space, measuring 58.4 × 14.6 m. and enclosed by walls; as this area was neither floored, nor was there any evidence for partitions, it may have been a kitchen garden. Further to south was a long aisled building (Building H), now known to have measured 34.7 × 15.3 m., which was floored with rammed chalk and may have been used as stables and cattle-sheds. Immediately to south was found in 1969 a small detached structure (Building I); it measured c. 14 × 9 m. and contained three rooms, constructed of mortared flint, one of which was laid with an *opus signinum* floor. This building has been described as a bath-building, but it is difficult to accept this interpretation, for its plan does not suggest it, nor is there evidence of a stoke-hole. Moreover, there is no apparent need for a bath-house at this part of the site. A group of buildings (J) was located to south of Building C, but most of these structures survived as foundations only. The most substantial of these buildings measured at least 26.2 m. in length by 8.6 m. wide, and its floor of rammed chalk suggested a barn. Though the whole group of these buildings is imperfectly recorded, it is probable that their function was agricultural rather than domestic, and this suggestion is supported by their location at some distance from the main buildings. Another detached aisled building (Building K), probably approached from the main compound by a gravel track, was found in 1969 91 m. south-west of Buildings H and I. Originally measuring at least 28.7 × 6.1 m., it was later extended to more than 48.8 × 17.7 m. before it was drastically reduced in its final of five phases. At least ten rooms of this building, some laid with tiled floors, have been identified, ranged round a central hall; the insertion of two corn-driers at the south end of this building indicates again agricultural use and possibly for the housing of the farm's labour force.

The chronology of the Darenth villa-estate has been bedevilled by the methods of its nineteenth-century excavation.

Apart from the total lack of any recorded stratigraphy, there is a surprising dearth of pottery. Even allowing for the absence of any excavated rubbish pits, this cannot be accounted for by Payne's conclusion that the estate had been abandoned by its owners. It is indeed quite unique in excavations of Romano-British buildings of Darenth's size and complexity that so little pottery was recovered from the various modifications of the villa's buildings. However, on the basis of the 50-odd coins recovered during the 1894–95 excavations, it is clear that, though there was some first-century occupation on the outskirts of the villa, occupation of the site started soon after 100 and continued until the closing decades of the fourth century. This dating accords with that of Building K where coins and pottery indicate occupation from *c.* 170 to the fourth century.

Quite obviously from the recent excavations at least, there is still much more to be discovered at Darenth. Fortunately, the site of the main buildings is still preserved, and future selective re-excavation and re-examination of areas not explored in the nineteenth century may elucidate the problems presented by this large agricultural and industrial estate.[28]

Further south in the Darenth valley itself, two villa-estates have so far been identified, one at Farningham and another at Lullingstone. Farningham I (Fig. 15) was located 273 m. south-west of the village church. This villa-estate had a substantial house, consisting of a main range and two flanking wings, with fronting and rear corridors and a detached bath-house. At the height of its prosperity, the house was 54.9 m. long and 15.3 m. wide. The original house, built *c.* 80, was the usual strip-house of nine rooms and two passages, measuring 43.9 × 8.2 m., with a separate wing projecting to south. It was entered through the south wall of this wing. During the second century corridors were added to the front and rear of the house, which was itself extended to north by the addition of at least two more rooms, one of which was hypocausted; a new entrance portico was now constructed through the fronting corridor and the original entrance through the south wing was blocked. In the course of the fourth century the house was modified and reduced in size. It now consisted of four main rooms with tessellated floors, at least two of which had mosaic panels at their centre, though very little of them survived *in*

situ. The walls of the house were originally built on foundations of flint and mortar and carried upward in wall-plastered
clay. Internally, most rooms had been laid with *opus signinum*
floors and decorated with frescoes. The bath-house was
situated 76.3 m. east of the house's eastern wing but, except
for the partial examination of its cold plunge-bath, it has not
yet been excavated.

Occupation came to an end about the middle of the fourth
century when the house appears to have been abandoned and
demolished, though there are some traces of later occupation
north of the later house. There was no evidence for violent
destruction and the latest coin, dating to *c.* 337–350, supports
this suggestion.[29]

About 2¼ km. south-west of Farningham I, a villa-estate
was located at Lullingstone on the west bank of the Darent
(Fig. 21). The dwelling-house by itself is of fairly modest
proportions, but the luxury of its accommodation and the
baths, coupled with the agricultural and industrial buildings
as well as the temple-mausoleum and circular shrine, underline its status of a villa-estate.

The original house, built towards the end of the first
century, measured 28 × 11.9 m., and had walls of flint and
mortar; the accommodation consisted of a double range of
rooms and a corridor to the rear, and included a deep,
underground cellar which may have served as a grain store.
At the beginning of the second century a circular shrine (Fig.
19) was built on a terrace 24.4 m. north-west of the house. The
wall of this shrine was of mortated flint and its floor was
tessellated; the unknown cult object, probably on a *podium*,
may have stood behind a wattle-and-daub partition opposite
the entrance to the shrine which faced approximately to east.
This shrine was dismantled about 180 when the house was
expanded by the construction of a baths suite, the northern
cult rooms and detached kitchens. This new building brought
the overall dimensions of the villa to 38.1 × 20 m., including
the projecting stoke-hole and plunge-bath of the bath-house.

The baths suite was built adjacent to the south wall of the
house and was entered by means of a corridor running
alongside this wall and laid with a tessellated floor. The
accommodation provided was the usual sequence of *frigidar-*

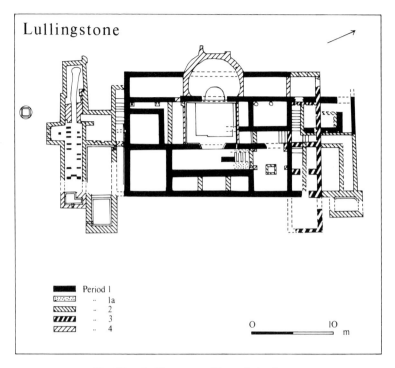

Fig. 21. Lullingstone: Plan of the house

ium, *tepidarium* and *caldarium* and a furnace at the west end of the unit. The cold room and tepid rooms had tessellated floors but the hot room was tiled, and both the cold room and the hot room had been provided with plunge-baths. Water was originally supplied by a well outside the south wall of the baths, which was later abandoned; it is not known how water was supplied to the baths from the fourth century onward. The bath-house was reconstructed and modified during its existence and was finally dismantled at the end of the fourth century. A small outbuilding was constructed during this second phase, 8.2 m. south of the baths, but little is known of its plan and purpose; it was not in use later than the third century.

The northern end of the house was radically modified *c*. 180 and the deep room converted into a cult room dedicated to the

worship of three water nymphs. The room was entered by a
flight of tiled stairs at its north-west corner. Internally, the
nymphaeum was laid with a concrete floor and its wall rendered
with white wall-plaster painted with panels and date-palms.
There was a niche in the south wall within which were painted
the three nymphs; the central figure was painted standing, the
other two seated. To north of the *nymphaeum* was constructed
an ambulatory. It had clay walls, was floored with pebble
concrete and enclosed a rectangular room. At the east corner
of the ambulatory a small compartment projected beyond the
east wall of the house; it was floored with *opus signinum* and a
tessellated pavement. The rectangular room was similarly
tessellated and its walls were finished with painted wall-
plaster displaying colours and *motifs* like those in the *nymphaeum*. The rectangular shape of this room, its surrounding
ambulatory and associated finds have led the excavator to
conclude that it was probably used as a temple contemporary
with the *nymphaeum* with which it shared identical schemes of
decoration, a connection further emphasized by their being
next to each other and linked by a central landing leading in
one direction downstairs into the *nymphaeum* and in another
two directions into the ambulatory.

The second century kitchens were built on a platform
levelled out of the chalk slope and 3 m. beyond the west wall
of the villa. The construction of this kitchen block was based
on ten large timbers placed vertically in post-holes and held
fast by pebble concrete. The walls were probably of clay and
the roof may have been thatched as no roofing-tiles were
found in the debris; inside this structure were two ovens,
mostly built of clay with some admixture of tiles. As the two
ovens were not contemporary, the kitchens were clearly in use
for a long time until they were converted early in the third
century into a tannery which was apparently not used for
long.

The next phase in the occupation of the villa is dated to *c.*
280, after the greater part of a century during which the house
is thought to have been abandoned. If so, then there must
have been some occupation to account for the conversion of
the external kitchens into a tannery, for even if this were the
work of a 'local inhabitant', he must have inhabited some-

where. However, during this new phase the bath-house was
re-built and the access into the *nymphaeum* blocked. Two
marble busts, thought to have belonged to the previous
occupants of the villa, were deposited on the flight of steps
formerly descending into the *nymphaeum*. Not only the *nymphaeum* was abandoned, but also the adjacent temple was
demolished and a new wall was built right across the northern
end of the house, which reduced its length by 4.3 m. Partition
walls, with arched flues, across this area divided it into three
rooms, with a fourth compartment projecting beyond the east
wall of the villa and interpreted as a stoke-hole. These new
rooms have been interpreted as a heated apartment, though
no clear evidence was found to indicate how the floor had been
supported; moreover, the absence of any evidence of fire has
suggested that the underfloor heating was not in fact used.

A large granary (Fig. 16) was erected during this phase 21.4
m. from the north-east corner of the villa and within 16.5 m. of
the present river-bank. This measured 24.4 × 10.1 m. and was
later externally buttressed. Its walls were of flint and mortar,
which were also used for the construction of the supports for
the granary's wooden floor; access into this building was
afforded by entrances through its north and south walls. This
granary continued into use until 380 when its wooden floors
were removed from most of its area. Some of the area was now
used as stables and for the storage of farm carts and elsewhere
as a pen for small animals.

Consequent upon the demolition of the *nymphaeum* and the
temple next to it, a new temple was constructed on the slope
above and to west of the villa soon after its presumed
re-occupation in 280 (Fig. 23). First, an excavation was made
into the chalk for the deposition of two burials in lead coffins.
Next, the *cella* was built over these burials; its walls were of
mortared chalk and internally decorated with painted wall-
plaster. Finally, the ambulatory wall was constructed of
mortared flint and a floor of *opus signinum* was laid. The
presence of tufa *voussoirs* in the debris suggests that the *cella*
was vaulted, and the absence of tile debris in the ambulatory
may mean that it had a wooden roof. The temple measured
12.2 m. sq., and continued in use as a place for worship until
the last quarter of the fourth century when the villa's occu-

pants were converted to Christianity. No evidence has been
found of the ritual practised in the temple, but its construction
over the double grave has suggested that the ritual may have
been connected with the burials and led to its description as a
temple-mausoleum.

The central part of the villa was reconstructed about the
middle of the fourth century when a reception room and a
dining-room occupied the centre of the house (Fig. 22). The
reception room was entered through an entrance corridor to
its east, which had originally led to the deep room; it was
separated from the dining-room by a mosaic step. The
reception room was rectangular; it measured 6.1 × 5.2 m. and
was laid with a mosaic pavement, which consisted of several
elements subordinate to the central panel. These subordinate
panels contained various decorative *motifs* including leaves,
crosses, swastikas, geometric designs and *guilloche*. The main
panel at the centre of the mosaic depicted Bellerophon,
mounted on his winged horse Pegasus, in the act of slaying the
Chimaera, surrounded by dolphins and shells; this design was
enclosed by a cushion-shaped *guilloche* border. The four

Fig. 22.   Lullingstone: The dining-room mosaics

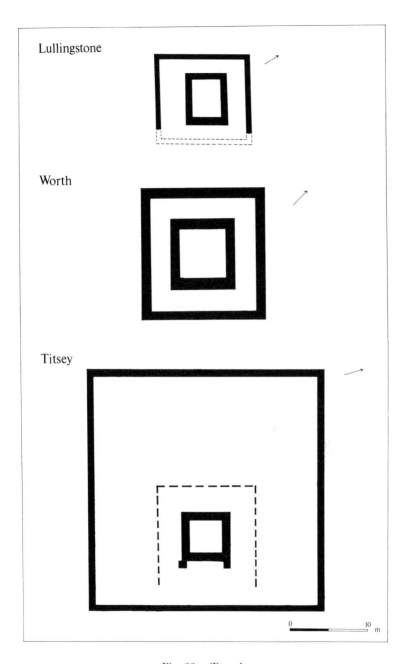

Lullingstone

Worth

Titsey

0   10 m

Fig. 23. Temples

corners of this mosaic were occupied by conventional repre-
sentations of the four seasons, of which Summer was virtually
destroyed. The whole mosaic was enclosed on three sides by
Greek meander borders. The dining-room was apsidal in
shape, with its apse projecting 2.1 m. to west and beyond the
original rear corridor of the house which had been partly
breached to allow for the construction of this new room.
Another mosaic floor had been laid in this dining-room,
surrounded by plain red tessellation. The mosaic panel depicted the abduction of Europa by Jupiter in the guise of a bull
and was enclosed by a simple *guilloche* consisting of a chain of
alternating red and white discs. Between the ends of this
border, at the top of this panel and forming the upper part of
the step down into the reception room, was a two-line
inscription reading, INVIDA SI TA[VRI] VIDISSET
IVNO NATATVS / IVSTIVS AEOLIAS ISSET ADVS-
QUE DOMOS, a somewhat garbled reference to the Aeneid.

At about 385 the bath-house was dismantled and filled in
with rubbish. This appears to have coincided with the conversion of the villa's occupants to Christianity and may not be
unconnected with the deteriorating economic situation in the
province. The westernmost room of the probable heated suite
of rooms was again converted and became the ante-chamber
to the Christian house-church; a new wooden floor was
constructed and the walls given a fresh coating of painted wall
plaster. Reconstruction of the collapsed wall-plaster showed
that the main motif of the decoration of the south wall was a
large *Chi-Rho* monogram. The room immediately east of this
ante-chamber may have served as a priest's room. The area
above the early deep room became the house-church, with
walls richly decorated in painted wall-plaster. Reconstruction
of the collapsed plaster showed that again it consisted of
Christian symbols, including a large *Chi-Rho* monogram within a floral wreath and parts of praying figures standing within
niches and columns consisting of fish instead of the usual
fluting. These praying figures are thought to have probably
represented members of the family living in the house.

Comparing it with other villa-estates in the canton and
elsewhere, the Lullingstone dwelling-house remained of modest size from its construction in the late first century until its

final destruction by fire at the beginning of the fifth century. However, a number of questions remain for which there are no convincing explanations. The original building is clearly an unpretentious farm-house, which was later enlarged by the provision of a bath-house and the construction of the cult-rooms at its northern end. This has been interpreted as evidence for a change in ownership of the house, and the presence of the marble busts as an indication that the new owner was 'a Roman, possibly of Mediterranean origin.' This interpretation, however, has not met with general acceptance, partly because of the difficulty of distinguishing, in social terms, between a Roman and a Romano-Briton. The suggestion that the house lay derelict for most of a century, notwithstanding the activity of the tannery during this period, is also open to question. There is no clear evidence to support the suggestion that this abandonment may have resulted from a possible involvement of its owner in the Clodius Albinus episode. Moreover, other sites in the canton (e.g. Farningham I and Eccles) show not only unbroken occupation, but also increasing prosperity. Then, though it is not impossible to accept that pagan ritual may have continued in the deep room whilst Christian worship obtained in the house-church immediately above it, it is less easy to accept that the house continued in occupation and had a house-church built on it, yet the baths suite was no longer in service. According to Meates' interpretation the house was used intermittently from the middle of the fourth century onward, perhaps left in the charge of a bailiff as farming continued on the estate. If so, it is difficult to understand the great expenditure involved in the reconstruction of the central rooms and the laying of the mosaic floors. What is clear, however, is that the villa-estate at Lullingstone was concerned with considerable farming activity as denoted by the storage capacity of its granary, and this must account for the continued prosperity exhibited at least by the mosaic pavements at such a late stage in the occupation of the villa-estate.[30]

A villa-estate was located at Northfleet. Excavations in 1909–11 and re-examination of the site in recent years have established at least three buildings, most of which had been extensively robbed or are inaccessible to further examination.

Only part of the likely dwelling-house is known and most of the structure lies under an industrial coal-tip. The surviving portion of this building appears to be a wing of the house, consisting of three rooms and parts of a corridor, measuring 18.7 × 8.9 m. Though much of the walls had been robbed, they were quite substantial and constructed of flint, ragstone and chalk. Wall-plaster and tessellation debris indicate that this house may have been of some substance. About 18 m. north of this house was a detached building, whose very slight foundations measured 26.2 × 12.7 m. It consisted of a large compartment at the rear which may have been sub-divided by timber partitions, though no evidence survived, with a number of rooms round three sides of this area. The incomplete plan suggests a farm building probably with provision for stalling of animals and accommodation for farm-workers. North of the northern corner of this structure a detached bath-house was recently found, though not yet completely excavated. The dimensions so far established of this bath-house were 15.4 × 6.1 m. It consisted of a hypocausted *caldarium*, projecting beyond the north wall of the building, with some evidence for a stokehole, adjacent to the *tepidarium* likewise heated by a hypocaust and having its own plunge-bath. The *frigidarium* was next to this room and had been paved with a mosaic, remnants of which survived *in situ*. Beyond this cold room were at least two more rooms, one of which had a tessellated floor and the other a bath at its east corner. The purpose of these two rooms is not clear as they are additional to the normal plan for a bath-house.

In general and within the limitations of the available evidence, it is clear that a substantial villa-estate was sited at Northfleet. It was probably concerned mainly with farming though, as there is a mention of a lime-kiln in the 1913 excavation report, it may also have carried out industrial activities.

About 6 km. to east another villa-estate is indicated in the village of Chalk but, once more, the evidence is fragmentary; however, evidence of occupation has been recorded over an area of about ¾ ha., which points to a large site. Unconfirmed reports of masonry remains at the north of this area suggest a building there; to south-west, part of a ploughed-out building, with hypocaust, was excavated in 1959. About 36 m. west of this site, a small building, measuring 12.7 × 3.6 m., was excavated in 1961. An excavation had been cut *c*. 2 m. into the chalk for the construction of this building, which had two storeys. Its walls were founded directly on solid chalk and rendered with mortar; as this rendering was not carried down to the chalk, it is probable that the basement had a wooden floor. There was an entrance at the north-east corner and five niches were in the east wall, 1.4 m. above the chalk subsoil, which may have held lamps. The upper floor was probably timber-framed and internally decorated with painted wall-plaster; its roof was similarly timber-framed and probably tile-hung. The construction of this building has not been dated, but there was evidence to suggest that it was not the earliest structure on the site. Originally, this building was probably used for the storage of oil or wine in its basement with residential accommodation on the upper floor, perhaps for the farm bailiff. Before the end of the third century, however, the building was altered by the lowering of its floor to the chalk subsoil and the blocking of the niches by a new coating of wall-plaster; a new upper floor would have also been constructed as the building is thought to have provided living quarters above and below this floor. However, by *c*. 300 the basement had perhaps become quarters for slaves and the upper floor converted into a store before it was finally burnt down soon afterwards. About 30–40 m. east of this outbuilding, a bath-house was excavated in 1974–75 (Fig. 24), measuring overall 12.4 × 13.9 m. with a furnace-room projecting to west; it had been built of mortared ragstone on flint foundations. Internally, a channelled hypocaust heated a room probably used as an *apodyterium;* the hot and tepid rooms were heated by pillared hypocausts. Both the *tepidarium* and the *frigidarium* had been provided with plunge-baths. The bath-house was probably built in the early second century and altered later in that century, though robbing has prevented a clear interpretation of these modifications. The building appears to have ceased serving as a bath-house late in the third century. A corridor was also partly recorded running to north from the western side of the baths, perhaps towards the main house. Finally, in 1979 a tiled wall-corner, containing a

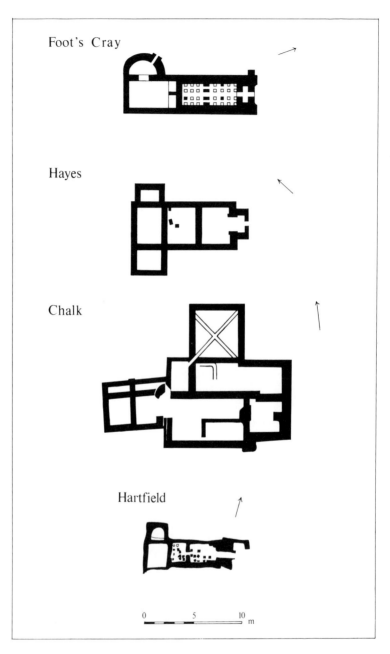

Foot's Cray

Hayes

Chalk

Hartfield

0   5   10 m

Fig. 24.   Bath-houses

tiled floor, was recorded in a restricted area about 100 m. west of the bath-house, but modern housing prevents further examination of the area. Until further opportunities for excavation in this area arise in the future, it is not possible to consider the economic background of the Chalk villa-estate, though there probably was a connection with the manufacture of pottery in its vicinity.[31]

Further to east in the Medway valley a villa-estate is strongly suggested by various buildings close to the west river-bank at Snodland. At the northern part of the site was part of a hypocausted room with ragstone walls; the debris filling this room indicates that the suspended floor was tessellated and its wall decorated with painted wall-plaster. Just to west of the hypocaust was recorded part of an apse built of chalk blocks with an outer skin of vertical bonding-tiles set in mortar. Internally, this apse was floored with *opus signinum*, which was later covered by a second floor of the same material. It was impossible to examine the remainder of this area, but it is very likely that the hypocaused room and the apse belonged to the villas's bath-house. The quarter-round moulding at the junction of the latter's wall and floor strongly indicates that it may have been the plunge-bath of the *caldarium* next to the hypocausted *tepidarium*. About 6 m. south-west of the apse was a rectangular structure built of mortared bonding-tiles and measuring 3.4 × 3.7 m. overall. Internally, this structure was laid with *opus signinum* ending in a strip of quarter-round moulding. This is clearly a water-cistern for the supply of the baths probably by means of wooden piping which has not survived.

The main building of the estate lay further to south-west but most of it lies beneath concrete yards. Sections of ditches at this part of the site indicate occupation before the building was constructed. Part of a corner and length of wall of the earliest building have been recorded with remnants of plain tessellation; a second and larger wall-corner has also been found. In its final phase, the main house had a tessellated fronting corridor and a projecting wing to west. The western corner of this wing contained a hypocausted room, probably served by a stoke-hole to its east. At least two more rooms projected to north-east beyond this hypocaust. This wing has been interpreted as a probable corn-drying compartment, but this appears improbable. A garden may have been situated beyond this wing. The fronting corridor had been further extended to south-east and a wall-corner was recorded. The building materials used for these walls were chalk blocks, ragstone, flint and bonding-tiles set in mortar; the associated floors were of rammed chalk or *opus signinum* and enough *tesserae* survived in the debris to indicate plain tessellations. In its final stage the front of the house had a total length of 30.2 m. Another building lay 122 m. to north of the main house but only a short length of two parallel walls, built of chalk blocks, could be recorded.

The occupation of this villa-estate began about the end of the first century and continued probably into the late fourth as suggested by pottery and the few late coins found. Nothing can be adduced as to the economic background of this villa until more of its buildings can be examined in detail.[32]

Across the river from Snodland and just over 2 km. to south-east lay the major villa-estate of the Medway valley at Rowe Place Farm, Eccles. The existence of Romano-British remains on the site had been noted over the last century and excavations undertaken in 1962–76 established the continued occupation of this villa-estate from the middle of the first century to the end of the Romano-British period (Fig. 25).

Following Iron Age settlement on the site and some earlier structures still to be studied in detail, the earliest house is provisionally dated to *c.* 65. This dwelling consisted of a strip of 12 rooms behind a fronting corridor; built of mortared ragstone, it measured overall 75 × 12.8 m. Five of these rooms at the north-western end of the house had tessellations surviving. These may have been borders to destroyed mosaic panels at the centre of at least three of these rooms as indicated by gaps in the tessellation and lumps of mosaic fragments used as hard core in later foundation trenches. The fronting corridor had a wooden floor and its roof was probably supported by timber uprights placed upon a low cill-wall. To south-west of the fronting corridor and 11.6 m. away from it was a long, ornamental water-basin, constructed approximately centrally to the house and measuring 51.1 × 5 m.; it was built of ragstone and mortar and rendered internally with

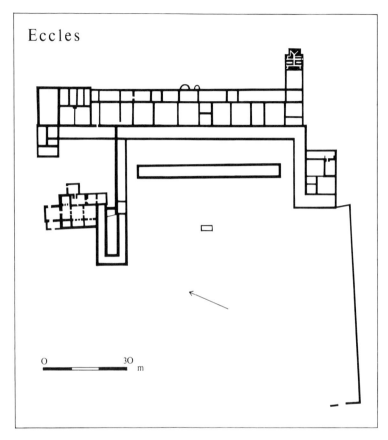

Fig. 25. Eccles: Final plan of the site

a waterproof coating of *opus signinum*.

To west of the house was a detached bath-house, similarly constructed and measuring overall 32 × 24 m., excluding the projecting *laconicum*. This bath-house, whose plan is reminiscent of military baths, originally consisted of the usual range of cold and heated rooms served by a furnace provided with a *testudo* (Fig. 26), a projecting circular *laconicum* with its own stoke-hole, fuel stores and a *palaestra*. Two modifications had been carried out during the existence of the baths and these affected the central range of hot rooms and the *laconicum* which

Fig. 26.   Eccles: The first baths (*praefurnium* and *caldarium*)

was provided with a second furnace. Internally, the bath-house was decorated with painted wall-plaster showing decorative schemes mostly of panels and floral medallions. Most of the rooms were laid with *opus signinum*, either as underfloors for the hypocausts or for tessellations which were mostly destroyed in the later wholesale demolition of the building. The *frigidarium* and its cold plunge-bath had polychrome mosaic floors as shown by several *tesserae* surviving *in situ* at the junctions of walls and floors. Following the demolition of the baths, these mosaics had been salvaged and stored for re-use. Study of the recovered fragments suggests that the mosaic at the bottom of the plunge-bath may have had a marine theme with a large fish or mammal at its centre, and that the main mosaic in the *frigidarium* consisted of *guilloches* bordering a geometric perspective box-pattern and a central panel possibly containing human or animal figures. This bath-house was destroyed by fire about 120 and thoroughly demolished to allow for the erection of its successor baths.

The destruction of the first bath-house brought about not only the construction of new baths, but also additions to the

Fig. 27. Eccles: The tessellated rear corridor of the house

main house. The fronting corridor of the villa was now extended to south-west and part of it re-laid with a tessellated floor. A new wing of four rooms was also built at the south-western end of the corridor and the frontage of the house extended to 94.8 m. The second bath-house was built just south of the new wing, partly over the site of its predecessor and behind a wall masking it from the front of the villa. The baths suite was a substantial structure containing several cold and heated rooms, with their own furnaces and had undergone several additions and modifications during its use. In its final reconstruction, this bath-house measured 27.1 × 21.7 m.

Major extensions were made to the villa about 180. A rear corridor was added to its plan and widened the central range of rooms to 17.3 m. The south-western end of this new corridor was laid with a tessellation of alternating strips of red and buff *tesserae* (Fig. 27) and the remainder with a tiled floor. A new range of seven rooms was also built next to the corridor; one of these was a large room, probably serving for storage, and the rest were kitchen and servants' bedrooms. At

the north-eastern end of the rear corridor, two rooms projected 13.6 m. to east. The easternmost of these rooms was
provided with a channelled hypocaust and used for the drying
of corn to be stored in the room to its west. The fronting
corridor of the villa was also extended to west at its south-east
end to serve a new wing, which had a hypocausted room and
furnace and was used for the parching and storing of grain. A
new bath-house was also constructed during this period and
incorporated some rooms belonging to the second baths. This
new bath-house consisted of ten hypocausted rooms, two
furnaces, a fuel store and a swimming-bath enclosed on three
sides by a corridor (Fig. 28). To afford access to the baths, the
villa's fronting corridor was also continued to west and
connected with the *piscina* of the baths. The corridor fronting
the house and its two wings were decorated with painted
wall-plaster and its penthouse roof supported by short Bath-
stone pillars. Between the two wings and at the centre of the
courtyard was also constructed a small ornamental basin,
measuring 3.8 × 2 m. The courtyard area was enclosed by a
garden wall, beginning at the south corner of the south-
eastern wing and continuing for 69.8 m. before it turned to
south-west.

   Further modifications were made to the villa about the
beginning of the fourth century. The rear corridor was divided
by partition walls into a series of ten rooms, one of which had
a channelled hypocaust inserted below its re-laid tessellation.
A horse-shoe shaped latrine was also built and washing
facilities, projecting beyond the rear corridor. The south-
eastern wing was also altered and divided into smaller
compartments, one of which had a wooden floor placed over
air-channels and was clearly used as a granary.

   In their final aspect (Fig. 25) during the fourth century the
buildings of the Eccles villa measured overall 105.5 × 73.2 m.,
including the wings projecting to front and rear and its garden
wall enclosed an area in front of the house of 89 × 116 m. or
rather more than 1 ha. In all respects a major villa-estate, the
Eccles villa has invited comment from the early years of its
excavation. Firstly, the occupation of the site soon after the
Roman invasion, the building of the earliest house and its
baths suite with its mosaics and the military affinities of its

ECCLES

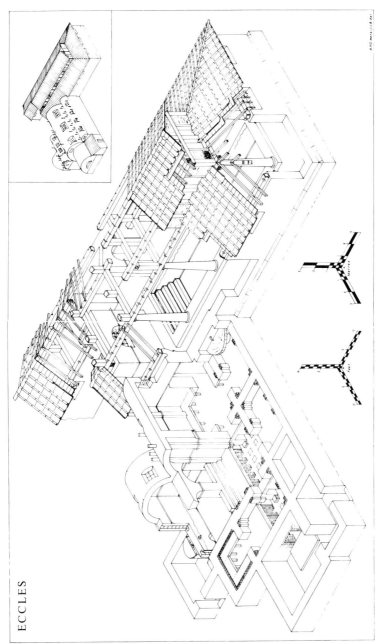

Fig. 28. Eccles: Reconstruction of the fourth-century baths

plan have suggested perhaps official promotion of a local philo-Roman aristocrat, perhaps even Adminius returning to Britain in the wake of the army. Be that as it may, the discovery of pottery manufacture very close to the villa site, perhaps producing for the army, makes it clear how was acquired at least some of the wealth expended in the construction of the dwelling-house and its baths suite. Secondly, the extensive provision of bathing facilities, out of proportion with the likely needs of those housed in the villa, and their running costs throughout the history of the estate indicate that the Eccles baths may have been used by people living beyond the estate and open up questions on the social organisation in the area. Thirdly, the Eccles villa-estate demonstrates not only continuous occupation, but also constantly increasing prosperity denoted by the frequent reconstruction of its baths, the alterations to the main house and the extension of its agricultural buildings. Even before the publication of the definitive report on the site, it is clear that the estate prospered on a mixed economy of large-scale farming of the fertile land above the Medway coupled with pottery and tile manufacture.[33]

A substantial villa-estate (Maidstone I) was situated on the east bank of the Medway at the Mount, Maidstone (Fig. 29), but once more the record is far from complete. Parts of this house were examined in 1844 and further excavation has recently been undertaken in advance of re-development on the site. The plan of the 1844 excavations shows a range of rooms, measuring some 10.7 × 19.8 m., at the southern end of the site; the walls were built of ragstone and had been externally buttressed to south and east. Work in 1970–71 and since has located a long corridor fronting onto the river and a northern range of rooms, probably facing the southern rooms across an open courtyard. This appears likely as short lengths of two parallel walls have been recorded at the western corner of the corridor, but the whole of the courtyard area and the probable site of the villa's main block to the east of it are now occupied by army installations. The second room of the western range was rebuilt in the fourth century and had a hypocaust inserted in it. A corridor, laid with an *opus signinum* floor, was also built to east of this heated room and its furnace. To east of this

Maidstone I

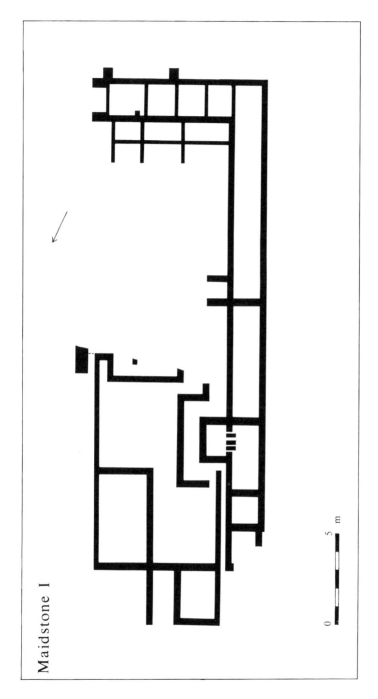

0   5   m

Fig. 29.   Maidstone I: Plan of the site

range, substantial building had also been undertaken during the first half of the third century when a number of large compartments was constructed, though their function is not yet fully elucidated.

The known buildings of Maidstone I occupy a fairly large area, though it is clear that more remains to be found to east of the probable courtyard. Nothing can be added so far about the economy of the estate, but its location practically on the water edge suggests connections with river transport.

A short distancce to south-east was situated Maidstone II (Fig. 30), another large villa-estate which was partly examined in 1870. The partial plan of the house shows the usual strip of rooms facing west and ranged in front of a rear corridor; the walls of the building were of ragstone and had tufa quoins. The east wall of the corridor extended to south to enclose a suite of seven rooms. Nearest to the central range and projecting to east was a long and narrow room, which had an apsidal end and contained a tessellated floor of red and white *tesserae* laid in herring-bone pattern. To south of this room were two heated rooms with their own stoke-holes. One of these rooms had the standard pillared hypocaust, but the other one, which was octagonal in shape and externally buttressed, was served by a channelled hypocaust. At the northern limit of the excavated area at least one room projected to east of the fronting corridor and may have been at the centre of the house or the beginning of another range of rooms, which is suggested by a hypocaust at the north end of the corridor. There is no information on which to judge whether the house was of one build; likewise, nothing is known of the date of its construction or the period of its occupation. However, the known overall dimensions of this house (greater than 50.8 × 29.3 m.) clearly point to a villa-estate of some size and opulence.[34]

East of the Medway valley, three villa-estates are so far known on the fertile land below the Downs at Boxted, Hartlip and Faversham. A large building was traced in 1882 at Boxted, 1.2 km. north of Watling Street; it measured overall 66.2 × 22.9 m., but it is not known whether the plan of the house as published is the original building or its final shape. This house had been constructed with walls of ragstone, flint

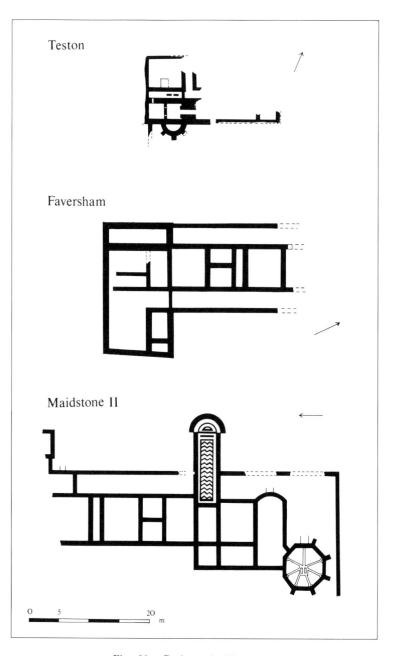

Teston

Faversham

Maidstone II

0 5   20
            m

Fig. 30. Baths and villa-estates

and tufa, but ploughing had removed most of the floors. The plan (Fig. 15) shows a dwelling with a central range of many, rather small rooms flanked by corridors to front and rear and had two larger rooms projecting to east beyond the front of the house. Some rooms were internally decorated with painted wall-plaster and others had tessellated floors. About 55 m. east of the eastern wing foundations were also found of two other rooms, one of which had a tessellated floor. It was not possible to determine whether these rooms belonged to a separate building or were connected to the house beyond them. From the pottery descriptions and the coins found, occupation of the site appears to have begun towards the end of the first century and continued at least throughout the second. It is clear, however, from this sketchy evidence and the recent discovery of a temple about 275 m. to south-west that a substantial villa-estate was located here.

South of Watling Street and 3.5 km, south-west of Boxted was situated the Hartlip villa-estate, consisting of at least eight buildings covering an area of 1.4 ha. However, the piecemeal examination of this large site during the last two centuries does not allow for a coherent appreciation of the estate. The main dwelling-house appears to have been located to south-west and at about the centre of the site; only a portion of it has been examined, occupying an area of 32 × 20.8 m. overall. In plan, this dwelling-house appears to consist of the usual central range of rooms, with a rear corridor; there is also some evidence for a fronting corridor beginning at the east corner. The walls were built of flint and rubble and also had tile courses. Internally, the walls were finished with painted wall-plaster, and the floors were of *opus signinum*, though there is no mention of tessellations. A two-room cellar projected to west beyond the rear of the house and was entered by a flight of tiled steps. Internally, the passage into the cellar had its wall-plaster painted white, and the cellar rooms were painted red. Finds of a large quantity of wheat and other cereals indicate that this cellar was used as a grain store. East of the dwelling-house, several sections of walls were recorded, but insufficient is known of the plan of these structures to allow for their interpretation; however, it is clear from the angle of these walls that they did not belong to the main house on the site. At the eastern end of the site and *c*. 70 m. from the house was a small, detached bath-house, measuring 15.3 × 21.4 m. This bath-house consisted of a cold room, with its own plunge-bath, next to two rooms heated by hypocausts whose floors were supported on box flue-tiles as at the Darenth villa. The *tepidarium* had its own plunge-bath, the *caldarium* was provided with a small, apsidal plunge and both rooms were served by two furnaces adjacent to the hot room. A large (21.4 × 15.3 m.) aisled building, buttressed both internally and externally, was adjacent to the bath-house; in fact, the west corner of this building overlaps the east corner of the baths *frigidarium*, but the excavation report does not indicate which of these two buildings was the earliest. It seems likely, however, that the bath-house must have been out of commission by the time the aisled building was constructed as a granary; for obvious reasons, it is most improbable that, if the area of the baths cold room had been reduced by the construction of the granary, a hypocausted building could have continued in use in physical contact with the grain store. A drainage ditch ran south-west from the baths and two buildings of incomplete plan and unknown purpose were sited nearby. The largest of these structures measured 19.2 × 13.7 m., and looks agri-cultural in plan; the other is shown as a wall-corner only and may have been part of the larger structure. About 58 m. north of the main house were recorded parts of another building, measuring overall *c*. 15.3 × 16.5, which preclude interpreta-tion.

Once again, the finds have not been published in detail, nor is it possible to date the several structures present on this site. However, coins and pottery suggest a general period of occupation from the end of the first century to the close of the Roman period. In general terms, the Hartlip villa-estate appears to have consisted of a main dwelling-house, with farm buildings flanking it to north and south, and the barn(s) on the site indicate agriculture as its main economic activity.

Further east another villa-estate was excavated in 1965 *c*. 1.2 km. north of Watling Street at Faversham during re-development of the site. Though it has been considered as the residence of a small farmer, and the house is only partially known, it shows features which indicate that, in its later stages at least, it may have developed into a villa-estate.

The original house had been built close to and partly over an Iron Age ditched enclosure; all its walls and floors had been completely robbed and the foundations surviving in robber trenches present problems of structural interpretation. However, it is very probable that the original building consisted of a range of at least six rooms, with a passage or stairway to an upper storey between three of them, enclosed within fronting and rear corridors, measuring overall 14.7 × at least 30 m. In the excavation report, it is considered that the corridors and the larger room at the south end of the house were additional to its original plan on the grounds that a verandah, supported on timber uprights, may have first fronted the house and that a butted joint was observed at the south end of the house. This interpretation is not convincing. It is not certain that butted joints observed in remains of foundation flints mean more than a temporary and very brief halt in building, and the line of flint-packed post-holes that suggested a verandah not only would make for an unnecessarily wide corridor at c. 4 m. but also and more important, stops short of the house at the northern end of the excavated area. Moreover, the narrow passage, which is integral to the plan of the house, clearly indicates that the fronting and rear corridors were also part of the original building and at c. 2.8 m. wide more in keeping with such corridors in Romano-British buildings. A wing was added to the south end of the house after c. 150, projecting to east of the fronting corridor and consisting of four new rooms and a fifth made by a partition blocking the south end of the corridor. One of these new rooms was internally apsidal and opened onto the room to its west which was heated by a channelled hypocaust; it is likely that these two rooms served as a dining-suite of the villa. This wing was finally modified during the third century by the construction of new walls, enclosing and slightly extending it. Though this dwelling-house was extensively robbed, enough evidence survived in the debris filling the robber trenches to show that at least some of the rooms were decorated with painted wall-plaster. None of the floors had survived *in situ* and they may have been of clay; tessellation debris indicates that the corridors may have had tessellated floors. Additionally, *tesserae* of five colours, found in the ruins of the dining-rooms, strongly suggest that the dining-suite had a mosaic floor.

The known plan of this house in its final stage (Fig. 30) shows a house with overall dimensions of 22 × more than 33 m.; clearly, more rooms lay to north beyond the excavated area, perhaps also another wing at the northern end of the house. Built during the second century, which accords better with the pottery found in a pit ante-dating the construction of the house, this villa-estate appears to have continued in use, as a modest agricultural estate, perhaps at a reduced scale, until the late fourth century, though this is not certain.[35]

There is a strong probability of a villa-estate to east of Canterbury at Wingham, close to Watling Street, where excavations in 1881–82 revealed a detached bath-house, which was re-examined in 1966. Though the main house has yet to be located, the luxury of the baths clearly argues the case of a villa-estate on this site.

The bath-house originally consisted of a suite of six rooms fronted by a vestibule, probably flanked by two small rooms and having the entrance to the baths at its centre. The *frigidarium* was at the east end of the baths and its walls were painted with dark red wall-plaster; it was floored with a mosaic pavement, showing a geometric design of black and white *tesserae*. Opening off this room and projecting to south was a shallow *piscina*, with a tessellated floor and its wall faced with black *tesserae*. West of the cold room were the hypo-causted *tepidarium*, *caldarium* and *laconicum*, served by a furnace at the west end of the baths. The original plan of this bath-house was later modified by the demolition of the vestibule and related rooms and the construction of two rooms, projecting to north from the two ends of the building. The eastern room may have served as an *apodyterium* and was laid with a mosaic floor, consisting of a design of Greek meanders in black and white *tesserae* and enclosed by black-and-white borders. The floor of the western room had been destroyed by later alterations and its purpose is uncertain. During this second phase (Fig. 31), the bath-house measured overall 12 × 19.2 m. Drastic modifications were subsequently made to the heated rooms. They were reduced to two and

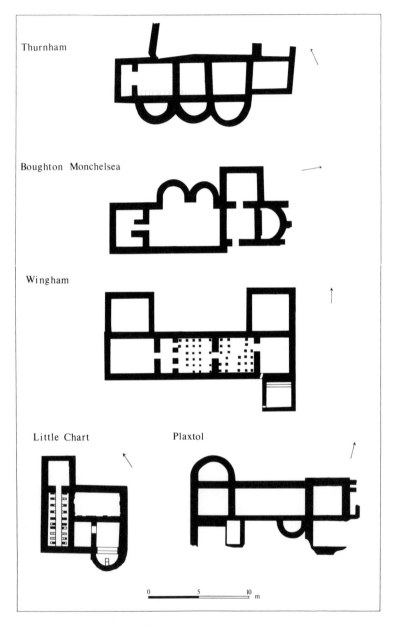

Fig. 31. Bath-houses

enlarged by the suppression of the *laconicum*, and their pillared hypocausts removed and replaced by channelled hypocausts. An apsidal room was also built, projecting south from the re-modelled *caldarium*, with which it shared the same furnace beyond the apsidal room. Later still, hot water-tanks had been inserted in the western projecting room and adjacent to the later hot room. Though disturbance during the nineteenth-century excavations makes interpretation of the later phases of the baths very difficult, it is not improbable that they had been converted to industrial use as underlined by the provision of much greater heating capacity than in their earlier phases and the channelled hypocausts which recall the combustion chamber of a tilery. Finds of pottery and coins suggest a general period of occupatiom from the second to the middle of the fourth centrury.

North of the bath-house and 46.6 m. from it was located an aisled building (Fig. 16), measuring 27.5 × 15.9 m. and aligned on the same east–west axis as the baths; another structure probably stood in this space, but this remains to be securely established. The walls of this aisled building had been robbed and only flint foundations and stone bases survived. At the centre of the building was a main hall, with an earthen floor, enclosed by aisles sub-divided by partitions into small compartments. Extensive alterations were noted, but there was a dearth of dating material in association with this building to indicate its construction and period of occupation. However, it is clear that this building, which was probably agricultural, survived late in the Romano-British period as some sherds of Anglo-Frisian pottery were found in an occupation layer within its north-eastern corner and fragments of Anglo-Saxon glass at a short distance from the building.

At about 91 m. south-west of the baths, remnants of walls and occupation debris, which included red and blue *tesserae*, suggest where the main dwelling-house may lie, whose excavation in future years should aid the interpretation of what was probably a villa-estate of some size and importance.

A large building complex was excavated in 1924 facing the Channel on the edge of East Cliff, Folkestone, and has since collapsed into the sea below the cliff (Fig. 32). The original

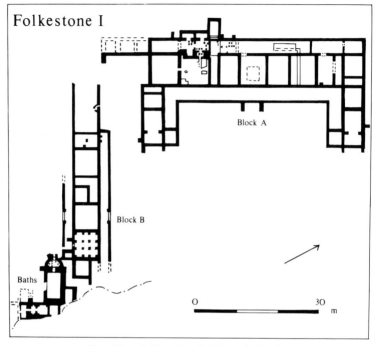

Fig. 32.   Folkestone I: Plan of the site

house is not kown in detail as it was completely built over by
the later building, but it was probably built in the early
second century. In plan, this house appears to have had a
main range of rooms behind a fronting corridor and two
projecting wings ending in bow-fronted rooms looking east;
the walls of this structure were built of tufa on flint and
ironstone foundations, and its overall dimensions were 26.1 ×
52.6 m. The secondary structures, built on the site during the
second century, consisted of two separate houses, facing east
(Block A) and north (Block B); their walls had been built of
grey sand-ragstone, chalk and pebble foundations, tiles and
re-used materials from the earlier house.

Block A, which measured overall 64.7 × 28.9 m., was the
usual design of a central range of rooms, with a rear corridor,
partitioned into smaller compartments, and two projecting

wings and a fronting corridor. The central range was symmetrically arranged with two pairs of three rooms each flanking another room. The outer room in each pair was a passage, and all the rest had remnants of tessellated floors, perhaps even central mosaic panels, only one of which survived though badly mutilated. The entrance into the house was at the centre of the fronting corridor and immediately behind this entrance was situated the main room of this house, which was floored with a mutilated, polychrome mosaic panel surrounded by tessellation. The design of this panel was geometric and consisted of five medallions, one in each corner and the fifth at the centre, and rectangular lozenges filling the spaces between the corner medallions; other rectangular panels filled with *guilloche*, ivy leaves and floral *motifs* filled the rest of the field. The corner medallions were filled with stylised flowers surrounded by two-strand *guilloche*, but nothing survived to suggest the decoration of the central medallion, except for a remnant of its *guilloche*. Two of the lozenges were filled with ivy leaves, but the decoration of the other two is uncertain. This range has been interpreted as the main living-rooms as they had tiled hearths, with the bedrooms perhaps occupying the projecting wings. In the western corner of the house was located its baths suite, which occupied part of the rear corridor and showed signs of reconstruction. The end room was originally hypocausted and may have been used by servants; the room adjacent to it appears to have initially acted as both kitchen and boiler room until its tiled hearth was removed to the southern corner and the hypocausted room filled in. The bathing accommodation comprised the usual provision of heated and cold rooms, with their own plunge-baths, and a *sudatorium*, probably heated by its own projecting furnace, at the north-west end of the suite. The *frigidarium*'s plunge-bath projected beyond the wall of the rear corridor, had two steps descending into it and was 0.92 m. deep. The south-west end of the building was not completely excavated as it passed under a modern road.

Block B appears unfinished to west. What survived the collapsed eastern end of this structure shows a central range of rooms, with fronting and rear corridors, and the surviving remnants of a detached bath-house to its south. Block B, which was built at the same time as Block A, measured overall at least 45.1 × 11.7 m. and ended to west in what has been interpreted as an open yard giving access to the garden occupying the area between Blocks A and B. The eastern end was partly lost by the cliff fall, but most of its accommodation has survived. The end room was probably used by servants and next to it was a large hypocausted room whose destroyed floor was suspended on stone piers; it was heated by a stoke-hole at the eastern end of the rear corridor. To west of this room were five more rooms, the end one of which was clearly a kitchen with a clay floor and two large tiled hearths; the room east of this kitchen was probably a dining-room. At the west end of the fronting corridor outside the kitchen a hearth and a forge had been inserted clearly at a late stage in this block's occupation. The bath-house south of Block B had considerably suffered through subsidence of the cliff edge and parts of its eastern rooms had collapsed. This bath-house consisted of a furnace to south heating a hypocausted *sudatorium* and the *caldarium* next to it. Both these rooms had been decorated with painted wall-plaster and floored with mosaics only one of which survived. To north were two cold rooms, mostly destroyed in the cliff fall, one of which must have been the *frigidarium* of the suite. Other rooms to west of the *caldarium* were not fully excavated, but the west end of the suite was occupied by a large *tepidarium* and apsidal plunge-bath, both heated by a furnace outside the latter; the floor of the *tepidarium* had not survived, but finds in the debris filling clearly show that its walls were internally faced with marble.

Following a pre-Roman occupation in the vicinity of the site, the site at Folkestone was developed about 100 when the earliest house was built. Later during the second century, Blocks A and B and the baths were constructed and occupation lasted until *c.* 370. As the baths suite in Block A is clearly a reconstuction of the west end of the house, it is almost certain that the bath-house south of Block B served both houses. Of the two houses, Block A was undoubtedly the main residence, not only because it is the largest but also because of the luxury of its accommodation. The site was obviously chosen because of its commanding prospect over the Channel; clearly, the earliest building and its succeeding structures must have been located somewhat further inland than when discovered as considerable cliff erosion has occurred since Romano-British times. There is no evidence to suggest the economic background of the earliest house, though it may have been connected with agriculture; certainly, this was most likely the case with the farm located at a short distance to east. However, the secondary buildings on the site may have been those of an official residence rather than belonging to a large villa-estate. Tiles, stamped CLBR, were used in the construction of these buildings, and this has led to the suggestion that the buildings were the residence of the commander of the *Classis Britannica*; attractive though this hypothesis is, it has not met with universal acceptance. The stamped tiles, which were not re-used from a demolished earlier building, very probably came from Dover where such tiles were used in the construction of the naval installations there. By themselves, these tiles obviously indicate a connection with the fleet, but do not conclusively prove the status of the buildings in which they were used. The expenditure involved in their construction and the recurring cost of their maintenance and servicing are so great that they seem inconsistent with the needs of a naval commander and his retinue who, by the nature of their employment, cannot have been in continuous occupation of this residence; perhaps significantly there are no finds of military equipment. Moreover, the Folkestone buildings continued in occupation well after the disappearance of the *Classis Britannica* or its removal from the Dover base. If the Folkestone buildings were an official residence, it is not inconceivable that they may have continued in use at a later stage by the Count of the Saxon Shore. Clearly the site lacks the agricultural buildings that would normally associate it with the economy of a villa-estate, unless such buildings were sited to east of Block A and since lost in the subsequent coastal erosion. The only evidence of economic activity is that of the forge sited at the west end of Block B, but this is clearly not conclusive of general industrial activity on the site.[36]

(iv)   *Bath-houses*

A number of bath-houses are known in the *civitas* and, because they do not appear to be connected with any other buildings, have been described as 'isolated bath-houses'. Their existence may be explained in three ways: (1) These baths may have been erected, on the model of town public baths, as a sort of rural public baths as well as meeting places; in this case, such bath-houses would have been 'isolated'. This would obtain in areas where local small farmers could not afford the costly luxury of building and maintaining private baths suites.[37] (2) Built of less flammable, hence more durable materials as they contained hypocausts, these bath-houses have survived and been recorded whereas the less solidly built, timber-framed farm-houses that they may have belonged to have so far escaped archaeological detection. (3) Some of these bath-houses were clearly built in industrial areas to serve as the equivalent of modern 'pit-head' baths.

The westernmost of these bath-houses was recently excavated on the edge of the canton at Garden Hill, Hartfield (Fig. 24). It was a small structure, measuring *c.* 7.5 × 4.7 m. overall, built with walls of mortared sandstone and looking very makeshift; it had the standard three rooms, with a stoke-hole to east of the hot room. The cold room had an apsidal cold plunge-bath projecting to north and drained by means of a lead pipe found *in situ*. Built during the second century, this rudimentary bath-house was clearly intended for the use of the labour force engaged in iron-working on the site and its vicinity.

At the north of the *civitas* a small, detached bath-house was recently excavated at Baston Manor, Hayes (Fig. 24). It consisted of a suite of five rooms, with a furnace to east, had walls of chalk blocks and tiles and measured overall 12.1 × 9.1 m.; two of these rooms were heated and the cold room had rooms projecting to north-east and south-west, one of which may have contained a plunge-bath. This bath-house was first dated from *c.* 70–140, but a reconsideration of the pottery indicates construction during the second century. No evidence has been found for other nearby buildings and this bath-house may have served the farmsteads known in this area.

Further north-west another small bath-house was recorded in 1956, on the west bank of the Cray at Foot's Cray. It measured 13.7 × 5.9 m. and its plan (Fig. 24) is strongly reminiscent of the Hartfield baths, though the construction here is much more substantial and regular. This bath-house

had two hypocausted rooms and a cold room, with a projecting, apsidal plunge-bath. Dated too early, the Foot's Cray
bath-house is more likely to have been built during the second
century and dismantled *c.* 180, perhaps because of the
ground's instability. Again, there is no known evidence to
account for its use, though a number of farmstead sites are
known in the Cray valley.

About 3.5 km. to south another bath-house was located at
Orpington, some 800 m. south of the farm-house at Orpington
Station, but its full plan and dimensions are not known; an
apsidal room, a rectangular bath and three other rooms, with
opus signinum-bonded flint walls, have been cleared, but it is
not known whether this bath-house was detached or part of a
larger structure. Likewise, its date of construction is uncertain, though finds in the area suggest occupation from the
second to the late fourth century.

Further inland there is a probable bath-house at Kemsing
where several hypocausted rooms of a building were examined
in 1949. It is quite possible, of course, that these heated rooms
may have been part of a dwelling-house rather than a baths.
At Plaxtol remains of foundations were recorded in 1857–58
(Fig. 24). Built of ragstone and tiled courses, the excavated
building measured overall at least 17.7 × 9.7 m. and is shown
as comprising a cold room at its west end, with an apsidal
plunge-bath projecting to north and another probable plunge-
bath to south. To east was a large room with traces of
hypocaust and an apsidal compartment projecting to its
south. It is probable that this large room was in fact sub-
divided. If so, this room would have contained the *tepidarium*
and the *caldarium*, with its apsidal plunge-bath, heated by a
stoke-hole to east where wood ashes and charcoal were
recorded. Though no pottery has been published, the presence
of decorated samian ware clearly points to at least the second
century. In the debris were found several box-tiles bearing a
roller-stamped inscription giving the maker's name (Cab-
riabanus), which has also occurred on tile fragments found in
recent excavations at the Darenth villa-estate. It is clear that a
tilery supplying both Darenth and Plaxtol remains to be
located. From what is known of this site and other finds in its
immediate area, it is very likely that the Plaxtol building must

have been the baths of a farm-house, which is yet to be discovered, rather than an 'isolated' bath-house.

Much the same can be said of the site at Teston above the north bank of the Medway where a partial excavation in 1872 revealed what may well be the baths suite of a dwelling-house awaiting further examination (Fig. 30). The incomplete plan shows the west corner of a building, measuring overall 9.9 × 14.2 m., constructed of ragstone masonry and containing two, possibly three, hypocausted rooms: a *caldarium*, heated by a furnace to its east, with a projecting, buttressed, apsidal plunge-bath; and to west another heated room, probably the *tepidarium*. Further to north was a large, flagged area, probably a *palaestra*. A long wall to east, beyond the heated rooms, may have contained other rooms of the baths or been part of the dwelling-house. The site was certainly occupied during the second century.

East of the Medway, there is a possibility of bath-houses at Borden, near Sittingbourne, and Buckland, near Faversham, but the record is very confused, and the structures at these two sites may belong to farm-houses rather than baths. A detached bath-house was excavated in 1841 at Boughton Monchelsea (Fig. 31); it measured 18.3 × 9.2 m. At the centre of the building was a large, hypocausted room, with two apsidal plunge-baths, served by a furnace to its south; it is likely that a partition wall divided this room into the normal *caldarium* and *tepidarium*. To north was a rectangular *sudatorium* and to its east the *frigidarium* with its own apsidal, cold plunge-bath. Though other foundations, with painted wall-plaster surfaces, were thought to exist east of the cold room, this is not certainly established. The site has produced coins suggesting occupation in the early first century, but the bath-house is likely to have been constructed, conveniently close to a stream, during the second century and continued in use into the fourth. Unless a farm-house remains to be found nearby, this bath-house would seem to have served the needs of the small farming community in its area.

Parts of another bath-house were recently found in the course of road-works at Thurnham where foundations were recorded in 1833. Excavations in 1958 brought to light part of a building, which is clearly a bath-house (Fig. 31). It had been built upon an earlier structure and had walls of ragstone and flint; it measured overall 16.9 × 6.5 m. The accommodation consisted of a *caldarium*, a *tepidarium* and a *frigidarium*, each provided with projecting, apsidal plunges. Additionally, the cold room had a small compartment to its west which may have served as a changing room. Parts of the *opus signinum* flooring of the cold room and the probable undressing room had survived *in situ*, but the floors and hypocausts of the heated rooms had been completely demolished; likewise, the furnace had been destroyed, though it must clearly have lain to east of the *caldarium*. Built in the late second century or early in the third, this building seems to have been destroyed at the end of the third century. It is probable that this bath-house was part of the farm-house destroyed in the nineteenth century to which probably belonged a small agricultural outbuilding found *c*. 39 m. east of the baths.

A compact bath-house was excavated in 1947 at Little Chart, near Ashford; it was built of ragstone, with some tile, and measured 10. × 10.8 m. overall (Fig. 31). The accommodation included an *apodyterium*,floored with a plain tessellation, and a *frigidarium* with a tessellation containing a central panel with a geometric pattern of black and white *tesserae*. To south of this cold room steps led into an apsidal cold plunge-bath. To west was a small *tepidarium* and a larger *caldarium*, both laid with at least plain tessellations. The *tepidarium* was not hypocausted and must have been heated by heat reaching it from the *caldarium*. The *caldarium* had a sort of channelled hypocaust, reminiscent of tileries, and a large furnace to its north. At a later stage, an apsidal plunge-bath was built against the west wall of the *caldarium*. Evidence to suggest the date of construction was scanty; late first century pottery found in a pit *c*. 79 m. from the west corner of the baths need indicate no more than earlier occupation on the site. However, a few coins suggest that this bath-house was in use *c*. 250 and that alterations, affecting the furnace and the *caldarium*, took place during the fourth century. Once more, it is not certain that the Little Chart bath-house was 'isolated' as parts of another building were demolished by quarrying in 1947–48 14.6 m. north-west of the baths. Another bath-house is suggested by records of foundations, which included apses, under the church and in the churchyard at Lyminge.

The southernmost 'isolated' bath-house was discovered in 1970 at Beauport Park, on the high ground above Hastings, in a known iron-working site. The structure was in a remarkable state of preservation and some of its walls had survived to a height of *c.* 2 m. An original suite, consisting of a *frigidarium* and its cold plunge-bath, three heated rooms and a stoke-hole, had been built about 175; it was repaired and extended, during the first half of the third century, by the addition of three more rooms and another stoke-hole. One of these new rooms was a *caldarium*, with a hot plunge-bath adjacent to the furnace and an apsidal hot-water basin. In its final phase this bath-house measured 14 × 15.4 m. Heating was provided by both pillared and channelled hypocausts, and the walls were decorated with painted wall-plaster, some surviving *in situ*. This bath-house was probably abandoned *c.* 250, though the site apparently was occupied into the fourth century. Over 600 tiles, stamped CLBR, found in fragments in the debris and others intact and incorporated in its structure, clearly demonstrate the connection between the fleet and this bath-house, which was very probably intended as 'pit-head' baths for the use of the iron-working workforce.[38]

Temples

Several rural temples have so far been recorded. Some of these were part of a villa-estate, e.g. the temple and shrine at Lullingstone (Figs. 23 and 19), or connected with the army as at Richborough; others were built on hill-tops and on or near roads. In Celtic Gaul, temples often lay on tribal boundaries and afforded shelter to refugees or a location for inter-tribal contacts; in Roman Britain, this can be argued for temples of pre-Roman foundation (the Worth temple is precluded because of its location), but it cannot apply to rural shrines in general. Apart from the circular Lullingstone shrine, temples were of the usual Romano-Celtic rectangular, concentric plan, with a *cella* enclosed within an ambulatory.

A road-side temple probably stood at Greenwich Park close to the line of Watling Street where a short section of wall and,

at a higher level, remnants of a tessellated floor were examined in 1902. The numerous finds included an inscribed
fragment of white marble, and parts of columns and statuary,
as well as an inscription, the first line of which probably refers
to Aesculapius, all of which are indicative more of a temple
than a dwelling. This is further supported by the large
number of coins, about 300, found scattered in the small area
examined and suggesting occupation from the middle of the
first century to the late fourth.

A temple was located on the western edge of the canton at
Titsey and close to the Roman road from London towards
Lewes. Only the flint foundations of this temple survived, but
it was clearly of the normal Romano-Celtic plan (Fig. 23).
The nearly square *cella* (6.2 × 6.5 m.) was surrounded by an
ambulatory within a *temenos*, occupying an area of 31.2 × 30.1
m. It is not certain when this temple was built, but it is
thought that its construction was contemporary with the
building of the Roman road, which is dated to the late first
and early second centuries. It may have been connected with
the villa built nearby at about the same time, though the
temple site is at some distance (*c.* 800 m.) and appears to have
become disused, much earlier than the dwelling-house, at the
end of the third century.

Another temple site is strongly indicated by circumstantial
evidence on Blue Bell Hill, Aylesford. It is located on high
ground close to and east of the Roman road from Rochester
towards Hastings and overlooks the Eccles villa-estate.
Nineteenth-century finds on an oval mound, measuring 27.4
× 14.6 m. and over 4 m. high, of 'extensive buildings' and part
of a tiled floor, much building debris and numerous small
objects and coins have strongly suggested a temple site. Many
coins found on or near the site, including three Belgic ones,
support this possibility, and indicate occupation from the first
to the late fourth century. Certainly, the location of the site
has much to commend it and, if the pre-Roman coins suggest
its religious use before the Roman conquest, it may well be
that some sort of a shrine already existed here, perhaps on the
boundary of a tribal sub-division.

A temple was excavated in 1969 at Boxted *c.* 275 m. to
south-west of the villa site and half-way between it and the

line of Watling Street. The structure, of the usual concentric plan, had been badly robbed and only flint foundations survived, though there was also evidence for tile quoins; the *cella* measured 6.7 m. sq. and the ambulatory 13.4 m. sq. Dating evidence was scanty, but occupation appears likely during the second century. The location of this temple suggests that it may have served in the dual capacity of a road-side shrine and for the worship of the villa's inhabitants.

The basilican building on the Hartlip villa-estate (pp. 130–1) has also been suggested, on grounds of analogy, as a possible religious building, but this is not convincing. Another probable temple site was trial-trenched at Barham in 1970 to confirm air photography, which showed a rectangular enclosure of *c.* 65.5 × 85.5 m., but no further details are available. The easternmost temple was at Worth, the site of an earlier Iron Age occupation, possibly a shrine. Excavations in 1925 uncovered evidence of a Romano-Celtic temple (Fig. 23), built of mortared chalk blocks and measuring overall 16.1 × 15.8 m., with a *cella* of 5.7 × 5.6 m. Parts of a statue suggested that this temple may have been dedicated to a war god and in use throughout the Roman period.[39]

Though there are several temples and shrines, both in towns and other urban settlements and in the countryside, little is known of the religion of the Cantiaci; what is known, moreover, is more often than not a matter for conjecture rather than established fact. Some of the finds associated with the Springhead temple precinct have suggested curative powers attributed to the gods worshipped there, and it is possible that the cult was connected with the nearby springs. Water is again associated with nymphs worshipped in the first Lullingstone house. Aesculapius may have been the deity of the probable temple in Greenwich Park and Mars, or his Celtic equivalent, at Worth. Beyond these tentative connections, there is no direct evidence to indicate either the deities, publicly worshipped in the *civitas*, or the form of the ritual their worship took. In private life, some indication of the beliefs current in the canton can be seen in the clay statuettes of Venus and mother-goddesses, both fertility symbols, that have frequently been found in towns and country alike. Likewise, there is only a little direct evidence for the exotic

religions imported into Roman Britain by the army and
merchants, consisting of casual finds such as a bronze statuet-
te of Osiris probably in a Roman context at Swanscombe, and
the head of a terracotta figure again of Osiris recently found in
Rochester.

Leaving aside the problem of whether the element *Eccles-* in
place-names may denote the existence of a fourth-century or
later Romano-British church, which has now been seriously
questioned, direct evidence for Christianity in the countryside
is restricted to the fourth-century house-church at Lullingstone (p. 114). In any case, Christianity is likely to have had
more adherents in urban settlements and its presence is
attested in Canterbury. Apart from references by Bede to
Christians in Canterbury under Roman rule and the recent
find outside the city-wall of a silver hoard, which contained a
spoon and a *ligula* incised with the *Chi-Rho* monogram, it is not
improbable that a church existed on the site of the cathedral
and was completely removed in 1067. Moreover, it is now
thought that the early St. Pancras may have been a late-
Roman extra-mural Christian church. On the other hand, it
has been persuasively argued that St. Martin's, long suspected as the site of a late-Roman church, is likely to have
been a mausoleum. There are also strong reasons for believing
that a Christian church existed within the fort at Richborough
in the late fourth or early fifth century. In any case, Christianity in the *civitas*, as in the rest of Roman Britain, is likely to
have remained a minority religion, despite Constantius II's
order for the destruction of pagan temples. It is not possible to
demonstrate archaeologically that a resurgence of Celtic
religion took place during the fourth century parallel with the
gradual breakdown of Romano-British institutions; however,
the evidence of substantial repairing at the Worth temple after
Constantine's death may not be an isolated pointer.

Rural burials

Burial took place in family mausolea, barrows, cemeteries
connected with urban settlements, or single grave-groups
which abound in the countryside of the *civitas*. Both inhumation, in wooden coffins and stone or lead *sarcophagi*, and

cremation were practised, and cemeteries are known where both practices obtained.

Apart from the mausolea connected with the villa-estates at Keston and Lullingstone, a mausoleum was recently excavated beneath the ruins of the church at Stone, near Faversham, to north of Watling Street. The building (Fig. 19) was constructed of ragstone with string courses of bonding-tiles; it had an *opus signinum* floor, was internally decorated with painted wall-plaster and measured 5.8 × 6.1 m. overall. The interpretation of the structure as a mausoleum rather than the *cella* of a standard road-side Romano-Celtic temple rests on the absence of an ambulatory wall, which does not appear demolished in post-Roman re-building. No building is so far known within reasonable distance of this mausoleum, but much settlement is known in the general area. There was little dating evidence and the few coins recovered suggested original construction in the fourth century. Other mausolea may have existed at St. Martin's, Canterbury, and at Folkestone II where there were two ill-recorded structures, one of which had a deep, sunken floor suggestive of a tomb rather than a dwelling.

Several Roman barrows are known in the *civitas* and have been discussed by Dunning and Jessup. These burial chambers may occur singly, e.g. at Holborough, or in groups of two or more, e.g. in Canterbury, usually near a Roman site or beside Roman roads, and are conical, steep-sided and surrounded by a ditch. Such barrows contained a cremated burial, rarely a secondary one, and appear to have been erected mainly during the first half of the second century.

The westernmost barrow may have been located at West Wickham where excavations in 1889 found evidence for a probable, ploughed-out barrow, but the evidence is inconclusive as in the case of the ploughed-out barrow probably sited near the building at Plaxtol, which may have contained an inhumation. The barrow at Holborough stood 5.5 m. high and was more than 30 m. in diameter. It contained a primary cremation burial in a wooden coffin, and a secondary inhumation of an infant in a decorated lead *sarcophagus*. Amongst the finds was an iron folding-stool, a piece of silk damask, and a worn coin of Antoninus Pius as well as much pottery,

especially amphora fragments. The pottery evidence suggested that the barrow was erected during the first quarter of
the third century and was soon followed by the secondary
burial not later than *c.* 250; recent reconsideration of the
amphora fragments, however, indicates a late third-century
date. Though there was no evidence to suggest the status of
the primary burial, the grave furniture, and in particular the
luxury item of a purse lined with silk damask, has suggested
an official from Rochester, perhaps residing in the house at
Snodland slightly more than 1 km. to south-east.

Other barrows, of probable Roman date, have been located
in the eastern part of the *civitas*, apparently aligned on main
Roman roads. A probable barrow at Chartham Downs was
situated close to the Canterbury–Ashford road and two
groups of three large barrows each, aligned on Watling Street,
have been recorded at Boughton-under-Blean and Kingston.
Another barrow of probable Roman date at Stowting is
aligned on the Canterbury–Lympne road. Three more barrows in a row were excavated in 1882 or 1883 at Bishopsbourne close to the Canterbury–Dover road; they contained
cremated bones in stone cists. The three aligned barrows at
Shepherdswell are said to have produced 'Celtic, British,
Saxon and Roman remains' and their dating must be re-
garded as doubtful. The easternmost barrow was located near
the west gate of the Richborough fort; there a low mound
covered an inhumation in a wooden coffin, which was deposited in a pit cut 2.5 m. below the level of the chamber during
the third century.

The greatest concentration of barrows was, however, in
Canterbury (Fig. 8). Four barrows, known as the Dungill
Hills, are known: the Dane John, the Little Dungill about 275
m. further north-east, a third one, destroyed in 1860, near the
east station and a fourth, again destroyed, *c.* 90 m. south-east
of Dane John. A probable fifth barrow was on the site of Salt
Hill where an inhumation burial was found in 1867–68. The
surprising feature of the Canterbury barrows is that they were
all necessary in view of the several cemeteries linked with the
city; an explanation may be that they were groups of tombs
belonging to socially prominent families.[40]

Cemeteries abound in the *civitas*, either as single or multiple

grave-groups dotted all over the countryside or more extensive
burial grounds connected with urban settlements (e.g. Canterbury, Fig. 8) or rural establishments, but it would seem
profitless to discuss more than a random selection. Such
cemeteries naturally indicate settlement in the vicinity which
is at times archaeologically elusive (e.g. Ospringe).

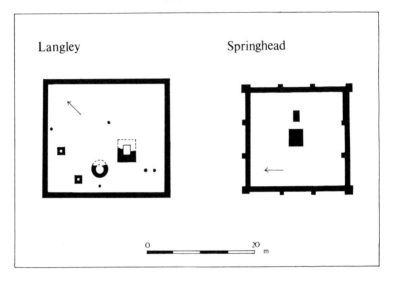

Fig. 33. Walled cemeteries

Apart from the cemeteries at Canterbury, large cemeteries
must have existed at Rochester, probably on Boley Hill, but
lack of space may have forced burial across the Medway at
Strood where the number of burials found seems dispro-
portionate to the ribbon development along Watling Street.
Cemeteries on high ground above and near Dartford indicate
a sizeable settlement in the area. In the countryside there are
cemeteries close to Maidstone and at Otford, both areas of
considerable settlement, and another large cemetery is said to
have been found at Petham. Oddly enough, no cemeteries
have so far been found connected with some of the large
villa-estates (e.g. Darenth and Eccles), but this is clearly due
either to unrecorded destruction during industrial development, as probably at Eccles, or lack of excavation. The best

recorded cemetery was excavated in 1920–25 close to Watling Street at Ospringe; the 387 inhumations and cremations recorded were about one-half of the total and burial had taken place over a long period, from the second to the fourth century which clearly implies a sizeable, perhaps road-side settlement in the area, probably *Durolevum*, (Ch. 3) which is still to be located. A feature of rural cemeteries is that some of them were enclosed by a wall. At Langley (Fig. 33) the walled enclosure on a hill-top, close to the Rochester–Hastings road, measured about 25 m. sq. and contained a square tomb, with ragstone walls, 1.2 m. thick, a tower-like monument, rising perhaps to about 6 m. high, and another circular tower which had an external diameter of 3.5 m.; a general second-century date has been proposed for this cemetery. Another walled

Fig. 34.   Eccles: Graffito on the bowl of a spoon

cemetery at Sutton Valence was close to the branch road from the Maidstone area to Lympne and occupied an area of 18.3 × 4.6 m.; again, the associated finds suggest a date in the second century. Another rectangular enclosure at Borden, with walls of loose flint, was aligned on Watling Street; it had a circular tower, with an external diameter of 6.9 m., and was dated from the second to the fourth century. At Springhead (Fig. 33) on Watling Street, the walled enclosure measured 17.7 × 16.9 m. and had walls 0.9 m. thick. The central burial was deposited within an oolitic *sarcophagus*, and three more coffins, two of undecorated lead and one of stone, were also found. A second-century date is likely. Other walled cemeteries have been recorded at East Barming and, prob- ably, at Plaxtol.[41]

Fig. 35.   The Eccles *defixio*

Summary

In general terms, the river valleys and the lower ground below the Downs to the north of the canton where most settlement took place appear to have been dominated by a comparatively small number of large villa-estates. Keston in the west, Darenth in the Darent valley, Eccles in the lower Medway valley, would seem to be the *haupt* villa-estates of their respective areas. Within the ambit of neighbouring urban settlements, these villa-estates must have been related to the farm-houses and farmsteads in their area. Lullingstone may have been a special case and the houses in Maidstone clearly dominated the upper Medway valley. Settlement in the Sittingbourne/Faversham area may have depended on the settlement at *Durolevum*. The location of the *civitas* capital at Canterbury apparently influenced the settlement of the eastern part of the canton, though future excavation may show that either Boughton Aluph or, more probably, Wye was the chief villa-estate of the Stour valley.

Most of the sites examined to date display varying degrees of wealth which attracted elements of what would now be considered literacy, even culture, as shown not only by the literary references in the Lullingstone mosaics and the Otford wall-plaster fragment, but also on the ubiquitous graffiti of names, etc. (Fig. 34), and the as yet undeciphered Eccles *defixio* with its *boustrophedon* inscription (Fig. 35). Yet, the overall aspect must perforce remain fragmentary until the available evidence on the multitude of sites can be studied in detail as a whole rather than as individual sites.

5

Industry and the Economy

The economy of the *civitas*, when both documentary sources and the archaeological evidence are taken into account, can best be described as a mixture of agriculture and light industry. Developing from its Iron Age predecessor[1] under the impetus of the better tools imported by the Romans and the consequent clearance of forest land, agriculture flourished on the lighter soils of the chalk uplands, the river valleys and the coastal belt, as clearly demonstrated by the evolution of Iron Age farmsteads into Romano-British farms and villa-estates on some of which cottage industries, such as metal-working, were practised. The main industrial activity, however, was concentrated close to the sources of raw materials. Pottery and tile manufacture developed to a large scale on the banks of the Medway, on the Thames foreshore, the Medway marshes, and the Canterbury area, and the iron-working sites already exploited in the Weald were expanded. Elsewhere, there is evidence for salt-extraction, metal-working, the development of the oyster-beds in the Thames estuary, perhaps also for fulling or dyeing.

Farming was well established before the Claudian invasion. Strabo, writing in the period between Caesar's expeditions and the landing at Richborough but drawing his material from Pytheas's visit to Britain in the fourth century B.C., refers to corn being grown as well as gold, silver and iron being extracted. Caesar mentions farming and was struck by the frequency of farm-buildings and the large number of cattle.[2] This well-established tradition of farming and animal husbandry must clearly have greatly developed under Roman rule; yet, the only direct evidence is the development of the farms and villa-estates which, drawing their prosperity from the land, proclaim its profitable exploitation – large barns, for instance at Lullingstone and Horton Kirby, and corn-driers at Wye and Eccles show that ample surpluses of cereals must have been produced for trading.

Little is so far known of the methods used in farming; Pliny mentions marling the heavier soils with chalk,[3] but few agricultural implements have been found on excavated sites. Even less well established are the fields belonging to farms, and there is very meagre evidence for the cereals produced, though bread wheat, barley and oats have been found on a number of sites.[4] Though stock raising was clearly undertaken as early as Caesar's time, the evidence of animal bones from excavated sites allows no general conclusions on the extent of this activity; one possible indication is the kite-shaped enclosure at Mangravet Wood, near Maidstone, where an area of 10.4 ha. of arable land may have been converted into a pasture ranch.[5]

Potteries

Pottery manufacture was undertakn in the canton on a broad belt stretching from west to east mainly along the shores of the Thames, the Medway estuary and the Stour, with a number of kiln sites further inland. The large number of sites and the vast amount of the pottery they must have produced clearly indicate that pottery-making was not carried out solely for the satisfaction of local markets and that much of it must have been sold beyond the boundaries of the *civitas*.

The most westerly industrial site is at Charlton where the possibility of a pottery kiln has been suggested by a shallow pit, with burnt wood and clay, but the absence of kiln furniture (apart from a fragment of a clay bar) and wasters indicates that this is more likely to a have been a salt-panning site. Inland, at Joyden's Wood, near Bexley, a late second century kiln excavated in 1951–53 has since been uncritically accepted as a pottery kiln in spite of the excavators' caution. The kiln lacks a firing-pit (though an adjacent ditch may have served as such) and, more important, any evidence for kiln furniture or wasters. It seems more likely that this kiln was a corn-drier which the excavators themselves put forward as an alternative interpretation. A kiln was found in 1904 at Galley Hill, Swanscombe, in the course of chalk extraction, but only the combustion chamber and the flue into the firing channel were recorded. There was no evidence for any kiln furniture or pottery associated with this kiln. A probable kiln-site is shown on the Ordnance Survey *Map of Roman Britain* (1956 edition) at Stonehill Green, south of the Joyden's Wood site, and the distinctive pottery found at Stone Castle Quarry, Greenhithe, has suggested the likelihood of a kiln near the site, which may have been lost together with virtually all the Romano-British site during wartime large-scale quarrying. Close by at Stonewood on Watling Street another kiln was reported, though no other details survive. Another pottery kiln was found in 1921–22 during road-works along Watling Street at Springhead (Fig. 14) and partly destroyed before recording; however, the pottery found in it dates it to the second century. Further inland, an odd-shaped kiln was found close to the building at Otford and seems to have produced mainly flagons dateable to the late first century.

Considerable pottery-making activity has been established at a site on the parish boundary between Chalk and Shorne. Unfortunately, the site was badly destroyed in the course of quarrying for gravel, which allowed only for partial recording. However, discounting workmen's claims for more, at least five kilns were investigated. One of these was circular with a central pedestal and dated by the pottery found in its filling to the late second century; the remnants of a second kiln were examined nearby and it appeared to be of similar type, though no dating evidence survived. Two more kilns were found close to each other in the same area and one of these was of up-draught type. No pottery was found in these two kilns, but finds in the area suggest a second-century date. A fifth kiln was destroyed by the cutting of a gas trench, and no structural or dating evidence remained. Some 914 m. north-east of this site another kiln was found in 1926 in a gravel-pit at Hoo Junction; it was probably circular or oval and its filling contained wasters and kiln bars. The activity of this kiln was not established, but a reconstructed vessel in its rubbish filling

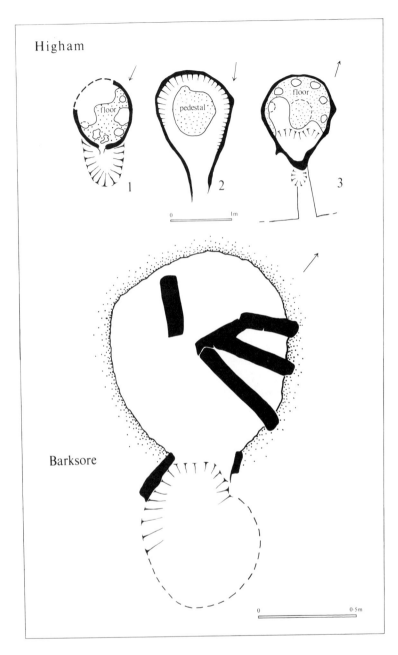

Fig. 36.   Kilns

suggests the second century.[6] Further east the cutting of a gas-main trench in 1978 has uncovered evidence for four, possibly five, kilns in the parish of Higham[7] producing black-burnished wares. The earliest of these kilns (Fig. 36, no. 1) had a double oval chamber, measuring internally 0.8 × 0.9 m., with a free-standing pedestal supporting a permanent floor pierced by vent-holes. Some inconclusive evidence was also found that this kiln may have been constructed upon the remnants of an earlier one; its activity has been dated to 160–180. Close to this kiln three more kilns were located. Of these, the largest, with an internal diameter of 1–1.1 m., was found beneath kiln 3 and may have been active between 180 and 220. Kilns 2 and 3 (Fig. 36) lay close to each other on opposite sides of the gas-main trench and about 7 m. west of kiln 1 and are both dated to 220–240. Kiln 2 had a single, oval chamber, 1.3 m. long × 1.3 m. wide, whilst kiln 3 (Fig. 38) was double-chambered, oval (measuring 1.25 m. long × 1.1 m. wide) and its central pedestal supported a floor pierced by vent-holes. The activity of the industry centred on this site has been dated from at least

Fig. 37.   Higham: Kiln 2

Fig. 38.   Higham: Kiln 3

160–240, as the inconclusive evidence for the earlier kiln below kiln 1 does not allow for an earlier dating. Another kiln site had long been suspected further to east at Broomhey Farm, Cooling, where there is much loose, burnt soil and considerable amounts of pottery have been recovered. Indeed, a kiln was mentioned in 1932 and tentatively dated to the second century, but the site has not been adequately published. Recent work has shown that industrial activity extended over a large area, though it is not yet clearly established what sort of activity this may have been. However, the presence of much building debris and *briquetage* in the area suggests a building nearby and salt-panning as well as possible pottery manufacture.

The area to north and west of Cliffe appears to have been another centre of pottery making. On West Cliffe Marshes, soil erosion of the bank exposed 'kilns', another kiln was found under the eroded bank at Cliffe Marshes, 'connected with at least one other kiln' and third–century pottery, and 'kilns were found $\frac{1}{4}$-mile N.E. of Cliffe.' However, as none of these sites and the associated pottery have been adequately published, it is impossible to conclude on the nature of this activity and its dating. At the western extremity of the Hoo peninsula, a kiln was found on the Isle of Grain, close across the Medway estuary to sites of several potteries. The find on the salt marshes off Hoo St. Werburgh of a large quantity of flagons suggests another kiln nearby.[8]

Another large concentration of potteries was located on the marshland area north-east of Upchurch and its products have long been known as 'Upchurch ware'; however, the rise in the sea-level since Roman times[9] and the consequential burial of the sites under several feet of alluvium have precluded methodical excavation of the sites concerned, and only chance finds or examination of eroded banks at low tide have allowed the discovery of a number of kiln sites. Payne records, in a letter from C.H. Woodruff, 'the clearest traces of kilns' on the right bank of Otterham Creek, though the mention of 'portions of bricks covered with a vitrified glaze' may suggest, if not a salt-panning site, a tilery rater than a pottery kiln. There are several finds of pottery and wasters from the marshes north-east of Upchurch from which it was concluded that pottery-making began in the area *c*. 40 and continued until the end of the second century when it may have been transferred to the more sheltered area of Otterham Creek. Remains of a kiln at a short distance from the sea-wall of Slayhills Saltings were also found in 1894, but no other evidence survived. In recent years, two kilns were partly recorded in the Slayhills Marsh; one of these was of circular, up-draught type, the other rectangular. The associated pottery, containing wasters, suggests activity for both kilns in the latter half of the first century. Another pottery kiln was recorded in 1972 on marsh-reclaimed land at Barksore (Fig. 36); it was a circular, up-draught type (0.9 m. internally), with two pre-fabricated and elongated pedestals supporting clay fire-bars and in production after *c*. 50. Further east, on the saltings at Bedlam's Bottom, there was recorded another circular, up-draught kiln, with a central pedestal and pre-fabricated fire-bars. A 'poppy-head' beaker found embedded in the pedestal suggests activity in the second century, but no other pottery was found in association.

Pottery manufacture was also undertaken on the east bank of the Medway very close to the villa at Eccles; the whole area, where much industrial activity had taken place, has been almost completely destroyed by modern waste-pits and no kiln(s) survived, except for parts of a waste-dump. The pottery from this deposit, consisting largely of wasters and a few items used in pottery-making, indicates production of jars and bowls, flagons, mortaria, imitations of imported lead-glazed wares, Gallo-Belgic platters and rouletted butt-beakers, ending about 65 (Fig. 39). It is very likely however, that manufacture continued longer elsewhere on this site as suggested by a tilery operating at the end of the second century near the site of the kiln waste.[10]

Another major area of pottery production was centred around Canterbury where no less than nine pottery kilns have so far been identified. In 1939 an oval-shaped pottery kiln was found in the Municipal Gardens close to the Dane John mound and many wasters were recovered, including bowls, dishes, jars, flagons and mortaria, dating from the first to the second century. In 1949 a circular kiln was found in Reed Avenue with late first-century pottery in association. At St. Stephen's outside the town, an oval-shaped kiln was found in 1954; it was associated with and used the same stokehole as a tilery (Fig. 41, no. 6). The pottery kiln had a tongue-like projection supporting the oven floor and was of the up-draught type. The products of this kiln range from flagons, jars and reeded bowls to dishes and cooking-pots. The dating of the activity of this kiln to 130–140 relies on two pieces of samian recovered from the stoke-hole pit, but a fragment from a flanged dish was found at the same depth; this and other pottery from the same deposit indicate a later date. Moreover, as the earlier pottery illustrated in the excavation report was found in the filling of the kiln's furnace, i.e. after it ceased to operate, it cannot suggest the kiln's period of production, whereas the stoke-hole pit was receiving rubbish at a much later period. In the circumstances, it seems more likely that this kiln is dated too early. About 64 m. east-north-east of the tilery was found another kiiln, roughly circular in plan and measuring 1 m. internally. Its floor was supported by three clay pilasters reinforced with tiles and a short central wall of

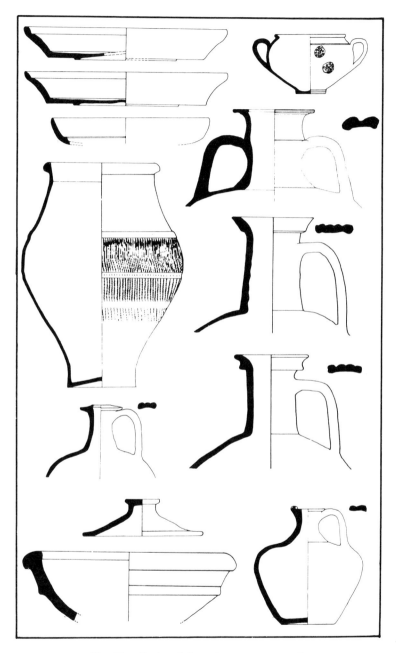

Fig. 39. Eccles: Selected pottery types ($\frac{1}{4}$)

broken tiles (Fig. 40, no. 2). The kiln products included imitation Gallo-Belgic platters, combed wares, carinated beakers, jars, bowls and flagons, which indicate a mid first-century date. Two more pottery kilns were found in Whitehall Gardens. One of these was of up-draught type, oval-shaped and measured 1.5 m. long and 1 m. wide; its clay floor was pierced by vent-holes (Fig. 40, nos. 4a and b). The pottery found associated with this kiln consisted of flagons, jars and reeded, carinated bowls and dates its period of production to *c*. 130–160, perhaps rather earlier. The second kiln (Fig. 40, no. 3) was of up-draught type and circular, with an internal diameter of 0.9 m., and its floor was supported by a free-standing tongue; the pottery found in the furnace chamber suggests a date of *c*. 150–180. A third kiln found in the same area was circular, of up-draught type, and wasters of jugs, two-handled amphorae and mortaria date it to the middle of the second century. Two more kilns were recently recorded during building work. One was found in 1978 outside the city walls in North Lane. This kiln was of up-draught type with two fire chambers and appeared to have been destroyed after firing. The associated pottery, mostly jars and bowls suggests production about the end of the first century. The second kiln was found during the construction of the Canterbury by-pass. Though the structure was partly destroyed by bulldozing, it appears to have also been of up-draught type, possibly with two flues, and produced necked jars, bowls, lid-seated jars or bowls and strainers probably during the period 60–80.[11]

Further east from Canterbury, evidence was found in 1872 at Preston for what may well have been a shallow, horizontal-draught pottery kiln; other potteries may have also been located close to the Margate building, at Ospringe and Dymchurch, though in the latter case salt-panning is more probable. Pottery-making was also undertaken in the iron-working area of the Weald as indicated by wasters found at Bardown, but 'the Bardown kilns have not been found.'[12]

Pottery manufacture in the *civitas* was undoubtedly on a mass-production scale, and the number of kiln-sites so far known as well as their large output underline this aspect of the industry. Production was concentrated west of the Medway, apart from the Eccles site, on the Thames foreshore from

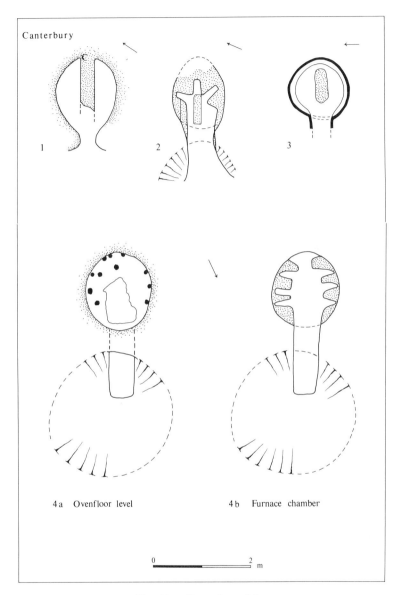

Fig. 40. Canterbury kilns

Springhead to Cooling where kilns were producing throughout the second century and up to about 240. It is unlikely that
it will ever be known how long the Eccles industry continued,
but at least part of it was in production from soon after the
conquest to about 65. In the Medway Marshes production
again began about 50 and lasted certainly into the third
century at least. The other major pottery producing area was
centred round Canterbury from about 50 to 180. Though the
numerous kilns at Canterbury can be accounted for by the
needs of its population, even so a proportion of its production
must have been marketed beyond the cantonal area as can be
shown in the case of stamped Canterbury mortaria.[13] The
same must clearly apply to the western potteries; the number
of kilns on the Medway Marshes, the Thames foreshore and
elsewhere, though obviously catering to the needs of Rochester, other settlements and the countryside, again indicates
marketing further afield, probably even supplying army requirements, as is likely with early potteries such as Eccles.
However, only future mineralogical studies and comparisons
of factory pottery with vessels found at marketing points will
establish this strong probability beyond doubt.

Tileries

Another class of kiln was used for the manufacture of the
various tiles used in building, yet, in spite of the numerous
buildings in towns and the countryside, only three tileries
(and a probable one at Springhead) have to date been
positively identified in the whole of the *civitas*, two at Canterbury and a third one at Eccles. The smaller of the Canterbury
tile-kilns (Fig. 41, no. 5) was a regular, rectangular structure,
measuring 2.4 × 1.8 m., and had three cross-walls and
cross-flues between them; the products of this tilery seem to
have been roofing-tiles (*tegulae*), though box flue-tiles may also
have been made during the second century. The second
Canterbury tilery had an unusual T-shaped plan (Fig. 41, no.
6), with a main flue (5.9 m. long) but without cross-walls to
support a floor, and it seems that the firing of tiles took place
within this long flue. Production in this tilery consis. d of

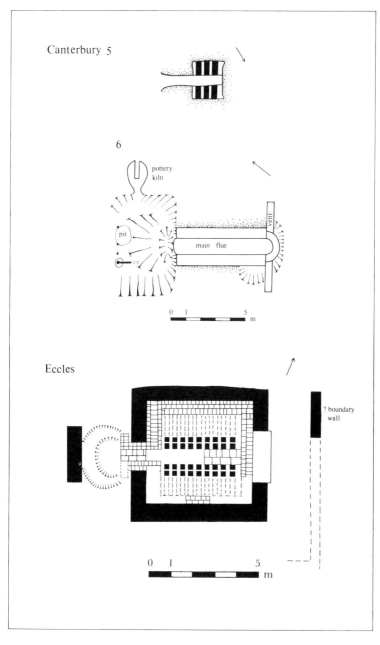

Canterbury 5

6

pottery kiln

pit

main flue

vent

0 1 5
m

Eccles

? boundary wall

0 1 5
m

Fig. 41.   Tileries

tegulae and *imbrices*, though a suggestion has recently been made that this kiln may have been used for drying tiles before they were actually fired in a standard tile-kiln. The dating of this tilery has not been established, though it is probable that it operated at the same time as the second-century pottery kiln adjacent to it. A tilery was excavated at Eccles in 1966 (Fig. 42) after it had been almost detroyed by bulldozing which removed all its superstructure; it was a nearly-square tilery (Fig. 41) and its firing chamber measured 4.9 × 4.7 m. which makes it 'the largest civilian tile-kiln so far recorded in Britain.' The central flue, crossed by nine walls, opened out into the stoke-hole pit to the rear of which was a short length of wall, probably to prevent an uncontrolled surge of flame into the flue; destruction of this tilery was so complete that it was impossible to be sure that the tiles found associated with it (bonding-, bridging- and *pila*-tiles as well as one *imbrex*) were actually fired in it, though stratified pottery suggests a date in the late second or third century. There is also a probability of a tilery somewhere in the vicinity of Cranbrook; many tiles, some unused and others bearing the CLBR stamp of the *Classis Britannica*, were recently found at a site with evidence for iron-working. On the other hand, apart from these finds, little as yet is positively known of a 'building (which) was sited not later than the second century'. The presence of these tiles at this site need not indicate local manufacture as this material could have been stored for building, and the incorporation of CLBR-stamped tiles in the baths at the Beauport Park iron-working site is a probable pointer to such use.[14] A very probable tilery in the Plaxtol area has already been mentioned (Ch. 4).

Other Building Materials

Burning of chalk in kilns for the production of lime used in building and internal wall-plastering must have been undertaken on a large scale but, so far, few lime kilns have been positively identified. Two were located outside the Richborough fort *c*. 88 m. north of the wall; they were both circular and about 1.8 m. in diameter. Another possible lime-kiln was

Fig. 42. Eccles: The tilery

found at Canterbury and a fourth close to the Northfleet
building. This was a substantial kiln constructed of chalk
blocks and measured 3 m. in internal diameter. There is also a
possibility of another kiln on the Isle of Sheppey, but this may
have been used for the burning of oyster-shells rather than
lime.[15]

Another industrial activity which was greatly expanded
under the Romans concerned itself with the provision of
building materials. Timber was plentiful and widely used, but
the exploitation of forest land has left, of course, no archaeological traces. Apart from timber, Kentish ragstone was mainly
used, alongside tiles, for building, with quarries located in the
neighbourhood of Maidstone at Boughton Monchelsea, Loose
and Allington. As a building material ragstone was used
extensively in the canton and exported by barge via the
Medway and the Thames as far afield as Essex and London.
Other building materials used were tufa, a calcareous stone,
which was particularly used for *voussoirs* in the vaulting of
hypocausted buildings, and chalk which was widely incorporated in buildings.[16]

Salt production

Another industry that flourished on the extended coastline of the *civitas* was concerned with the extraction of salt from sea-water. The method, already referred to by ancient authorities as used in Gaul, was to allow salt crystals to form from sea-water fed into evaporating vessels placed over hearths or in bonfires. Local clay, often tempered with straw, was used for making simple containers and their lids, the remnants of which, usually known as *briquetage*, litter salt-panning sites. The hearths, often in groups of two or three, were normally oval-shaped, shallow troughs scooped out of the surrounding soil and lined internally with puddled clay as at Cliffe Creek and Funton. The fuel used for firing these hearths must have been wood, and large deposits of ash surrounding them amply demonstrate their continuous use. The heat generated in these hearths was sufficiently high to cause some vitrification of both the internal lining, which had in some cases to be renewed, and of the evaporating vessels placed on them supported by the characteristic wedge-shaped firebars. This vitrification had the additional advantage of rendering these poorly made vessels completely impervious.

The salt industry was broadly concentrated on the low-lying ground of the Thames and Medway marshes, though there are a few probable outliers. This concentration in areas producing pottery has often brought about some confusion resulting from which salt-panning sites and their adjoining deposits of burnt clay and ash have been mistakenly interpreted as pottery kiln-sites. The westernmost of these salt-panning sites may have been located at Charlton but the evidence is inconclusive. The large majority stretches on a broad belt, facing across the Thames the well-known Essex Redhill sites, from Chalk and Higham to the Hoo peninsula and the Medway marshes, where there is a large concentration of sites and undoubtedly many more still to be recognised, as far as east of Upchurch. *Briquetage* on the prison grounds at Eastchurch on the Isle of Sheppey suggests salt-panning there, too, rather than 'a small farmstead'. There are also some indications at the extreme east of the canton at Dumpton Gap, Broadstairs, and Dymchurch, but coastal changes make the evidence inconclusive. It is not improbable, however, that salt-panning was also undertaken along the southern coast of the *civitas*, particularly on the creeks and inlets of the Romney Marsh area where conditions similar to those of the Thames and Medway marshes obtained. Salt-panning certainly was carried on along the Sussex coast beyond the borders of the Cantiaci, with the nearest sites being at Eastbourne, and an analogous situation is likely to have developed further east on the shores of the English Channel.[17]

Dating of the salt-panning industry is not easy. On most sites the pottery recovered is not stratified and the nature of most of these low-lying areas is such that there has been considerable mixture of pottery from different chronological contexts. There is, however, evidence from some sites of activity in pre-Roman times developing into large-scale industry during the second century, perhaps beginning to decline during the third century when changes in the sea level probably brought about the abandonment of low-lying marsh sites. To link the fortunes of the salt industry on the Thames and Medway marshes with an apparent decline in the pottery industry, however, is premature when so little is so far known of the organisation and production of this industry in the later years of the Roman period. Both pottery and salt would need to be produced locally for local needs rather than be imported from farther afield and, though the loss of other markets may have brought about a smaller production, it is at least probable that salt-panning and pottery industries on the marshes continued throughout the Roman period.

The Iron Industry

Iron-working in Britain was known to the Romans and is referred to by Caesar and Strabo.[18] Within the area of the later *civitas*, there is direct evidence for iron-working in Belgic times from sites like Canterbury and Swarling[19] though, no doubt, iron was extracted and processed at several other sites, too, especially in the hinterland of Hastings.

However, during the Romano-British period the heaviest concentration of iron-working was in the Weald of Kent and

Sussex, for in this area the sideritic ores of the Wadhurst Clay provided an easily-worked source of raw materials. The iron ore occurs in carbonate nodules enclosed by limonite, and the deposits in discontinuous layers at the base of the clay beds were naturally exposed in the sides of deep streams and gills running through the Weald or in pits especially dug for the purpose; moreover, the hardwoods of the Wealden forest, mostly birch and oak, provided an excellent supply for the charcoal needed in the smelting process.

A number of iron-working sites on the northern fringes of the Weald may have been connected with some of the late Iron Age hill-forts and population of the area. At Garden Hill, Hartfield, the site of a hill-fort covering about 2.7 ha., bloomery cinder and slag as well as the baths[20] clearly indicate iron-working in the vicinity of the site. On the southern limits of the Weald, only the sites at Crowhurst Park and Footlands in the Battle-Sedlescombe area were probably at work before 43. There are no settlements of the period known so far that can be connected with these sites, but their small output may have been transported inland or by sea-routes to the settled areas beyond the Weald.[21] However, the Roman conquest and the rapid integration of the south-east into the Roman world brought about in its train a considerable expansion of the iron industry similar to that of the potteries. A larger and more accessible market, owing to the construction of a road network in which iron-working played a part in the use of slag for building,[22] meant much greater exploitation of the clays for iron-smelting as well as for pottery making. Though the centre of the industry now shifted from the fringes to the High Weald and occupied an area stretching for some 48 km., the coastal sites, over a belt of 9.5–16 km., were expanded, too, so that by the end of the first century, about a dozen sites were in full production. The first half of the second century saw a further expansion of the industry, with new sites, such as Bardown and Chitcombe, coming into production, as older sites were being exhausted and new ones were found, bringing the total of iron-working sites and their satellites to more than 20 production areas. The industry began to decline about 250 and only two sites, Oldlands and Footlands, appear to have continued in production,[23] perhaps because their location very

close to main Roman roads made it economically worthwhile
to continue working the dwindling ore deposits. Production
must have reached enormous levels and indicates the demand
for iron during the two centuries the industry continued in full
production. At Bardown and its satellite sites, it has been
estimated, on the basis of the slag-heaps, that between 8,000
and 10,000 tons of iron were produced, representing an
annual output of 160–200 tons. Enormous quantities of iron
slag were removed in the mid-nineteenth century from the
Beauport Park and Oaklands sites, and a recent estimate of
the volume contained in Beauport Park refuse heaps puts it
over 100,000 tons, i.e. a production of some 50,000–60,000
tons of iron ore over a period of 160–170 years.[24]

The whole question of the iron industry in the Weald, its
expansion and decline are connected with the activities of the
Classis Britannica, a connection cautiously advanced some
twenty-five years ago by Richmond and later supported by
Cunliffe. It has since been further amplified by Cleere in a
number of recent papers.[25] The whole thesis is based on the
discovery of stamped tiles of the *Classis Britannica* not only at
coastal establishments such as the forts at Lympne, Dover and
Richborough and the Folkestone building, but also at the
Bodiam harbour installations, the iron-working sites at Bardown, Beauport Park and the probable site at Cranbrook. The
clay used for the manufacture of these stamped tiles came
from the Fairlight area,[26] but the location of the tilery is not so
far known. It is not unlikely, however, that this site may have
been in the Cranbrook area where a number of stamped tiles
in mint condition were recently found. The site is incomplete-
ly examined and published, but the presence of *tuyère* fragments and the iron slag used near Cranbrook in the construction of the Rochester–Hastings road and the branch road to
Ashford and Canterbury suggest iron-working. The Cranbrook stamped tiles may have been intended for or surplus to
the needs of a building, such as the Beauport Park baths, still
to be found. As Richmond put it 'no administrative or
working centre for the Weald is known'[27] and to suggest that
'Cranbrook appears to have been an administative centre of
some kind,'[28] is to go beyond the available evidence. A better
candidate for such a function seems to be Beauport Park

where at least 1300 stamped tiles were found,[29] some of them incorporated in the structure of the substantial bath-house. All these stamped tiles and their find-spots clearly demonstrate the connection of the fleet and the iron industry, but the thesis that the *Classis Britannica* brought about the expansion of the industry, controlled it to the extent of seeing the Weald as 'an Imperial mining estate'[30] and that iron-working in the eastern Weald declined after the removal of the fleet from its Channel ports, though plausible, is not entirely convincing in that it does not take into account several other factors. Cleere's thesis, a development of Margary's examination of the road-system in the eastern Weald,[31] postulates a 'government-administered undertaking rather than a native industry' because of the vast increase in the scale of iron production which, according to this thesis, local communities of iron-workers would be incapable to sustain in order to supply army needs. Yet, if they were not 'capable of such a large-scale conception', who would have carried out this grand design? Certainly not the inexperienced sailors of the fleet. But, even assuming that the fleet could have provided the necessary manpower, if not the expertise, which the existing iron-working communities may have lacked, it is not reasonable to expect it to do so at a time, certainly in the latter part of the first century, when all the fleet's resources must have been earmarked for its support role for the advancing army. Moreover, even at sites such as Beauport Park or Bardown, which was excavated over a number of years, no items of military equipment have been found. At Bardown the only structural remains discovered consist of the post-holes for timber buildings, possibly the shacks and sheds of a temporary population of mineworkers. An expansion, parallel to that of the iron industry in the eastern Weald and contemporary with it, did take place in the native pottery industry for the supply of the army, as demonstrated by the potteries at Eccles and on the Medway marshes, without any direct military involvement or control and consequently the diversion of the iron produced to army requirements ignores the need of iron supplies in the development of towns and other urban settlements and the countryside, which clearly was at its highest during the *floruit* of the Wealden iron industry.

Whether the exploitation of the Wealden iron 'was *essentially* (my italics) a sea-based operation'[32] is also open to debate. Cleere's argument, stemming from the need to explain the role of the *Classis Britannica* in the development of the iron industry, is again largely based on Margary's examination of the roads in the eastern Weald and, in particular, the Rochester–Hastings road which he considers as likely to have been built in two stages, a northern section from Rochester to Hemsted being added to an already-existing road serving the iron-working sites further south. There is no dating evidence for this argument, which relies exclusively on the southern alignments of the road to suggest that it was not of military origin and built in two stages. There is no reason to suppose that this road was built by the army as it was not built in the wake of the advancing legions, which was clearly the case with Watling Street, nor did it connect a major Channel port with the hinterland of the province. On the other hand, its essential purpose appears to have been to provide a link between the Wealden iron industry and the Thames via Rochester by avoiding the more hazardous sea-voyage; the indirectness of some of its southern alignments can be explained by local topography and the location of the sites it served. Likewise, that both land and sea transport must have been used for the iron products of the eastern Weald, apart from its being reasonable to expect it, is further shown by the branch road from the Hemsted junction ultimately aiming at Canterbury. This road not only skirted the Roman coastline but also had short road sections descending to the very edge of the coastal inlets in the area as if to emphasize water-borne transport of iron products, particularly if there were a smelting site near Cranbrook. All in all, the roads and the harbour installations at Bodiam, perhaps also elsewhere, suggest that the iron industry was served both by land and sea, and it seems that the necessity to support the fleet's *control* for the iron industry brought about the concept of an 'essentially . . . sea based operation.'

In the present state of our knowledge, it seems reasonable to suggest that, soon after the Roman invasion, the existing pre-Roman iron industry (and it could not have been all that small to attract the attention of Caesar and Strabo) was greatly expanded, with the aid of the *Classis Britannica,* to meet the demands for iron of a much larger market, both military and civilian. A practical expression of this aid was the building of at least one 'pithead' baths at the major Beauport Park site where military engineering, at least in the design of the structure, is evident.[33] Another was the manufacture of tiles for building purposes, though stamping these tiles does not necessarily prove that they were made *by* sailors of the fleet.[34] The distribution of stamped tiles suggests at present that the interest of the fleet was confined to iron-making sites close to its Lympne base across the estuarine waters of the present Romney Marsh, with Bardown being farthest inland, and that sites further west, which are in the majority, may not have been involved (there is clearly no military influence at Hartfield). The Dover fort of the *Classis Britannica* was finally abandoned at about 210,[35] and the fleet may have transferred its base to Lympne until its disappearance from the archaeological record about 250. At about that time, the Bardown and Beauport Park sites appear to have ceased production.[36] These two facts have been taken as heralding the decline and collapse of the iron industry as if it depended solely on the military market. Yet, other iron-making sites, some in the vicinity both of Bardown and Beauport Park, appear to have continued in production into the fifth century. Though, undoubtedly, both the end of the direct military involvement and the over-exploitation of some iron-producing sites brought about a recession in the iron industry, it is wondered whether recent advances in pottery dating, upon which the period of production of most sites is based, and further discoveries may not in future significantly alter this generalised picture of the Wealden iron industry.

Although the iron industry was concentrated in the Weald, iron-making was also undertaken in other parts of the *civitas.* There is a possibility of smelting at the Charlton site and on a site at Smarden, near Ashford, where iron slag has been found. More recently, iron-smelting hearths, dating from the late-first to the early-third century, were found near Wye. At Brenley Corner, Boughton, the site of a mainly industrial road-side settlement excavated in advance of motorway construction, sufficiently large quantities of iron slag and ironstone suggest that smelting was undertaken there, the ore originating from a deposit of ironstone from the Woolwich Beds of the Forest of Blean close to the site.[37]

Minor Industries

At several sites, both urban and rural, evidence has been recovered for crafts which would now be termed 'cottage industries'. The tradition of bronze casting and enamelling practised in Belgic Swarling was continued at Springhead where there is also evidence for iron- and lead-working, and at Canterbury.[38] An iron crucible at the Eccles site suggests metal-working of a hitherto indeterminate nature. The manufacture of military belt-buckles and fittings, and *ballista* bolts, as well as pewter-making and the milling of corn using water power has been recently identified at Ickham.[39] Fulling and tanning have been demonstrated at Titsey and Lullingstone, and fuller's earth was probably extracted at Bearsted.[40] Ornamental hair-pins from antler or bone were manufactured in the Chalk building and at Eccles. Lastly, mention must also be made of the oyster beds at the extreme west corner of the canton whose products were celebrated by Roman authors.[41] The ubiquitous shells occur either as domestic rubbish on virtually all sites or crushed as admixture in clays used for pottery-making.

Fig. 43. Carnelian intaglio from Eccles: *left*, wax impression (2:1)

6

The late Fourth and Fifth Centuries

The conditions prevailing in the *civitas* during the fourth century, especially in the final decades between the *conspiratio barbarica* of 367 and Honorius' rescript, are not altogether clear. This is partly because the evidence, both documentary and archaeological, when not entirely lacking, varies from the secure to the very fragmentary. What happened to the Cantiaci during this period cannot be more than conjecture in the light of conditions in Roman Britain. Even so, there is no evidence in the form of destruction or abandoned sites to suggest that events in the province beyond the canton had an immediate and direct effect on the life of its inhabitants; the decline was much more gradual. But, indirectly, the political instability of the period was reflected in the defensive disposi-tions against external threat; the intention to defend the province was there, but unforeseen events in the rest of the empire made it impracticable.

Faced with the likelihood of ever-increasing raids from across the North Sea and undoubtedly aware of the ease with which the army had landed in 43, the imperial government sought to strengthen the coastal defences of the Saxon Shore and its forts. Thus, by an ironic twist of history, the original invaders were to become the defenders of the most exposed part of the canton. The role of the Saxon Shore forts under-went a strategic reconsideration: instead of being used as quarters for troops in sufficient numbers to guard likely landing places such as river estuaries and to cut off retreating parties of raiders, the forts were now intended to withstand a concerted attack, even a prolonged siege. Manpower was clearly required to garrison the forts and to undertake any refurbishing or additional work necessitated by their new role; and it is precisely at this time that the manpower resources of the Roman army, both in Britain and elsewhere, were depleted and over-stretched.

According to the *Notitia Dignitatum*, the troops manning the Saxon Shore forts in the canton during the latter part of the fourth century were the *Cohors I Baetasiorum* at Reculver; the *Legio II Augusta* transferred to Richborough from its Caerleon base, though some detachments may have been serving elsewhere; the *Milites Tungrecani* at Dover, and the *Numerus Turnacensium* at Lympne, the last two units probably drafted into Britain at the time of the Theodosian restoration in 369.[1] Even so, these troops had to be reinforced by the importation of Germanic mercenaries from northern Gaul. The pattern had already been established on the Continent where *laeti* or *foederati* had been settled behind the frontier with grants of land in exchange for military service. If the fort at Lympne was abandoned about 350 and its garrison transferred to Pevensey,[2] additional troops would have been needed to guard the gap between Richborough and Pevensey. The stationing of *foederati*, who probably arrived with Theodosius, is attested at Richborough by their weapons, ornaments and the distinctive metalwork of their buckles and strap-ends. Moreover, other finds of such metalwork, some of it British-made copies, from a number of sites in Britain indicate that some *foederati* may have also performed guard duties in towns and the countryside.[3] Though no such metalwork has so far been found at Canterbury, finds at Lullingstone, Snodland, Milton near Sittingbourne and two other unknown Kentish sites suggest the stationg of *foederati* in the countryside.[4] Whatever works may have been needed in the forts are difficult to identify, except in the case of Richborough where the bastion at the south-west corner was added to the original plan of the fort,[5] but such works would no doubt have been intended to prepare the forts in advance of an imminent threat to the province.

However, the instability of the imperial government, in the face of invasions from barbarians in northern Gaul and the rebellious army in the West, imposed a constant drain of troops from Britain, first under Magnus Maximus in 383, then by Stilicho in 401 and finally by Constantine III in 407. This gradual depletion of the Roman army in the province undoubtedly affected its civilian administration; it also engendered a feeling of insecurity which manifested itself in an accelerating drift away from the countryside into the defended towns. Thus, by about 408 when a serious Saxon invasion took place, there was practically nothing that Rome could do to protect Britain, and the Britons' reaction was in effect to anticipate Honorius' rescript. The rebellion that followed the Saxon invasion not only freed the country from the invaders, but also culminated in the expulsion of the remaining Roman administrators.[6] Whether this was a peasant revolt, as has been recently argued,[7] and the upper classes of the towns were appealing to Honorius for his intervention in order to restore the *status quo*, and with it their privileged position, is academic and does not alter the fact that by 410 Honorius was grating legal sanction to a situation that obtained in fact, a unilateral declaration of independence and the end of Roman Britain.

As town and country were closely related in times of prosperity, their relationship broke down as the economy of the province ground to a halt. Towns continued to be occupied into and beyond the fifth century, even though their occupation would have certainly been of a different order and scale; on the other hand, country estates declined towards the end of the fourth century.

Of the two walled towns in the *civitas*, Rochester can offer little other than pits with fourth-century coins and pottery to indicate some continuity of occupation. Canterbury provides evidence, in the fate of its buildings, of the fluctuating circumstances of their owners who, in turn, reflect their increasing concern for their protection in the measures adopted for the defence of the town. Some of the houses in Canterbury continued into use in the fourth and early fifth centuries; others, burnt down or fallen into disrepair, had not been rebuilt. Yet, the concern felt by the citizens of Canterbury is shown by the bastions for the deployment of defensive *ballistaria* which were added to the walls in Theodosian times.[8]

In the countryside, life continued to prosper until the latter years of Roman rule. The fourth-century coins from various

sites, despite the relative paucity of late-Roman coinage in
Britain, attest this continuing prosperity. Coins of Magnen-
tius were found at Wingham and Folkestone; coins of Honorius and Theodosius or Arcadius are present at the Hartlip
and Farningham II buildings, respectively, whilst Springhead, Lullingstone, Darenth and Eccles, with considerable
proportions of post-367 coins, testify to continued and thriving
occupation. This coin evidence is further reflected in the
building taking place at various sites. At Lullingstone the
house was continuously occupied until its final destruction by
fire, perhaps in the fifth century; new rooms, laid with mosaic
floors, were built about 330–60 and a Christian chapel was
founded about 380–85.[9] At Darenth, there was much reconstruction after 350 when the swimming-pool was converted
into a new bath-house and other buildings were probably
erected.[10] The living quarters at Eccles were reconstructed
also in the fourth century when the rear corridor of the house
was subdivided into separate rooms, laid with new tessellations and a hypocaust, and the south-east wing was rebuilt,
providing further evidence for the unbroken prosperity of this
estate.[11]   The end of the large country estates, where this can
be shown by modern research, resulted from decay, after they
were abandoned, rather than violent destruction. After the
collapse of the economy based on the supply of coin, which
was drastically reduced from the fourth century onward,[12] the
landowners were unable to afford the upkeep of these large
houses and abandoned them during the last years of Roman
rule for the comparative security of the towns.[13] Deprived of
the economic benefits of the countryside and perhaps becoming overcrowded with the influx of people seeking the protection of their walls, the towns themselves began to decay.[14]

   The political situation in the canton in the early years of the
fifth century can only be pieced together in the context of
sub-Roman Britain. After the expulsion of the Roman of-
ficials, clearly some sort of local administration will have
supervened, and this can only have been supplied by the
landowning nobility. Yet, not all the links with the Roman
world were severed, even if Rome proved incapable of recover-
ing the province. Certainly, the Church in Gaul continued to
take an active interest in Britain. Hence, the first visit of St.

Germanus in 429 to combat Pelagianism and the graphic account in Constantius' *Vita Germani* of Germanus' meeting at St. Alban's with the impressively arrayed British nobles, which suggests that at any rate some of the trappings of Roman rule were still surviving. Germanus visited Britain a second time in 446–47, perhaps as a result of the Britons' appeal to Aetius. But, failing direct archaeological evidence, it can only be conjectured that sub-Roman Britain fragmented into regional factions of usurpers[15] vying with each other for ascendancy until, out of the resulting disorganisation, there emerged, perhaps about 425, the *superbus tyrannus* figure of Vortigern. Whatever his background and intentions, Vortigern sought to buttress his authority, which may have been weakened by the first visit of Germanus, by the importation in 449 at Ebbsfleet of more Germanic mercenaries under Hengist and Horsa, who had probably served under the Romans on the Continent as *laeti*. Vortigern was attempting to fill the vacuum caused by the absence of the Roman army and to create a policing force for his overlordship; in effect, he introduced a Trojan horse. For this policy worked well enough as long as the aspirations of the *foederati* concerning land and payment could be satisfied. Soon enough, however, these *foederati* became aware that they could seize for themselves the land they had come to protect. This is precisely what they proceeded to accomplish with the aid of reinforcements from across the North Sea, causing the Britons to address one final, though unfruitful, appeal to official Rome in the face of surrounding enemies, the *gemitus Britannorum* of 446–54. The situation was one of confused intrigue and fighting, between Vortigern and his opponents amongst the Britons on the one hand, and the encroaching Saxons on the other, culminating in 455 in the battle at Aylesford and the consolidation of the Saxons east of the Medway.

There is so far little archaeological reflection of this situation and most of it comes from the extreme eastern part of the canton where a distinctive class of pottery, quite unlike anything produced in late-Roman Britain, appears about the middle of the fifth century. This is the so-called Anglo-Frisian pottery, a grey ware, with burnishd exterior and grooved or twisted-cable decoration, and it has been identified at Wingham and Lullingstone, in both cases in layers dating to the end of the Roman occupation of these sites and hinting at Saxon settlement. The evidence for such settlement is much more secure at Canterbury, however, for, apart from a number of sherds of Anglo-Frisian pottery, six huts of the well-known sunken *Grubenhaus* type were found within the ruins of Roman buildings and in such orderly arrangement alongside a Roman street as to suggest a settlement in one of the *insulae*. One of these huts belongs to this period, though the rest may be of sixth-century date.[16]

West of the Medway, the evidence of settlement during the fifth century is likewise very sparse. It consists mainly of a group of early cemeteries on the south side of the Thames at Orpington, Horton Kirby, Northfleet, Higham and Cliffe, where both cremation and inhumation were practised, which suggests that penetration of the area had taken place from the Thames and inland along the Darent and the Cray and their tributaries. Orpington, the most recently excavated of these cemeteries, provided evidence for a total of 70 graves and is provisionally dated from the middle of the fifth century.[17]

When all this piecemeal evidence is marshalled together the picture that remains is very blurred and underlines how little is still known of the conditions obtaining amongst the Cantiaci before they were finally submerged in the Saxon kingdom of Kent. The prosperity of the late fourth century seems to have gradually dissolved, and the geographical situation of the canton brought it once again to the forefront of the next wave of invasions. With the breakdown of the economy, the apparent loss of traditional skills,[18] and the movement away from the country into the towns and other settlements, the Roman order was succeeded by disorganisation approaching chaos and the emergence of regional rivalries. A society soldered together by the Roman administration and its institutions broke down and lost its identity until the arrival of the Saxons provided it with a new social focus. No doubt, some of the Roman institutions did survive for a time, especially where this was in the interests of the privileged and wealthy classes. But for the majority of the Cantiaci the years to the middle of the fifth century would appear to have been little more than a return to the fragmentation of the pre-Roman period.

The record, both documentary and archaeological, of the period from about 370 to 450 is so far too sketchy to allow for more than this general outline of a prosperous *civitas* regressing into the kind of primitive condition from which it had emerged under the Romans. In the end, the Cantiaci faded out of history, leaving like the Gaulish Parisi their only imprint in the modern name of their cantonal capital.

Glossary

Civitas peregrina:	A self-governing community of non-citizens
Croisillon:	A cruciform part of an iron window *grille*
Potin coin:	An Iron Age coin cast in a mixture of tin and bronze
Quadrifrons:	A building in the shape of a cross with four arched entrances
Sacellum:	The shrine of the regimental standards
Testudo:	The semi-cylindrical boiler in the furnace of a bath-house
Vexillatio:	A body of troops on detachment from the main unit

Notes and References

References to British journals use the abbreviations recommended by the Council for British Archaeology, which are those of the American Standards Association (list Z39, 5-1963, revised 1966). Other abbreviations used are:

JRS Journal of Roman Studies
RIB R.G. Collingwood and R.P. Wright, *Roman Inscriptions of Britain*, i (Oxford 1965)
VCH *Victoria County History*

1. TRIBAL TERRITORY AND THE PRE-ROMAN IRON AGE

1. *B.G.*, V, 22.
2. An attempt to define their territories (Rodwell *1976*, 213) on the basis of the distribution of Gallo-Belgic coins only is debatable.
3. *B.G.*, V, 9. For a recent discussion of the situation, see Cunliffe *1982*. I am very grateful to Professor Barry Cunliffe for kindly allowing me to consult a draft of his paper before publication.
4. Borden: *Archaeol. Cantiana*, lxi (1948), 148–55; Broadstairs: Hurd *1909*, 433; Highstead: *Archaeol. Cantiana*, xcii (1976), 236–8; Fordwich: Jenkins *1962*, 12; Greenhithe: Detsicas *1966*, 139–41; Faversham: Philp *1968*, 65–6.
5. Rochester: *Archaeol. Cantiana*, lxxvii (1962), li; Canterbury: *Archaeol. Cantiana*, lxx (1956), 247; lxxii (1958), 198, and recent work by the Canterbury Archaeological Trust, *Archaeol. Cantiana*, xcvi (1980), 403; xcviii (1982), 224.
6. Rodwell *1976*, 263.
7. Webster *1980*, 57.
8. Rivet *1958* and *1964*, 144.
9. *Geography*, IV, 3, 3, and IV, 5, 1.
10. *History*, V, 21, 3.
11. *B.G.*, V, 22.
12. e.g. Caesar's Cenimagni, Segontiaci, Ancalites, Bibroci and Cassi (*B.G.*, V, 21).

13. *Geography*, II, 3, 12–3.
14. If the variant 'Κάντικοι' were unobjectionable on other grounds, it may be due less to a scribal error in transcription than a deliberate attempt to render the Celtic suffix *-acus* by its Greek equivalent – ικος. Holder's observation (Holder *1896*, col. 21) on the suffix *-acus*, 'Die Kelten bildeten damit personennamen (nicht patronymica), völker- und ortnamen . . .', is relevant here.
15. In this respect, Ptolemy's mistake in including London within the tribal territory may illustrate the accuracy of his information.
16. *RIB*, 192. I am indebted to Professor A.L.F. Rivet, who refers me to the curious equivocation in Collingwood and Myres *1937* between *Cantii* and *Durovernum Cantiacorum* on the map and p. 167; Wacher *1978*, 113, 124.
17. Rivet *1958* and *1964*, 144; Frere *1967*, 204.
18. *B.G.*, V, 22. It is clearly anachronistic to refer to the Cantiaci in an Iron Age context (Cunliffe *1974*, 77; Rodwell *1976*, fig. 10; Webster *1978*, fig. 2; Laing *1979*, map 2; Webster *1980*, map 1).
19. Cunliffe *1973*, 23.
20. Evans *1954*, 103–46.
21. If the site on Blue Bell Hill, immediately to the east of the Roman road from Rochester (VCH (Kent) *1932*, iii, 104), is indeed that of a temple, which is likely, it may delimit the western boundary of the Canterbury *pagus,* just as the Titsey temple may be located on the western boundary of the *civitas.*

2. HISTORY: A.D. 43–367

1. Dudley and Webster *1965*, 58.
2. Cassius Dio, LX, 19.
3. It is not impossible that to this early phase belong the two skirmishes fought in east Kent (Cassius Dio, lx, 20). It is also probable that a fortlet may have been established during this period at Reculver, perhaps to secure the mouth of the Wantsum Channel into the Thames estuary, a vital supply line for the army advancing west.
4. A landing further west, very probably in the Chichester harbour area, may have been made but in support of Vespasian's drive westward (Cunliffe *1973*, 24–6) after the battle of the Medway, at the earliest, or when the army had reached the Thames.
5. Frere *1967*, 64.
6. Dudley and Webster *1965*, 67; Burn *1953*, 105–15.
7. See n. 5.
8. Collingwood postulated a bridge at Belgic Rochester (Collingwood and Myres *1937*, 83), which could be supported by the town's Roman name, *Durobrivae* (= 'the walled town with bridges', Jackson *1970*, 72; Rivet and Smith *1979*, 346–8); against this, Frere has argued that the name was transferred to the town from an army fortlet (Frere *1971*, xvi–xvii), which he suspects below Rochester castle (Frere *1967*, 64).

9. It is worth noting that at the Eccles site there are ditches with a rudimentary box-gutter, filled with Claudian pottery and a few bronze items which could belong to military equipment.
10. Dudley and Webster *1965*, 67.
11. Cassius Dio, LX, 20.
12. Thornhill *1976*, 119–28.
13. *Britannia*, iii, 334–5; Dunnett *1975*, 41.
14. For Richborough, see Bushe-Fox *1926*, *1928*, *1932*, *1949* and Cunliffe *1968*, 234 ff.
15. Cunliffe *1968*, 238.
16. Bushe-Fox *1949*, 38 ff.; Strong *1968*, 41.
17. Strong *1968*, 53 ff., for detailed information.
18. *Ibid.*, 72.
19. *RIB*, 66.
20. Philp *1981a*, for detailed information.
21. Winbolt *1925*, 7.
22. Thompson *1953*, 55.
23. Philp *1969a*, 223.
24. VCH (Kent) *1932*, iii, 20.
25. Information based on brief references in *JRS*, *Britannia* and *Archaeol. Cantiana*, and Philp *1969b*, 3–11.
26. Philp *1969b*, 10; however, baths are occasionally sited outside the fort, e.g. at Chesters on Hadrian's Wall. At Reculver, except to east, there is room for a bath-house outside the fort, and this may have been situated to the north where massive foundations were recorded (Battely *1745*, 53).
27. Cunliffe *1977*, 5.
28. Or its reconstruction (Hassall *1977*, 9).
29. Richmond *1961*, 225; Mann *1977*, 15; *JRS*, lv (1965), 220; Birley *1967*, 63–102.
30. Mann *1977*, 15; Cunliffe *1977*, 3; more specifically, 220–230 (Cunliffe *1968*, 261).
31. *Britannia*, i (1970), 310–1.
32. Bushe-Fox *1926*, 10; *1928*, 18–22; *1932*, 22–5; *1949*, 60–6; Cunliffe *1968*, 22–7, 244.
33. Cunliffe *1968*, 244.
34. Johnson *1970*, 246.
35. Johnson *1981*.
36. The south-west bastion is additional; Johnson *1981*, 30.
37. Cunliffe *1968*, 248–9.
38. Bushe-Fox *1932*, 34–6; Cunliffe *1968*, 248.
39. Philp *1977*, 20–1. See also Philp *1981a*.
40. Hassall *1977*, 8.
41. Cunliffe *1980*, but see also Philp *1981b*.
42. Cunliffe *1980*.
43. White *1961*; Johnson *1976*, Cunliffe *1977*, 2–6; Johnson *1977*.
44. It is possible that the *Notitia* drew on earlier sources, but these could not have been much earlier as the list was intended to show com-

mands, etc., at or about the time of its compilation (White *1961*, 45–55; Hassall *1977*, 7–10).

45. Eutropius, IX, 21.
46. That it could be interpreted as a shore both settled by and defended against Saxons (Johnson *1977*, 63) is further supported by the evidence at Portchester (Cunliffe *1975*).
47. White *1961*, 41 ff.; Johnson *1976*, 126 ff.
48. Reculver and Bradwell guarding the mouth of the Thames, Richborough the entrance to the Wantsum Channel, Dover on the Dour and at the start of the road to Canterbury and Lympne at the head of several inlets into the Weald.
49. The *Notitia* lists the *Classis Anderetiana* in Paris as well as the *Milites Anderetiani* at Mainz; Cunliffe *1975*, 426.

3. COMMUNICATIONS AND URBAN SETTLEMENT

1. Margary *1973*, fig. 1. Margary, in discussing the course of the road at Pine Wood, mentions 'a new alignment pointing towards Wickhambreaux' (Margary *1973*, 38), and evidence has recently been found for two sections of road in the area (Private information from Mr J. Bradshaw); Payne *1895*, 9–10; *1898*, 1–9; *JRS*, liii (1963), 158; Arnold *1921*, 130–1; VCH (Kent) *1932*, iii, 85; Dymond *1961*, 154.
2. Margary *1949*, 129, 131.
3. Margary *1973*, 41; Jessup *1936*, 191; a short road probably connected the Rochester–Hastings road with the Eccles villa-estate and industrial site as a section of road was recorded in a clay pit behind the site (VCH (Kent) *1932*, iii, 145, 153); Dymond *1961*, 149; *Archaeol. Cantiana*, lxxxiv (1969), 23; Lemmon and Hill *1966*, 86–102; Cunliffe *1968*, 258; Brodribb *1969*, 111.
4. Margary *1973*, 50.
5. *Ibid.*, 60.
6. Margary *1965*, 262–6.
7. Jackson *1970*, 73; Rivet and Smith *1979*, 353–4.
8. I acknowledge my debt to Mr T.W.T. Tatton-Brown, with whom I have discussed the available evidence. An opportunity has been taken to add recently found buildings to the plan (Fig. 9), but these are not discussed in the text.
9. Frere *1954*, 140. A ditch, 'possibly military', was recently found in the Castle site (*Archaeol. Cantiana*, xciii (1977), 213.)
10. A ditch at the Castle site 'may be one of the ditches of the Belgic *oppidum*' (*Archaeol. Cantiana*, xcii (1976), 240).
11. Frere *1970*, 85.
12. *Ibid.*, 84, fig. 1; Wacher *1975*, 182, fig. 39.
13. Tatton-Brown *1976*, 238, fig. 4, and private information from Mr T.W.T. Tatton-Brown.
14. Wacher *1975*, 189.
15. I owe this point to Mr T.W.T. Tatton-Brown.

16. *Pace* Wacher *1975*, 181.
17. Frere *1970*, 83–113.
18. Tatton-Brown *1976*, 238–40, fig. 4; *Britannia*, viii (1977), 423, fig. 29.
19. *Archaeol. Cantiana*, xcii (1976), 238–9; *Britannia*, viii (1977), 423–4. I owe the interpretation of a possible temple to Mr T.W.T. Tatton-Brown.
20. Urry *1978*, 1.
21. Williams *1947*, 68–87; Lewis *1966*, 78.
22. *JRS*, xxxvii (1947), 97; xl (1950), 113; xli (1951), 138; xxxvii (1947), 177; xxxix (1949), 110; xli (1951), 139; li (1961), 191; *Archaeol. Cantiana*, xciii (1977), 217; xciv (1978), 272; Williams and Frere *1948; Archaeol. Cantiana*, xcii (1976), 217; xciv (1978), 272; Williams and Frere *1948; Archaeol. Cantiana*, xcii (1976), 240; see also Frere and Stow *1983*, and *Archaeol. Cantiana*, xcviii (1982), 222–5.
23. Frere *1970*, 110.
24. *JRS*, lii (1962), 190; xlvi (1956), 144; xlv (1955), 143; li (1961), 191.
25. *Britannia*, v (1974), 458–9; *JRS*, xlvi (1956), 144; lii (1962), 190; *Archaeol. Cantiana*, lxxxiii (1968), 273; *JRS*, xlvi (1956), 144; xliv (1954), 102; xlv (1955), 143; *Britannia*, iii (1972), 351.
26. Jackson *1970*, 72; Rivet and Smith *1979*, 346–8.
27. Frere *1971*, xvi.
28. *Archaeol. Cantiana*, lxxvii (1962), 1; *JRS*, liii (1963), 158. A full report has not yet been published and detailed dating information is not available.
29. Harrison and Flight *1968;* Harrison *1970*; Harrison *1972*.
30. Harrison and Flight *1968*, 57; Arnold *1889*; Payne *1895;* Harrison and Flight *1968*, 57, 70; Harrison *1970*, 95–8; *1975*, 211–2; *1976*, 252–3; Detsicas *1972*, 132. Though purely conjectural, it is not unlikely that such a rebuilding of the east gate was contemporary with the building of the stone wall.
31. Harrison and Flight *1968*, 76; Mann *1977*, 15; Frere *1967*, 253–4.
32. VCH (Kent) *1932*, iii, 86; Harrison *1972*, 121 ff. (to speak of 'neglect' in this context (Rodwell *1976*, 338) is to show unawareness of recent work); *Archaeol. Cantiana*, xxii (1897), lxi; VCH (Kent) *1932*, iii, 87; Payne *1895*, 6; Flight and Harrison *1978*.
33. VCH (Kent) *1932*, iii, 86, 169; Payne *1895*, xxii, xlix, lii.
34. There is no evidence to connect Rochester with a naval unit to justify its description as a naval base (Wacher *1975*, 51) nor to suppose that there was an undefended *vicus* associated with this hypothetical base (Wacher *1974*, 23, fig. 1, and private information).
35. Rivet *1970*, 44–5.
36. The excavations were directed by Mr W.S. Penn (Penn *1952, 1957, 1958, 1959, 1960, 1962, 1964, 1967, 1968)* and later by Mr S.R. Harker (Harker *1970, 1971, 1972, 1973)* to whom I am indebted for the amended plan of the site on which my figure is based.
37. Penn *1965*, 116, 113.
38. *The pilae* referred to in the report (Penn *1968*, 171) are in fact the flues through the wall between the *caldarium* and the *tepidarium*.

39. VCH (Kent) *1932*, iii, 92.
40. Penn *1965*, 109, and *1958*, 80–1. The drawn section (fig. 3) shows these two surfaces and below them 'a chalk floor just over six feet wide', which is interpreted as part of a timber building, which is too difficult to accept in view of the narrow width of this 'floor' and the need to allow for enclosing walls, however slight, for which no signs are shown in the section.
41. It is clear that some timber buildings must have existed in view of the first-century material found, but the clearance must have completely removed them.
42. This accords well with the view that 'stone-founded dwellings do not appear in the minor settlements before about A.D. 120 at the earliest . . .' (Todd *1970*, 124).
43. Private information from Mr S.R. Harker.
44. As the floor of the entrance building was *c*. 0.9 m. above the level of the courtyard, such debris layers would be needed to raise it to the necessary height.
45. The measurements quoted here are based on the published plan (Penn *1959*, fig. 1) where there are some slight discrepancies between it and the figures given in the report, e.g. the temple is drawn as 10.8 × 10.5 m. and the *cella* as 5.5 m. square (= 18 ft. square, not '18 ft. 8 in. by 18 ft. 8 in.' as in the report).
46. Not unlike the Silchester temple in *Insula* XXXV. It is very odd to suggest that tessellated floors would not have survived under such a penthouse roof (Penn *1959*, 26), as they clearly did so in other Romano-British buildings.
47. However, the find-spot of this vessel, 'on N. wall of cella' (Penn *1959*, 47, and 5, fig. 1) makes it clear that it could only have been deposited there *after* the destruction of the *cella* wall, and there is no convincing reason to show that the vessel and the seeds it *may* have contained were in fact used for the suggested purpose (pp. 56–8).
48. Penn *1960*, 113; the dimensions taken from the plan are 8.7 × 5.8 m.
49. *Ibid.*, fig. 1, opp. 114, shows this 'layer' as a lump which is later (p. 117) likened to a lining.
50. The Springhead pottery, in general, can be shown to be dated too early.
51. If stone were used, some fragments might have survived and been recognised more readily than anonymous tiles.
52. Penn *1962*, 110, yet it was described as a temple. There is no mention of the 'larger building', unless this refers to Temple III.
53. *Ibid.*, 113. The plan (fig. 1, opp. 116) shows this base at *c*. 1.4 m. from the temple steps, but the general plan of the area (Penn *1965*, fig. opp. 108) places it at nearly 6 m., which appears a more accurate position.
54. Blagg *1979*.
55. It is unreasonable to suggest that ovens had been placed on the *wooden* floor and then collapsed through it (Penn *1957*, 60).
56. The pottery dating is generally unreliable; a sectional drawing (Penn *1957*, 62, fig. 6) shows a layer containing 'green samian' *(sic)*.

57. VCH (Kent) *1932*, iii, 42–55; *Archaeol. Cantiana*, lxiii (1950), xlv; Murray Threipland and Steer *1951*, 130–49; Murray Threipland *1957*, 14–37; Rahtz *1958*, 111–37; Rigold *1969*, 78.

58. Wheeler *1929*, 33, 39. The Boulogne *pharos*, of the same octagonal plan and with twelve or thirteen diminishing stages, is said to have risen to some 61 m.; it is not securely dated, but it may have been erected by Caligula in 40.

59. Philp *1973*. A bath-house is currently being excavated nearby.

60. Rivet *1958*, 145; *1964*, 145.

61. Scott Robertson *1883*, 68–80. Wacher classes Maidstone as an undefended *vicus* without giving grounds for this status (Wacher *1974*, 23, fig. 1).

62. VCH (Kent) *1932*, ii, 98–9.

63. Rivet *1958*, 145; *1964*, 145.

64. VCH (Kent) *1932*, iii, 88; Spurrell *1889*, 312; *Archaeol. Cantiana*, li (1939), xlvii; Tester *1956*, 253–4; *Archaeol. Cantiana*, lxxiii (1959), xlvii; lxxxvi (1971), 210–5; *Britannia*, v (1974), 459; vi (1975), 283, and information from Mr R.M. Walsh; *Archaeol. Cantiana*, xxii (1897), lii; Dunkin *1844*, 91 ff., and in 1965 (Information from Mr J. Ritson).

65. Jackson *1970*, 77; Rivet and Smith *1979*, 351.

66. VCH (Kent) *1932*, iii, 151; *Archaeol. Cantiana*, lxxvi (1961), xlvi; Tester *1963*, 179–80; Spurrell *1889*, 313; VCH (Kent) *1932*, iii, 104, 110.

67. The distance given in the *Peutinger Table* is actually 7 Roman miles, but as already shown 'the confusion between *X* and *v* applies to the Peutinger Table no less than to the Itinerary' (Rivet *1970*, 45).

68. VCH (Kent) *1932*, iii, 97–8; Whiting *et al. 1931*; Payne *1878*, 428–9; *1893*, 30–3; *Archaeol. Cantiana*, lxxx (1965), 271; Baxter and Mills *1978*, 239–47.

69. Sturry: *Archaeol. Cantiana*, lxii (1949), 145–6; Bodiam: Lemmon and Hill *1966*, 86–102; Cunliffe *1968*, 258; Brodribb *1969*, 111; Gravesend: *The Daily Telegraph*, 5th September, 1979.

4. RURAL SETTLEMENT

1. As seen at the Park Brow site of the Regni (Wolseley, Smith and Hawley *1927*, 1–40; Cunliffe *1973*, 96–8.)

2. In a paper I read at Attingham Park, Shrewsbury, in February 1969.

3. I am indebted to Mr. J. Bradshaw, for much information based on his field-work in the Stour valley.

4. Philp *1963a*, 76–7.

5. e.g. at Barham Downs (*Antiquity*, vii (1933), 292, Pl. II; *Britannia*, ii (1971), 286.)

6. e.g. at Fawkham (Philp *1963b*, 57–9), Greenhithe (Detsicas *1966*, 142–5) and Highstead (*Archaeol. Cantiana*, xcii (1976), 236–8; *Britannia*, vii (1976), 376.)

7. As at Shooters Hill, Greenwich (*Antiq. J.*, v (1925), 175; VCH (Kent)

1932, iii, 167) and Charlton (Elliston-Erwood *1923*, 227–39; VCH (Kent) *1932*, iii, 101).

8. Alexander *1961*, 23; Detsicas *1966*, 143–4; *Britannia*, vii (1976), 376; *Archaeol. Cantiana*, xcii (1976), 236.

9. *Archaeol. Cantiana*, lxxviii (1963), 179–80; lxx (1956), 263; *JRS*, xviii (1928), 208; VCH (Kent) *1932*, iii, 124; *Archaeol. Cantiana*, lxxxvii (1972), 236.

10. *Archaeol. Cantiana*, lxviii (1954), xlvi, 240; lxxii (1958), 210.

11. VCH (Kent) *1932*, iii, 119.

12. I am indebted to Lt.-Col. G.W. Meates, for much material on the settlement of the Darent valley.

13. Wilmington: Spurrell *1889*, 312; *Archaeol. Cantiana*, xci (1975), 212; *Britannia*, vii (1976), 377. I am indebted to Mr R.M. Walsh, for information and a plan of his excavations. Horton Kirby: *Kent Archaeol. Rev.*, 34 (1973), 113; *Britannia*, iv (1973), 322–3, and v (1974), 459.

14. Farningham Wood: Spurrell *1889*, 307. Farningham, The Folly: Priest *1931*, 66–73. Farningham II: *Archaeol. Cantiana*, lxi (1948), 181–2; lxxvi (1961), l–li, lxxii–lxxiii; lxxviii (1963), lv. Eynsford: *Archaeol. Cantiana*, lxxxvi (1971), 241–2. Shoreham: *Archaeol. Cantiana*, lxi (1948), 181; lxxii (1962), 202.

15. Otford (Progress Building): Pearce *1927*, 153–8; Pearce *1930*, 157–71. Twitton (Frog Farm): *Archaeol. Cantiana*, xlii (1929), xlviii–xlix; xliii (1931), xlviii–xlix; xlvi (1934), xliii; xlix (1937), 286; lxxx (1965), liii–liv. Otford (Charne Building Site): *Archaeol. Cantiana*, lxviii (1954), xliv–xlv; lxxxvii (1972), 241–2.

16. Ash: VCH (Kent) *1932*, iii, 103–4; *Kent Archaeol. Rev.*, 5 (1966), 10–12; 18 (1969–70), 17; 20 (1970), 13–20; *Britannia*, i (1970), 303–4; Smith *1963*, 28. Betsham: *Archaeol. Cantiana*, xxii (1897), 51; VCH (Kent) *1932*, iii, 113; *Archaeol. Cantiana*, lxx (1976), 261–2. Ightham: VCH (Kent) *1932*, iii, 119.

17. Stone Castle Quarry: Detsicas *1966*, 136–90. Stone: Spurrell *1889*, 307.

18. Tester *1961*, 88–109.

19. Frindsbury: VCH (Kent) *1932*, iii, 115–6. Cuxton: *Archaeol. Cantiana*, xxv (1902), lxvii; VCH (Kent) *1932*, iii, lll; Rigold *1972*, 39. Allington: VCH (Kent) *1932*, iii, 103. East Malling: *Archaeol. Cantiana*, lxix (1955), 208; lxxi (1957), 228–9; lxxx (1965), 257–8; *JRS*, lvi (1966), 217. Little Buckland: *J. Brit. Archaeol. Assoc.*, ii (1847),88; VCH (Kent) *1932*, iii, 99. East Barming: *Archaeol. Cantiana*, xiii (1880), 169; VCH (Kent) *1932*, iii, 104.

20. Chatham: VCH (Kent) *1932*, iii, 110, 149, 160. Borstal: VCH (Kent) *1932*, iii, 148. Wouldham: VCH (Kent) *1932*, 109, 149; Jessup *1956*, 170–1. Burham: Payne *1898*, 10–11. Eccles: Payne *1898*, 12–3; *Archaeol. Cantiana*, xxxiv (1920), 155. Tovil: *J. Brit. Archaeol. Assoc.*, ii (1847), 75; VCH (Kent) *1932*, iii, 99. East Farleigh: VCH (Kent) *1932*, 154; *Archaeol. Cantiana*, li (1939), 204.

21. Minster-in-Sheppey: VCH (Kent) *1932*, iii, 161. Otterham Creek: VCH (Kent) *1932*, iii, 164. Lower Halstow: VCH (Kent) *1932*, iii, 117. Milton-next-Sittingbourne: *Archaeol. Cantiana*, xii (1878), 428–9; VCH

(Kent) *1932*, iii, 96. Faversham: VCH (Kent) *1932*, iii, 93. Luddenham: VCH (Kent) *1932*, iii, 94. Buckland: *Archaeol. Cantiana*, xxiv (1900), liv; VCH (Kent) *1932*, iii, 94. Hog Brook: VCH (Kent) *1932*, iii, 118; Harty: VCH (Kent) *1932*, iii, 118. Borden: VCH (Kent) *1932*, iii, 105. Hollingbourne: *Archaeol. Cantiana*, lxxii (1958), 222; lxxiii (1959), 229–30; *JRS*, l (1960), 235–6. Chart Sutton: *Archaeol. Cantiana*, lxiii (1950), 155. Frittenden: VCH (Kent) *1932*, iii, 154. Charing: Detsicas *1975*, 107–10.

22. Crundale: VCH (Kent) *1932*, iii, 111. Boughton Aluph: Information from Mr J. Bradshaw. Wye: *Archaeol. Cantiana*, lxxxvii (1972), 233. Aldington: Information from Mr J. Bradshaw. Saltwood: VCH (Kent) *1932*, iii, 124. Folkestone: *Archaeol. Cantiana*, x (1876), 173–7; VCH (Kent) *1932*, iii, 114–5. Whitstable: *JRS*, lii (1962), 190. Chislet (Highstead): I am indebted for the information and a plan to Dr F. Jenkins. Hoath: *Kent Archaeol. Rev.*, 28 (1972), 240–50. Littlebourne: *Proc. Soc. Antiq. Lond.*, xxx (1917–18), 102–10. Ickham: VCH (Kent) *1932*, iii, 119, and information from Mr J. Bradshaw. Sandwich: *Archaeol. Cantiana*, xciv (1978), 191–4; *Kent Archaeol. Rev.*, 60 (1980), 232–47. Sholden: VCH (Kent) *1932*, iii, 152; O.S. Card Index. Margate: *JRS*, xiv (1924), 240; VCH (Kent) *1932*, iii, 121–2.

23. Collingwood *1930*, 113; Rivet *1969*, 177; Percival *1976* 14–5; Wacher *1978*, 112–3.

24. Fig. 29 in Wacher *1978*, which includes North Leigh, Woodchester *and* Little Milton, illustrates the point.

25. Rivet *1969*, 211–2.

26. Leveson-Gower *1869*, 214–37; Fox *1905*, 214–8.

27. VCH (Kent) *1932*, iii, 119–21; Piercy-Fox *1955*, 96–116; *JRS*, lviii (1968), 205; *Kent Archaeol. Rev.*, 11 (1968), 10–14; 14 (1968), 8–9; 15 (1969), 6; 21 (1970), 22; 49 (1977), 215–8.

28. Payne *1897*, 49–84; Fox *1905*, 12–26; VCH (Kent) *1932*, iii, 111–3; Philp *1973*, 119–54; *Britannia*, i (1970), 304; iv (1973), 322; Smith *1963*, 17. For a recent re-appraisal of the site, see Black *1981*.

29. *JRS*, xxxix (1949), 110; Meates *1973*, 1–21.

30. Meates *1979;* Rivet *1980*, 417–9.

31. Northfleet: Steadman *1913*, 7–15; VCH (Kent) *1932*, iii, 122; I am indebted to Mr A.C. Harrison, for information of the current excavations. Chalk: *Archaeol. Cantiana*, lxxiii (1959), xlviii, 207–8; Johnston *1972*, 112–48; *Britannia*, vi (1975), 282–3; vii (1976), 374–6; *Kent Archaeol. Rev.*, 61 (1980), 8–9.

32. *Archaeol. J.*, i (1845), 164; *Archaeol. Cantiana*, xl (1928), 79–80; VCH (Kent) *1932*, iii, 124; Ocock and Syddell *1967*, 192–217.

33. VCH (Kent) *1932*, iii, 153. Interim reports in *Archaeol. Cantiana*, lxxviii (1963) – xciii (1977); Frere *1967*, 269–70, 306; Branigan *1971*, 114; Wacher *1979*, 96; Detsicas *1979*, 313; Detsicas *1974*, 128–9; Detsicas *1977*, 19–29; Stevens *1966*, 123.

34. Maidstone I: *J. Brit. Archaeol. Assoc.*, ii (1847), 86–9; *Archaeol. Cantiana*, i (1858), 170–2; VCH (Kent) *1932*, iii, 99; I am grateful to Mr D.B. Kelly, for information and a plan of the recent excavations; *Archaeol.*

Cantiana, lxxxvii (1972), 217–9; *Britannia*, iv (1973), 323. Maidstone II: Roach Smith *1876*, 163–72; VCH (Kent) *1932*, iii, 99.

35. Boxted: *Proc. Soc. Antiq. Lond.*, ix (1882), 162–3; Payne *1883*, 104–7; Payne *1893*, 61–9; VCH (Kent) *1932*, iii, 106–9. Hartlip: Roach Smith *1852*, ii, 1–24; VCH (Kent) *1932*, iii, 117–8. Faversham: Philp *1968*, 62–72; Detsicas *1968*, 293; *Kent Archaeol. Rev.*, 21 (1970), 20.

36. Wingham: Dowker *1882*, 135, and *1883*, 351; VCH (Kent) *1932*, iii, 125; I am indebted to Dr F. Jenkins, for much information and plans of his recent re-excavation of the site; *JRS*, lvi (1966), 217; lvii (1967), 202; lviii (1968), 205–6. Folkestone: Winbolt *1925a;* Winbolt *1925b*, 209–10; Winbolt *1926*, 45–50; VCH (Kent) *1932*, iii, 114; Collingwood *1937*, 275; Cunliffe *1968*, 260; Rigold *1972*, 31–41.

37. O.S. Map of Roman Britain *1956*, 10. The size of the baths at Eccles, described as 'more . . . than is good for a normal villa' (Stevens *1966*, 123), strongly suggests that they may have been available not only to estate workers, but also to others living in the area, e.g. in the Burham farm. Stevens *1966*, 119; Percival *1975*, 142.

38. Hartfield: *Britannia*, iv (1973), 321; *Antiq. J.*, liv (1974), 278–80; I am grateful to Mr J.H. Money, for inviting me to visit the site and supplying interim reports on his excavations, Hayes: *Archaeol. Cantiana*, lxxx (1965), lviii; *JRS*, lvi (1966), 217; Philp *1973*, 80–93. Foot's Cray: *Archaeol. Cantiana*, lxx (1956), 263; lxxi (1957), xlv, 240; *JRS*, xlvii (1957), 223–4; *Kent Archaeol. Rev.*, 33 (1973), 85–8. Orpington: *Archaeol. Cantiana*, lxxxviii (1973), 223; lxxxix (1974), 220; xci (1975), 206. Kemsing: *Archaeol. Cantiana*, lxiii (1950), xliv–xlv. Plaxtol: Luard *1859*, 2–8; VCH (Kent) *1932*, iii, 122–4; *Britannia*, ii (1971), 297–8. Teston: *J. Brit. Archaeol. Assoc.*, xxix (1873), 45, 71; VCH (Kent) *1932*, iii, 125. Borden: VCH (Kent) *1932*, iii, 105. Buckland: VCH (Kent) *1932*, iii, 94. Boughton Monchelsea: *Archaeologia*, xxix (1842), 414–9; VCH (Kent) *1932*, iii, 105–6. Thurnham: VCH (Kent) *1932*, iii, 125; *JRS*, xxiv (1934), 217; *Archaeol. Cantiana*, lxxii (1958), 225; *JRS*, xlix (1959), 135; Pirie *1960*, 162–70. Little Chart: VCH (Kent) *1932*, iii 149; *Archaeol. Cantiana*, lv (1942), 76–7; *JRS*, xxxiii (1943), 77; Eames *1957*, 130–46. Lyminge: *Archaeol. Cantiana*, ix (1874), lxxviii; VCH (Kent) *1932*, iii, 121. Beauport Park: *Britannia*, iii (1972), 350; I am grateful to Mr G. Brodribb, for a plan of the excavations.

39. The Springhead temples have been discussed in Ch. 3; the probable location of a temple in Canterbury was established in 1980. Frend *1955*, 8–9; Rivet *1958*, 134. Wheeler *1928*, 317; Wright *1965*, 67–70. Greenwich: VCH (Kent) *1932*, iii, 116–7; *London Archaeologist*, 3 (1979), 311–7. Titsey: *Proc. Soc. Antiq. Lond.*, viii (1878–81), 213; *JRS*, xxvi (1936), 262; Graham *1936*, 84–101; Rivet *1958*, 145. Blue Bell Hill, Aylesford: *Archaeologia*, xxx (1844), 536; *Archaeol. J.*, i (1844–5), 264; VCH (Kent) *1932*, iii, 104; *Archaeol. Cantiana*, lxii (1949), 134; Lewis *1966*, 124. Boxted: *Kent Archaeol. Rev.*, 18 (1969–70), 9; *Britannia*, i (1970), 304; iv (1973), 321–2. Hartlip: Lewis *1966*, 95. Barham: *ex info*. Mr N.G. Macpherson–Grant. Worth: *Antiq. J.*, viii (1928), 76;

Archaeol. Cantiana, xlviii (1926), xliii; l (1928), xlvii; Klein *1928*, 76–86; VCH (Kent) *1932*, iii, 175; Lewis *1966*, 48.

40. Fletcher and Meates, *1969*, 273–94; *1977*, 67–72; Thomas *1980*, 149–50; Rigold *1972*, 32; Dunning and Jessup *1936*, 37–53; Jessup *1959*, 1–32; *1962*, 853–67. West Wickham: *Archaeol. J.*, lviii (1901), 103–5; VCH (Kent) *1932*, iii, 174. Plaxtol: *Archaeol. Cantiana*, ii (1859), 6–7; VCH (Kent) *1932*, iii, 163. Holborough: Jessup *1954*, 1–61; *Archaeol. Cantiana*, lxxx (1965), 246–50; Jessup *1970*, 112–6; Farrar *1973*, 90; Jessup *1962*, 861. Chartham Downs: VCH (Kent) *1932*, iii, 149; Dunning and Jessup *1936*, 53. Boughton: Dunning and Jessup *1936*, 53. Bishopsbourne: *Archaeol. Cantiana*, xv (1883), 311; *Proc. Soc. Ant. Lond.*, ix (1881–83), 163; VCH (Kent) *1932*, iii, 146–7. Shepherdswell: VCH (Kent) *1932*, iii, 167; Dunning and Jessup *1936*, 53. Richborough: Bushe-Fox *1932*, 5, 25–9; VCH (Kent) *1932*, iii, 34. Canterbury: *Archaeol. J.*, xxxii (1875), 370; lxxxvi (1929), 272–5; VCH (Kent) *1932*, iii, 77; Urry *1948*, 141–7; Jessup *1962*, 855.

41. Strood: *Archaeol. Cantiana*, ii (1854), xl; xxi (1895), lii; *J. Brit. Arch. Assoc.*, ix (1854), 359–60; *Archaeol. Cantiana*, xxix (1911), 217. Dartford: *Archaeol. Cantiana*, xxii (1897), liii; *JRS*, lvii (1967), 200. Maidstone: *Archaeol. Cantiana*, ii (1859), 143; VCH (Kent) *1932*, iii, 99–101. Otford: *Archaeol. Cantiana*, lxxxi (1966), lxi; *JRS*, lix (1969), 232. Petham: Payne *1893*, 197; VCH (Kent) *1932*, iii, 163. Ospringe: Whiting, Hawley and May *1931;* VCH (Kent) *1932*, iii, 95. Langley: *Archaeol. Cantiana*, xv (1883), 76–88; *J. Brit. Arch. Assoc.*, ii (1847), 86; *Archaeol. J.*, xx (1863), 392; VCH (Kent) *1932*, iii, 158–60; Jessup *1959*, 14–5, 26–7. Sutton Valence: *Archaeologia*, xxix (1842), 421–3; *Archaeol. Cantiana*, x (1876), 166; xv (1883), 88; VCH (Kent) *1932*, iii, 170–1; Jessup *1959*, 31–2. Borden: Payne *1893*, 54–8; VCH (Kent) *1932*, iii, 98; Jessup *1959*, 23. Springhead: *Archaeologia*, xiv (1808), 37–9; Dunkin *1848;* Jessup *1959*, 29–30.

5. INDUSTRY AND THE ECONOMY

1. A case in point is the Greenhithe site (Detsicas *1966*) where an Iron Age farm, with corn storage-pits (Diodorus Siculus, *History*, V, 21, 5) was superseded by a Romano-British site.

2. Strabo, *Geography*, IV, v, 2; *B.G.*, V, 12.

3. Pliny, *Natural History*, IX, lxxxix, 169.

4. An attempt to show the survival of Roman centuriation at Cliffe (Nightingale *1952),* preserved in modern roads and other boundaries, has not met with general acceptance (Bowen *1969*, 31, *pace* Applebaum *1966*, 106). Large-scale flour production is attested at Canterbury (Frere *1967*, 260–1). See Helbaek *1940–41*, 177, on the possible importation of oats into Britain by the Romans. E.g. at Little Chart (Cook *1936*, 234–5) amd Chalk (Johnston *1972*, 140–1.)

5. Crawford and Keiller *1928*, 255; Collingwood and Richmond *1969*, 179.

6. Charlton: Elliston-Erwood *1916*, 161; VCH (Kent) *1932* iii, 129. Joyden's Wood: Farrar *1973*, 100; Williams *1977*, 197–8; Tester and Caiger *1954*, 170; Detsicas *1978*, 239. Swanscombe: Youens *1905*, lxxiii–lxxiv. Greenhithe: Detsicas *1966;* Farrar *1973*, 100; Williams *1977*, 198. Stonewood: Peake *n.d.* Springhead: Jessup *1928*, 339. Otford: Pearce *1930*, 160–2. Shorne: Allen *1954*, 146; *1956*, 252–3; *1970*, 184; VCH (Kent) *1932*, iii, 130.

7. I am grateful to the British Gas Corporation and Mr P.D. Catherall for allowing me to examine and use the records of this excavation before their publication.

8. Cooling: *Archaeol. Cantiana*, xlv (1933), xliii; *ibid.*, lxxxi (1966), lix. Cliffe Marshes: *Archaeol. Cantiana*, lxxxi (1966), lv; *JRS*, lvi (1966), 217. Isle of Grain: *Archaeol. Cantiana*, lxii (1949), xlv. Hoo St. Werburgh: Blumstein *1956*.

9. Evans *1954*. Upchurch, cf. *Archaeol. Cantiana*, xcviii (1982), 27–50.

10. Otterham Creek: Payne *1893*, 79; Hume *1955*, 80. Slayhills: Evans *1950*, 146–7; Jackson *1962*, 194. Barksore: Jackson *1973*, 288–90; *Britannia*, iv (1973), 321. Bedlam's Bottom: *Archaeol. Cantiana*, lxxxi (1966), lix. Eccles: Detsicas *1977*, 19–29; *1974a*, 130–1; *1974b*, 305–6.

11. Webster *1940*, 109–36; *JRS*, xl (1950), 114; Jenkins *1956*, 40–56; *1960*, 151–61; *JRS*, l (1960), 236; *Archaeol. Cantiana*, lxxiii (1959), xlvi; Bennett *1979*, 166–8; *Archaeol. Cantiana*, xcvi (1979), 272–3.

12. Preston: Dowker *1878*, 47–8; VCH (Kent) *1932*, iii, 131. Margate: *JRS*, xiv (1924), 240; VCH (Kent) *1932*, iii, 161. Ospringe: Whiting, Hawley and May *1931*, 107. Dymchurch: *J. Brit. Archaeol. Assoc.*, ii (1847), 138; *Archaeol. Cantiana*, xiii (1880), 182. Weald: Cleere *1970*, 20.

13. Hartley *1977*, 11, 13.

14. Canterbury: Jenkins *1960;* McWhirr *1979*, 154–5. Eccles: Detsicas *1968*, 170–8; Cuomo di Caprio *1971–72*, 431; McWhirr *1979*, 158. Cranbrook: *Archaeol. Cantiana*, lxxii (1958), lx–lxii; *ibid.*, lxxvi (1961), lvi–lvii; *JRS*, xlvii (1957), 223; *ibid.*, xlix (1959), 137; Brodribb *1969*, 109–11; *Archaeol. Cantiana*, lxxvi (1961), lvi.

15. Richborough: Bushe-Fox *1932*, 36-8; Cunliffe *1968*, 249. Canterbury: VCH (Kent) *1932*, iii, 128. Northfleet: Steadman *1913*, 122. Isle of Sheppey: Payne *1898*, 98. Now (November 1983) also at Hartfield.

16. Ragstone was used in buildings in Essex (Williams *1971*, 172; Dunnett *1975*, 94.); Marsden *1967*, 36 ff.; e.g. chalk bricks found at Greenhithe (Detsicas *1966*, Pl. I), the apsidal plunge-bath (Room 2A) of the second bath-house at Eccles (Detsicas *1963*, Pl. IX) and the incorporation of chalk in buildings at Dover.

17. Pliny, *Natural History*, XXXI, 7; Tacitus, *Annals*, XIII, lvii. Cliffe Creek: Miles *1969*, 272–3. Funton: Detsicas, forthcoming. Charlton: VCH (Kent) *1932*, iii, 129. Upchurch: *Archaeol. Cantiana*, lxxxv (1970), 185; Miles *1975*, esp. fig. 15. Eastchurch: *Archaeol. Cantiana*, lxxxii (1967), 291–2. Broadstairs: Wilmer *1908*, 207–14. Dymchurch: Hurd *1909*, 427–32. Eastbourne: Bradley *1975*, fig. 9a.

18. *B.G.*, V, 12; Ptolemy, *Geography*, IV, 5, 2.

19. Jenkins *1962*, 17; Bushe-Fox *1925*, 52.

20. Tebbutt *1973*, 12; Money *1977*, 345–7.
21. To postulate 'an entrepreneurial group' (Cleere *1974*, 174–5) and allude to the Chichester *collegium fabrorum* in order to explain a local market for these sites is pure conjecture.
22. Iron slag has been found along the southern part of the Rochester–Hastings road near Bodiam and at its Cranbrook junction with the road skirting the Roman coastline towards Ashford and Canterbury; similarly, the London–Lewes road runs on iron slag for much of its length along the western border of the canton.
23. The evidence is reviewed in Cleere *1974*.
24. Cleere *1974*, 184, 191.
25. Richmond *1955*, 158; Cunliffe *1968*, 258.
26. Peacock *1977*, 239–42.
27. Richmond *1955*, 158.
28. Cleere *1977*, 18.
29. Brodribb *1979*, 211–3.
30. Cleere *1974*, 181 ff.; *1977*, 18.
31. Margary *1947*, 22–41.
32. Cleere *1974*, 182.
33. In contrast to the makeshift baths at Garden Hill, Hartfield.
34. The stamped tiles, made from local clay, could have neen made in an unknown government tilery or on contract by a civilian manufacturer, or in several tileries, as there are distinctions in the stamps (Brodribb *1979*, 215–6), which would have been authorised to use the CLBR stamp in order to distinguish them from other tiles made for general marketing. It is noteworthy that so far tileries have been established in the canton only at Canterbury and Eccles; clearly, other tile-works await discovery.
35. Philp *1981*, 99.
36. It is not clear why the Beauport Park bath-house is said to have been 'systematically stripped of re-usable materials' (Cleere *1977*, 19) *at* the time of its abandonment as this could have occurred later without any dateable traces of this robbing.
37. Charlton: VCH (Kent) *1932*, iii, 127. Smarden: *J. Brit. Archaeol. Assoc.*, xiii (1907), 160. Wye: *Archaeol. Cantiana*, xliii (1931), 82–3. Boughton: *Archaeol. Cantiana*, lxxxv (1970), 178; *Britannia*, ii (1971), 288. Forest of Blean: *Britannia*, iv (1973), 322, and private information from Dr F. Jenkins.
38. Swarling: Bushe-Fox *1925*, 53. Springhead: *Archaeol. Cantiana*, lxxi (1957), 70 ff.; Penn *1968*, 169; *Britannia*, ii (1971), 288. Two enamelled 'duck brooches' (Penn *1968*, Pl. II), made at Springhead, have been found, one there and the other at Rochester (Canterbury: *Archaeol. Cantiana*, xcv (1979), 276).
39. *Archaeol. Cantiana*, xci (1975), 190–1; Young *1981*, 37–8.
40. Titsey: Fox *1905*, 1–26; Rivet *1958*, 124; Frere *1967*, 300. Lullingstone: Meates *1979*, 105–8. Bearsted: *Archaeol. Cantiana*, lxxvi (1961), 191–2.
41. Pliny, *Natural History*, IX, lxxix, 169; Juvenal, *Satires*, IV, 141; Tacitus, *Agricola*, XII, 20; Ammianus Marcellinus, xxiii, 6, 88; Martial, xiv, 99.

6. THE LATE FOURTH AND FIFTH CENTURIES

1. Johnson *1976*, 68.
2. Cunliffe *1980*, 288.
3. Hawkes and Dunning *1961*, 41.
4. Hawkes and Dunning *1961*, 52 ff.
5. Johnson *1982*, 30. Also at Dover where there is evidence for additional bastions.
6. Zosimus, IV, 5.
7. Thompson *1977*, but cf. Salway *1981*, 444–5.
8. Frere *1967*, 357–9, and fig. 12.
9. Meates *1979*, 24.
10. Black *1981*, 166.
11. Detsicas *1969*, 106, and *1972*, 106.
12. To such an extent that troops may have had to be paid in kind rather than coin, which may account for the silver ingots found in the canton (Painter *1981*).
13. At Eccles such dereliction was gradual and some occupation continued, perhaps into the fifth century, as shown by the insertion of a tiled hearth on the tessellation of one living room, dated late in the fourth century by a cross-bow brooch and pottery associated with the hearth.
14. Wacher *1974*, 414 ff., draws attention to the possibility of epidemic diseases having also had a part to play in this decay, but cf. Todd *1977*, 319–25.
15. Procopius, I, ii, 38.
16. Frere *1966*, 91–3; other sunken huts have also recently been found, *Archaeol. Cantiana*, xcviii (1982), 227.
17. Tester *1968*, and *Archaeol. Cantiana*, lxxxiii (1968), 258. There is also a possibility of another early cemetery at Farningham (*Archaeol. Cantiana*, xlvi (1934), 157), but the evidence there is inconclusive.
18. Pottery manufacture, for instance, came to an abrupt end.

Bibliography

(a) *Ancient authorities*

Ammiamus Marcellinus, *Res Gestae*, Clark, C.U., (ed.), Berlin 1910–15.
Caesar, *De bello gallico*, du Pontet, R., (ed.), Oxford 1900 and 1901.
Cassius Dio, *Historiae romanae*, Boissevain, U.P., (ed.), Berlin 1895–1931.
Diodorus Siculus, *History*, Oldfather, C.H., (ed.), London and Cambridge, Mass., 1939.
Eutropius, *Breviarium ab urbe condita*, Droysen, H., (ed.), Berlin 1879.
Juvenal, *Satires*, Clausen, W.V., (ed.), Oxford 1959.
Martial, *Epigrams*, Lindsay, W.M., (ed.), Oxford 1929.
Pliny, *Natural history*, Beaujeu, J., Ernout, A., André, J., *et al.*, (eds.), Paris 1947–74.
Procopius, *De bellis*, Haury, J., and Wirth, G., (eds.), Leipzig 1914.
Ptolemy, *Geography*, Müller, C., (ed.), Paris 1883–1901.
Strabo, *Geography*, Aujac, G., (ed.), Paris 1969.
Tacitus, *Agricola*, Ogilvie, R.M., and Richmond, I.A., (eds.), Oxford 1967.
    Annals, Fisher, C.D., (ed.), Oxford 1906.
Zosimus, *Historia nova*, Mendelssohn, L., (ed.), Leipzig 1887.

(b) *Modern works*

Alexander, J., (1961), 'The excavation of the Chestnuts megalithic tomb at Addington, Kent', *Archaeol. Cantiana*, lxxvi, 1–57.
Allen, A.F., (1954), 'Roman and other remains from Chalk, near Gravesend', *Archaeol. Cantiana*, lxviii, 144–58.
Allen, A.F., (1956), 'Chalk, Gravesend – Roman remains', *Archaeol. Cantiana*, lxx, 252–3.
Allen, A.F., (1970), 'Chalk and Shorne', *Archaeol. Cantiana*, lxxxv, 184–7.
Applebaum, S., (1966), 'Peasant economy and types of agriculture', in Thomas, C., (ed.), *Rural settlement in Roman Britain* (London).
Arnold, A.A., (1889), 'On Roman remains found at Rochester', *Archaeol. Cantiana*, xviii, 193–5.
Arnold, A.A., (1921), 'The earliest Rochester bridge. Was it built by the Romans?', *Archaeol. Cantiana*, xxxv, 127–38.

Baxter, R., and Mills, R. (1978), 'The Romano-British site at Radfield, Sittingbourne', *Archaeol. Cantiana*, xciv, 239–47.

Battely, J., (1745), *Antiquitates rutupinae* (Oxford).

Bennett, P., (1978), 'A Roman building near Sandwich', *Archaeol. Cantiana*, xciv, 191–4.

Bennett, P., (1979), 'Excavations at 16–21 North Lane, Canterbury', *Archaeol. Cantiana*, xciv, 165–73.

Birley, A.R., (1967), 'The Roman governors of Britain', *Epigraphischen Studien*, iv, 63–102.

Black, E.W., (1981), 'The Roman villa at Darenth', *Archaeol. Cantiana*, xcvii, 159–83.

Blagg, T.F.C., (1979), 'The votive column from the Roman temple precinct at Springhead', *Archaeol. Cantiana*, xcv, 223–9.

Blumstein, M., (1956), 'Roman pottery from Hoo', *Archaeol. Cantiana*, lxx, 273–7.

Bowen, H.C., (1969), 'The Celtic background', in Rivet, A.L.F, (ed.), *The Roman villa in Britain* (London).

Bradley, R., (1975), 'Salt and settlement in the Hampshire-Sussex borderland', in de Brisay, K.W., and Evans, K.A., (eds.), *Salt: the study of an ancient industry* (Colchester), 20–5.

Branigan, K., (1971), 'Pavements and poverty in the Chiltern villas', *Britannia*, ii, 109–16.

Brodribb, G., (1969), 'Stamped tiles of the "Classis Britannica"', *Sussex Archaeol. Coll.*, cvii, 102–25.

Brodribb, G., (1979), 'Markings on tile and brick', in McWhirr, A., (ed.), *Roman brick and tile* (Oxford), 211–20.

Burn, A.R., (1953), 'The battle of the Medway', *History*, xxxix, 105–15.

Bushe-Fox, J.P., (1925), *Excavation of the late-Celtic urn-field at Swarling, Kent*, (Oxford).

Bushe-Fox, J.P., (1926), *First report on the excavations of the Roman fort at Richborough, Kent* (Oxford).

Bushe-Fox, J.P., (1928), *Second report on the excavations of the Roman fort at Richborough, Kent* (Oxford).

Bushe-Fox, J.P., (1932), *Third report on the excavations of the Roman fort at Richborough, Kent* (Oxford).

Bushe-Fox, J.P., (1949), *Fourth report on the excavations of the Roman fort at Richborough, Kent* (Oxford).

Cleere, H., (1970), *The Romano-British industrial site at Bardown, Wadhurst* (Lewes).

Cleere, H., (1974), 'The Roman iron industry of the Weald and its connexions with the *Classis Britannica*', *Archaeol. J.*, cxxxi, 171–99.

Cleere, H.,(1977), 'The Classis Britannica', in Johnston, D.E., (ed.), *The Saxon Shore* (London), 16–9.

Collingwood, R.G., (1930), *The archaeology of Roman Britain* (London).

Collingwood, R.G., and Myres, J.N.L., (1937), *Roman Britain and the English settlements*, 2nd edn. (Oxford).

Cook, N., (1936), 'Archaeology in Kent', *Archaeol. Cantiana*, xlviii, 234–5.

Crawford, O.G.S., and Keiller, A., (1928), *Wessex from the air* (Oxford).

Cunliffe, B., (ed.), (1968), *Fifth report on the excavations at the Roman fort at Richborough, Kent* (Oxford).

Cunliffe, B., (1973), *The Regni* (London).

Cunliffe, B., (1974), *Iron Age communities in Britain* (London).

Cunliffe, B., (1975), *Excavations at Portchester. I: Roman* (London).

Cunliffe, B., (1977), 'The Saxon Shore – some problems and misconceptions', in Johnston, D.E., (ed.), *The Saxon Shore* (London), 1–6.

Cunliffe, B., (1980), 'Excavations at the Roman fort at Lympne, Kent 1976–78', *Britannia*, xi, 227–88.

Cunliffe, B., (1982), 'Social and economic development in Kent in the pre-Roman Iron Age', in Leach, Peter E., (ed.), *Archaeology in Kent to AD 1500.* (London), 40–50.

Cuomo di Caprio, N., (1971–72), 'Proposta di classificazione delle fornaci per ceramica e laterizi nell' area italiana, dalla preistoria a tutta l'epoca romana', *Sibrium*, xi, 371–464.

Detsicas, A.P., (1963–77), 'Excavations at Eccles', *Archaeol. Cantiana*, lxxviii–xciii.

Detsicas, A.P., (1966), 'An Iron Age and Romano-British site at Stone Castle Quarry, Greenhithe', *Archaeol. Cantiana*, lxxxi, 136–90.

Detsicas, A.P., (1968), Review of Philp, B., *Excavations at Faversham, 1965* (1968), *Archaeol. Cantiana*, lxxxiii, 293.

Detsicas, A.P., (1972), 'The Roman east gate: a tentative reconstruction', in Harrison, A.C., 'Rochester east gate, 1969', *Archaeol. Cantiana*, lxxxvii, 132.

Detsicas, A.P., (ed.), (1973), *Current research in Romano-British coarse pottery* (London).

Detsicas, A.P., (1974), 'Finds from the pottery kiln(s) at Eccles, Kent', *Antiq. J.*, liv, 305–6.

Detsicas, A.P., (1975), 'A Romano-British building at Charing', *Archaeol. Cantiana*, xci, 107–10.

Detsicas, A.P., (1977), 'First-century pottery manufacture at Eccles', in Dore, J., and Greene, K., *Roman pottery studies in Britain and beyond* (Oxford), 19–36.

Detsicas, A.P., (1978), Review of Peacock, D.P.S., (ed.), *Pottery and early commerce* (London), 237–40.

Detsicas, A.P., (1979), Review of Wacher, J., *Roman Britain* (London), 311–3.

Detsicas, A.P., (ed.), (1981), *Collectanea historica* (Maidstone).

Detsicas, A.P., forthcoming, 'A salt-panning site at Funton', *Archaeol. Cantiana*.

Dowker, G., (1879), 'Roman remains at Preston, near Wingham', *Archaeol. Cantiana*, xii, 47–8.

Dowker, G., (1882), 'A Roman villa at Wingham', *Archaeol. Cantiana*, xiv, 134–9.

Dowker, G., (1883), 'The Roman villa at Wingham, part II', *Archaeol. Cantiana*, xv, 351–7.

Dudley, D.R., and Webster, G., (1965), *The Roman conquest of Britain, A.D. 43–57* (London).

Dunkin, A.J., (1848), *Memoranda of Springhead.*

Dunkin, J., (1844), *History and antiquities of Dartford* (Dartford).

Dunnett, R., (1975), *The Trinovantes* (London).

Dunning, G.C., and Jessup, R.F., (1936), 'Roman Barrows', *Antiquity,* x, 37–53.

Dymond, D.P., (1961), 'Roman bridges on Dere Street, County Durham; with a general appendix on the evidence for bridges in Roman Britain', *Archaeol. J.,* cxviii, 136–64.

Eames, J., (1957), 'A Roman bath-house at Little Chart, Kent', *Archaeol. Cantiana,* lxxi, 130–46.

Elliston-Erwood, F.C., (1916), 'The earthworks at Charlton, London, S.E.', *J. Brit. Archaeol. Assoc.,* xxii, 125–91.

Elliston-Erwood, F.C., (1923), 'A further report on the earthworks at Charlton, London, S.E.', *J. Brit. Archaeol. Assoc.,* xxix, 227–39.

Evans, J.H., (1950), 'Roman remains from Upchurch Marshes', *Archaeol. Cantiana,* lxii, 146–7.

Evans, J.H., (1954), 'Archaeological horizons in the north Kent marshes', *Archaeol. Cantiana,* lxvi, 103–46.

Farrar, R.A.H., (1973), 'Techniques and sources of Romano-British black-burnished ware', in Detsicas, A., (ed.), *Current research in Romano-British coarse pottery* (London), 67–103.

Fletcher, Sir E., and Meates, G.W., (1969), 'The ruined church of Stone-by-Faversham', *Antiq. J.,* xlix, 273–94.

Fletcher, Sir E., and Meates, G.W., (1977), 'The ruined church of Stone-by-Faversham – second report', *Antiq. J.,* lvii, 67–72.

Flight, C., and Harrison, A.C., (1978), 'Rochester Castle, 1976', *Archaeol. Cantiana,* xciv, 27–60.

Fox, G.E., (1905), 'Notes on some probable traces of Roman fulling in Britain', *Archaeologia,* lix, 218–32.

Frend, W.H.C., (1954), 'Religion in Roman Britain in the fourth century A.D.', *J.Brit. Archaeol. Assoc.,* xviii, 1–18.

Frere, S., (1954), 'Canterbury excavations, Summer, 1946', *Archaeol. Cantiana,* lxviii, 101–34.

Frere, S.S., (1956), 'The end of towns in Roman Britain', in Wacher, J.S., (ed.), *The civitas capitals of Roman Britain* (Leicester), 87–100.

Frere, S., (1967), *Britannia* (London).

Frere, S., (1970), 'The Roman theatre at Canterbury', *Britannia,* i, 83–113.

Frere, S.S., (1971), 'Editorial', *Britannia,* ii, xv–xvii.

Frere, S., and Stow, S., (1983), *Excavations in the St. George's Street and Burgate Street areas* (Maidstone).

Graham, J., (1936), 'A Roman-Celtic temple at Titey, and the Roman road', *Surrey Archaeol. Coll.,* xliv, 84–101.

Harker, S.R., (1970), 'Springhead – The well, F.19', *Archaeol. Cantiana,* lxxxv, 139–48.

Harker, S.R., (1971), *Archaeol. Cantiana,* lxxxvi, 236–7.

Harker, S.R., (1972), *Archaeol. Cantiana,* lxxxvii, 228–9.

Harker, S.R., (1973), *Archaeol. Cantiana,* lxxxviii, 225–6.

Harrison, A.C., (1970), 'Excavations in Rochester', *Archaeol. Cantiana*, lxxxv, 95–112.

Harrison, A.C., (1972), 'Rochester East Gate, 1969', *Archaeol. Cantiana*, lxxxvii, 121–57.

Harrison, A.C., (1975), *Archaeol. Cantiana*, xci, 211–2.

Harrison, A.C., (1976), *Archaeol. Cantiana*, xcii, 252–4.

Harrison, A.C., and Flight, C., (1968), 'The Roman and medieval defences of Rochester in the light of recent excavations', *Archaeol. Cantiana*, lxxxiii, 55–104.

Hartley, K.F., (1977), 'Two major potteries producing mortaria in the first century A.D.', in Dore, J., and Greene, K., *Roman pottery studies in Britain and beyond* (Oxford), 5–18.

Hassall, M.W.C., (1977), 'The historical background and military units of the Saxon Shore', in Johnston, D.E., (ed.), *The Saxon Shore* (London), 7–10.

Hawkes, S.C., and Dunning, G.C., (1961), 'Soldiers and settlers in Britain, fourth to fifth century', *Med. Archaeol.*, v, 1–70.

Helbaek, H., (1940–41), 'Studies on prehistoric and Anglo–Saxon cultivated plants in England', *Proc. Prehist. Soc.*, vi–vii, 176–8.

Holder, A., (1896), *Alt-celtischer Sprachschatz* (Leipzig).

Hume, I.N. (1955), 'Romano-British potteries on the Upchurch Marshes', *Archaeol. Cantiana*, lxviii, 72–90.

Hurd, H., (1909), 'On a late-Celtic village near Dumpton Gap, Broadstairs', *Archaeologia*, lxi, 427–32.

Jackson, I., (1962), 'Upchurch: two Roman pottery kilns', *Archaeol. Cantiana*, lxxvii, 190–4.

Jackson, I., (1973), 'Romano-British pottery kiln on the Upchurch Marshes', *Kent Archaeol. Rev.*, no. 30, 288–90.

Jackson, K., (1970), 'Romano-British names in the Antonine Itinerary', *Britannia*, i, 68–82.

Jenkins, F., (1956), 'A Roman tilery and two pottery kilns at Durovernum (Canterbury)', *Antiq. J.*, xxxvi, 40–56.

Jenkins, F., (1960), 'Two pottery kilns and a tilery of the Roman period at Canterbury *(Durovernum Cantiacorum)*, *Archaeol. Cantiana*, lxxiv, 151–61.

Jenkins, F. (1962), 'Romano-British clay figurines as indications of the Mother-Goddess cults in Britain', *Latomus*, lviii, 834–52.

Jessup, R.F., (1928), 'A Romano-British settlement at Springhead, Kent', *Antiq. J.*, viii, 337–43.

Jessup, R.F., (1936), 'Reculver', *Antiquity*, x, 179–94.

Jessup, R.F., *et al.*, (1954), 'Excavation of a Roman barrow at Holborough, Snodland', *Archaeol. Cantiana*, lxviii, 1–61.

Jessup, R.F., (1956), '"The temple of Mithras" at Burham', *Archaeol. Cantiana*, lxx, 168–71.

Jessup, R.F., (1959), 'Roman barrows and walled cemeteries in Roman Britain', *J. Brit. Archaeol. Assoc.*, xxii, 1–32.

Jessup, R.F., (1962), 'Roman barrows in Britain', *Latomus*, lviii, 853–67.

Johnson, J.S., (1970), 'The date of the construction of the Saxon Shore fort at Richborough', *Britannia*, i, 240–8.

Johnson, S., (1976), *The Roman forts of the Saxon Shore* (London).

Johnson, S., (1977), 'Late Roman defences and the *Limes*', in Johnston, D.E., (ed.),*The Saxon Shore* (London), 63–9.

Johnson, S., (1981), 'The construction of the Saxon Shore fort at Richborough', in Detsicas, A., (ed.), *Collectanea historica* (Maidstone), 23–31.

Johnston, D.E., (1972), 'A Roman building at Chalk, near Gravesend', *Britannia*, iii, 112–48.

Klein, W.G., (1928), 'Roman temple at Worth, Kent', *Antiq. J.*, viii, 76–86.

Laing, L., (1979), *Celtic Britain* (London).

Leach, Peter E., (ed.), (1982), *Archaeology in Kent to AD 1500* (London).

Lemmon, C.H., and Darrell Hill, J., (1966), 'The Romano-British site at Bodiam', *Sussex Arch. Coll.*, civ, 86–102.

Leveson-Gower, G., (1869), 'On a Roman villa discovered at Titsey', *Surrey Arch. Coll.*, iv, 214–37.

Lewis, M.J.T., (1966), *Temples in Roman Britain* (Cambridge).

Luard, Major, (1859), 'On the recent discoveries of Roman remains at Plaxtol in Kent', *Archaeol. Cantiana*, ii, 2–8.

Mann, J.C., (1977), 'The Reculver inscription – a note', in Johnston, D.E., (ed.), *The Saxon Shore* (London), 15.

Margary, I.D., (1947), 'Roman communications between Kent and the East Sussex ironworks', *Sussex Archaeol. Coll.*, lxxxvi, 22–41.

Margary, I.D., (1965), *Roman ways in the Weald* (London).

Margary, I.D., (1973), *Roman roads in Britain* (London).

Marsden, P.R.V., (1967), *A Roman ship from Blackfriars, London* (London).

Meates, G.W., (1973), 'Farningham Roman villa II', *Archaeol. Cantiana*, lxxxviii, 1–21.

Meates, G.W., (1979), *The Lullingstone Roman villa, I: the site* (Maidstone).

Miles, A., (1969), 'Romano-British salt-panning hearths at Cliffe', *Archaeol. Cantiana*, lxxxiii, 272–3.

Miles, A., (1975), 'Salt-panning in Romano-British Kent', in de Brisay, K.W., and Evans, K.A., (eds.), *Salt: the study of an ancient industry* (Colchester), 26–30.

Money, J.H., (1977), 'The Iron Age hill-fort and Romano-British iron-working settlement at Garden Hill, Sussex', *Britannia*, viii, 339–50.

Murray Threipland, L., (1957), 'Excavations in Dover', *Archaeol. Cantiana*, lxxi, 14–37.

Murray Threipland, L., and Steer, K.A., (1951), 'Excavations at Dover; 1946–1947', *Archaeol. Cantiana*, lxiv, 130–49.

Nightingale, M.D., (1952), 'A Roman land settlement near Rochester', *Archaeol. Cantiana*, xlv, 150–9.

Ocock, M.A., and Syddell, M.J.E., (1967), 'The Romano-British buildings in Church Field, Snodland', *Archaeol. Cantiana*, lxxxii, 192–217.

Painter, K.S., (1981), 'Two Roman silver ingots from Kent', *Archaeol. Cantiana*, xcvii, 201–7.

Parsons, J., (1973), ' "Isolated" Roman bath-houses', *Kent Archaeol. Rev.*, no. 33, 85–7.

Payne, G., (1878), 'On Roman remains in the churchyard at Milton next Sittingbourne', *Archaeol. Cantiana*, xii, 428–9.

Payne, G., (1883), 'On foundations of Roman buildings at Boxted, near Lower Halstow', *Archaeol. Cantiana*, xv, 104–7.

Payne, G., (1893), *Collectanea Cantiana* (London).

Payne, G., (1895), 'Roman Rochester', *Archaeol. Cantiana*, xxi, 1–16.

Payne, G., (1897), 'Researches and discoveries in Kent, 1895–96', *Archaeol. Cantiana*, xxii, xlix–lxii.

Payne, G., (1898), 'Roman discoveries', *Archaeol. Cantiana*, xxiii, 1–23.

Peacock, D.P.S., (1977), 'Bricks and tiles of the *Classis Britanica*', *Britannia*, viii, 235–48.

Peake, W.B. (n.d.), *Excavations on a Romano-British site in Stonewood* (Dartford).

Pearce, B.W., (1927), 'Roman site at Otford', *Archaeol. Cantiana*, xxxix, 153–8.

Pearce, B.W., (1930), 'The Roman site at Otford', *Archaeol. Cantiana*, xlii, 157–72.

Penn, W.S., (1952), 'The Romano-British settlement at Springhead', *Archaeol. Cantiana*, lxv, 171–3.

Penn, W.S., (1957), 'The Romano-British settlement at Springhead. Excavation of the bakery, site A', *Archaeol. Cantiana*, lxxi, 53–105.

Penn, W.S., (1958), 'The Romano-British settlement at Springhead. Excavation of the Watling Street, shop and pedestal', *Archaeol. Cantiana*, lxxii, 77–110.

Penn, W.S., (1959), 'The Romano-British settlement at Springhead. Excavation of Temple I, site C1', *Archaeol. Cantiana*, lxxiii, 1–61.

Penn, W.S., (1960), 'Springhead: Temples III and IV', *Archaeol. Cantiana*, lxxiv, 113-40.

Penn, W.S., (1962), 'Springhead: Temples II and V', *Archaeol. Cantiana*, lxxvii, 110–32.

Penn, W.S., (1964), 'Springhead: the temple ditch site', *Archaeol. Cantiana*, lxxix, 170–89.

Penn W.S., (1965), 'Springhead – map of discoveries', *Archaeol. Cantiana*, lxxx, 107–17.

Penn, W.S., (1967), 'Springhead: Temple VI/Gateway', *Archaeol. Cantiana*, lxxxii, 105–23.

Penn, W.S., (1968), 'Springhead: miscellaneous excavations', *Archaeol. Cantiana*, lxxxiii, 163–92.

Percival, J., (1976), *The Roman villa: an historical introduction* (London).

Philp, B.J., (1963a), 'Romano-British West Kent A.D. 43–100', *Archaeol. Cantiana*, lxxvii, 74–82.

Philp, B.J., (1963b), 'The Romano-British farmstead at Eastwood, Fawkham', *Archaeol. Cantiana*, lxxviii, 55–73.

Philp, B., (1968), *Excavations at Faversham*.

Philp, B.J., (1969a), 'The Roman fort at Reculver', *Arch. J.*, cxxvi, 223–5.

Philp, B., (1969b), *The Roman fort at Reculver*.

Philp, B., (1973), *Excavations in West Kent, 1960-1970*.

Philp, B., (1977), 'Dover', in Johnston, D.E., (ed.), *The Saxon Shore* (London), 20–1.

Philp, B., (1981a), *The excavation of the Roman forts of the Classis Britannica at Dover, 1970–1977.*

Philp, B., (1981b), 'Richborough, Reculver and Lympne: a reconsideration of three of Kent's late-Roman shore-forts', in Detsicas, A., (ed.), *Collectanea historica* (Maidstone), 41–9.

Piercy Fox, N., (1955), 'Warbank, Keston: a Romano-British site', *Archaeol. Cantiana*, lxix, 96–116.

Pirie, E., (1960), 'Thurnham Roman villa', *Archaeol. Cantiana*, lxxiv, 162–70.

Priest, S., (1931), 'Some results of the 1925 excavations at the Roman site at Farningham', *Trans. Dartford Antiq. Soc.*, i, 66–73.

Rahtz, P.A., (1958), 'Dover: Stembrook and St. Martin-le-Grand, 1956', *Archaeol. Cantiana*, lxxii, 111–37.

Richmond, I.A., (1955), *Roman Britain* (Harmondsworth).

Richmond, I.A., (1961), 'A new building inscription from the Saxon-Shore fort at Reculver, Kent', *Antiq. J.*, xli, 224–8.

Rigold, S.E., (1969), 'The Roman haven of Dover', *Arch. J.*, cxxvi, 78–100.

Rigold, S.E., (1972), 'Roman Folkestone reconsidered', *Archaeol. Cantiana*, lxxxvii, 31–41.

Rivet, A.L.F., (1958), *Town and country in Roman Britain* (London).

Rivet, A.L.F., (1964), *Town and country in Roman Britain*, 2nd edn., (London).

Rivet, A.L.F., (ed.), (1969), *The Roman villa in Britain* (London).

Rivet, A.L.F., (1970), 'The British section of the Antonine Itinerary', *Britannia*, i, 34–82.

Rivet, A.L.F., (1980), Review of Meates, G.W., *The Lullingstone Roman villa. I; the site* (Maidstone), *Archaeol. Cantiana*, xcvi, 417–9.

Rivet, A.L.F., and Smith, C., (1979), *The place-names of Roman Britain* (London).

Roach Smith, C., (1852), *Collectanea antiqua*, ii (London), 1–24.

Roach Smith, C., (1876), 'On a Roman villa near Maidstone', *Archaeol. Cantiana*, x, 163–72.

Rodwell, W., (1976), 'Coinage, oppida and the rise of Belgic power in south-eastern Britain', in Cunliffe, B., and Rowley, T., (eds.), *Oppida in barbarian Britain* (Oxford), 181–367.

Salway, P., (1981), *Roman Britain* (Oxford).

Scott Robertson, Canon, (1883), 'Traces of Roman occupation in and near Maidstone', *Archaeol. Cantiana*, xv, 68–80.

Smith, J.T., (1963), 'Romano-British aisled houses', *Arch. J.*, cxx, 1–30.

Spurrell, F.C.J., (1889), 'Dartford antiquities', *Archaeol. Cantiana*, xviii, 304–18.

Steadman, W.H., (1913), 'Excavations on a Roman site at Northfleet', *The Dartford Antiquary*, i.

Stevens, C.E., (1966), 'The social and economic aspects of rural settlement', in Thomas, C., (ed.), *Rural settlement in Roman Britain* (London), 108–28.

Strong, D., (1968), 'The monument', in Cunliffe, B., (ed.), *Fifth report on the excavations of the Roman fort at Richborough, Kent* (Oxford), 40–73.

Tatton-Brown, T., (1976), 'Excavations in 1976 by the Canterbury Archaeological Trust', *Archaeol. Cantiana*, xcii, 235–44.

Tebbutt, C.F., (1973), 'Wealden fortified camps and the iron industry', *Bull. Wealden Iron Res. Gp.*, no. 5, 11–2

Tester, P.J., (1956), 'First-century potterry from Temple Hill, Dartford', *Archaeol. Cantiana*, lxx, 253–4.

Tester, P.J., (1961), 'The Roman villa in Cobham Park, near Rochester', *Archaeol. Cantiana*, lxxvi, 88–109.

Tester, P.J., (1963), 'A Roman settlement between Bexley and Crayford', *Archaeol. Cantiana*, lxxviii, 179–80.

Tester, P.J., (1968), 'An Anglo-Saxon cemetery at Orpington', *Archaeol. Cantiana*, lxxxiii, 125–50.

Tester, P.J., and Caiger, J.E.L., (1954), 'Excavation on the site of a Romano-British settlement in Joyden's Wood, near Bexley', *Archaeol. Cantiana*, lxviii, 167–83.

Thomas, C., (1980), 'Churches in late Roman Britain', in Rodwell, W., (ed.), *Temples, churches and religion in Roman Britain* (Oxford), 129–64.

Thompson, E.A., (1977), 'Britain A.D. 406–410', *Britannia*, viii, 303–18.

Thompson, F.H., (1953), 'Excavations at Reculver, Kent, 1951', *Archaeol. Cantiana*, lxvi, 52–9.

Thornhill, P., (1976), 'A Lower Thames ford and the campaigns of 54 B.C. and A.D. 43', *Archaeol. Cantiana*, xcii, 119–28.

Todd, M., (1970), 'The small towns of Roman Britain', *Britannia*, i, 114–30.

Todd, M., (1977), '*Famosa pestis* and fifth-century Britain', *Britannia*, viii, 319–28.

Urry, W., (1948), 'Salt Hill: a lost Canterbury tumulus', *Archaeol. Cantiana*, lxi, 141–7.

Urry, W., (1978), 'A circular Roman temple discovered in the late seventeenth century at Canterbury', *Archaeol. Cantiana*, xciv, 1–6.

Wacher, J.S., (1974), 'Villae in urbibus?', *Britannia*, v, 282–4.

Wacher, J.S., (1975a), *The towns of Roman Britain* (London).

Wacher, J.S., (1975b), 'Village fortifications', in Rodwell, W., and Rowley, T., (eds.), *Small towns of Roman Britain* (Oxford), 51–2.

Wacher, J., (1978), *Roman Britain* (London).

Webster, G., (1940), 'A Roman pottery kiln at Canterbury', *Archaeol. Cantiana*, liii, 109–36.

Webster, G., (1978), *Boudica, the British revolt against Rome AD 60* (London).

Webster, G., (1980), *The Roman invasion of Britain* (London).

Wheeler, R.E.M., (1928), 'A Romano-Celtic temple near Harlow, Essex; and a note of the type', *Antiq. J.*, viii, 300–26.

Wheeler, R.E.M., (1929), 'The Roman lighthouses at Dover', *Arch. J.*, lxxxvi, 29–46.

White, D.A., (1961), *Litus saxonicum* (Madison, Wisconsin).

Whiting, W., Hawley, W., and May, T., (1931), *Report on the excavation of the Roman cemetery at Ospringe, Kent* (Oxford).

Williams, A., (1947), 'Canterbury excavations in 1945', *Archaeol. Cantiana*, lx, 68–100.

Williams, D.F., (1977), 'The Romano-British black-burnished industry: an essay in characterization by heavy mineral analysis', in Peacock, D.P.S., (ed.), *Pottery and early commerce* (London), 163–220.

Williams, J.H., (1971), 'Roman building materials in south-east England', *Britannia*, ii, 166–85.

Williams, A., and Frere, S., (1948), Canterbury excavations, Christmas 1945, and Easter 1946', *Archaeol. Cantiana*, lxi, 1–45.

Wilmer, H., (1908), 'Late Celtic remains on the coast of Brittany comparable with the Red Hills', *Proc. Soc. Antiq. Lond.*, xxii, 207–14.

Winbolt, S.E., (1925a), *Roman Folkestone* (London).

Winbolt, S.E., (1925b), 'Roman villa, Folkestone', *Archaeol. Cantiana*, xxxvii, 209–10.

Winbolt, S.E., (1926), 'The Roman villa at Folkestone', *Archaeol. Cantiana*, xxxviii, 45–50.

Wolsey, G.R., Smith, R.A., and Hawley, W., (1927), 'Prehistoric and Roman settlements on Park Brow', *Archaeologia*, lxxvi, 1–40.

Wright, G.R.H., (1965), 'The correlation of the 'Romano-Celtic' temples', *Man*, no. 60, 67–70.

Youens, E.C., (1905), 'Discovery of a Roman kiln at Galley Hill, Swanscombe', *Archaeol. Cantiana*, xxvii, lxxiii–lxxiv.

Young, C., (1981), 'The late Roman mill at Ickham and the Saxon shore', in Detsicas, A., (ed.), *Collectanea historica*, (Maidstone), 32–40.

Index